LUCIËNNE KOOPS

The Ripple Effect

Know how powerful you are

Design Cover: *Rosa Maria Marquez, Light Channel UK*
Editorial services: *Mark Broad, Middlemarch Ltd. UK*
Layout: *Iurii Matviienko, Icreate Agency*
Picture Author: *Unmask Photography*

ISBN: 978 90 83213392 paperback
ISBN: 978 90 83213330 E-book, PDF

To Claire, Julian and Valerie

for you,
your future
and
the future of humanity

Contents

Welcome

This book is written with one of the most important principles in mind:

there is no absolute truth
there are only perspectives
perspectives are not fixed
it is a choice.

I am sharing my experiences and journey, on how I view the world, how life works, and I invite you to explore yours. Perhaps on a deeper level or from a very different standpoint than you have done before. The intention of this book is not to be factual but to stimulate growth and expansion, to free ourselves from anything that limits us.

Over a few decades, now, I have been passionate about finding out how life really works. I have been deep diving into numerous subjects: the workings of our mind, new scientific viewpoints on our biology, our monetary system, power dynamics, spiritual ideas and more. As a result, I have become an expert in human dynamics, self-reflection and observation. As a natural sceptic, I applied everything I read, contemplated whether it felt true for me or not, and dismissed whatever was not applicable or too far-fetched. I also noticed that I wasn't always ready for some new perspectives, as well as that there are a lot of misleading ideas out there.

Probably, like many of you, I have been ignorant of things I share in this book, for most of my life. Changing the way I react, facing painful insights or applying new ways to be truly present, takes courage, time and practice. It requires a choice to make that effort and for many of us there needs to be an inner – often painful – push to even consider the choice.

In this book I take you with me on my journey to show you that I am not gifted with anything special. We can all expand our awareness. I encourage you to take the shortcut, by saying 'yes' to yourself and start exploring, being as open as possible. It is only uncomfortable for a little while, soon you will notice how much relief it gives. Trust me, it is the greatest gift to yourself, your loved ones and to humanity.

Our planet right now needs bright minds, empowered souls and courageous ones. There are many ways to explore this for yourself. Just as there is not one truth, there is not one way. Know that whatever holds truth or inspires you is a reflection of who you are today.

While I wrote this book, my awareness expanded with it — so many new insights, moments of release and growth in relationships. Honestly, it has been a living workshop, from which I hope you will receive a similar process of expansion.

It is my sincere wish that this book opens you up, activates your critical thinking, heightens your discernment, gives you clarity when some puzzle pieces fall into place and most of all, makes you feel motivated to raise your vibrational frequency.

I hope to meet you on my path, to express my gratitude for reading my work, elaborate on new ideas and exchange our gained perspectives.

Let's create huge ripples together that lift humanity to a new phase in our evolution.

Lucienne

Light Code

By Rosa Maria Marquez

The visual on the cover of this book is the "I AM" light code transmission, a universal code. The purpose of this code is to connect you to your true "I AM" presence and divine blueprint.

The light scripture that runs through the centre of this code echoes the frequency of the creator of this book, like a signature of her soul's essence and the intention of her message.

Light Codes are cosmically channelled frequencies that I refer to as light transmissions. These light transmissions are an ancient and futurist universal communication system, a forgotten multi-dimensional healing modality.

I believe light code transmissions are a master healing tool, a beautiful and sacred gift channelled to assist humanity at this pinnacle time in our evolution, to rise to a higher plane of unity consciousness. Awakening the remembrance of who we truly are and our divine purposes as we journey through this human existence.

Light transmissions bypass the logical mind and work deep within the subconscious.

The transmissions meet the receiver at the level at which they are ready to receive, sending vibrational messages and data to the physical body at a cellular level and working within the etheric field and beyond. Light codes work by shining a light on what once was hidden, awakening ancient knowledge and wisdom which is embedded within your DNA structure, unlocking your full potential, activating your divine blueprint, awakening your forgotten gifts, and upgrading your abilities. Connecting you to your true divine sovereignty.

Connect to your I AM sovereignty, where the impossible becomes possible.

www.lightchannel.co.uk

Some terminology

I use 'to **sense**' many times in this book. This is different from the five senses we know: sight, hearing, smell, taste and touch. Nor is it the same as intuition. With sensing I mean a physical observation of energy. Many would refer to this as awareness. But what is it that *registers* the awareness? To me, that is our ability to sense. It is best compared with touch – we can feel a surface with our fingertips, we can sense that which we cannot see in material form.

System is used, and depending on the context, it has different meanings. When I use 'system' in the context of our physical body, I mean to include all of our bodies, including the energy fields around our physical appearance. When I use systems in the context of our institutions and governmental bodies, I mean all of those organized institutions together that influence our daily lives.

Consciousness and **awareness** can create endless discussions. Although I have mixed the phrases here and there, the difference to me is this. Consciousness is what we are, our eternal presence, beyond our mortal body. Awareness is whether or not (and how) we are aware of this eternal presence (the Self). Awareness is also used in being aware of our own thoughts, feelings, senses and behaviour. Can we observe it within ourselves and in others without putting a meaning on what we are aware of? When we are unconscious, we are not *aware* of anything, we act, perceive thoughts and react on autopilot. (note: this is, for many, our normal state of being and acting 95–99% of the time.)

Energy: you are a living energy field. Your body is composed of energy-producing particles, each of which is in constant motion. So, like everything and everyone else in the universe, you are vibrating and radiating energy. **Frequency**: your energy field (your physical body and its toroidal field) is not consistently the same in every moment, but moves up and down, depending on the information you pick up with all your senses (five senses and intuition).

Your **vibrational frequency** is related to your level of awareness, as in a bandwidth. Take a barometer with a scale from 1–1000 as a metaphor. Some people vibrate between 100–300. In a normal state they are mainly around 240, under stress they drop to 100, when they are joyful they rise to 300. Other people vibrate between the range of 200–500. Their average is 350, under stress they drop to 200, and in joy they rise to 500. The higher our vibrational field is, consistently, the lighter life feels.

When we are in **alignment** (or aligned) with who we are, the deeper essence, our cells are aligned in the same direction. There is a vertical line from our feet, grounded in the energy of the earth, upwards beyond our seventh chakra, connected to the collective field of consciousness. We feel it when we are in alignment: everything feels completely right, highly energized, fully inspired and full of possibilities.

A few disclaimers

I am not a native English speaker or writer, nevertheless, English felt the most natural way to express these ideas. I do realize that my choice of words is limited.

I am writing from a western European experience and viewpoint.

When I discuss relationships and use expressions like 'free will', I realize that this is not the case for arranged marriages and other cultural dogmas.

I often use 'he' to describe persons in general, not excluding the other gender or to ignore gender neutrality.

When I describe intimate relationship dynamics, my personal experience of relationships is only in the heterosexual realm. I don't feel that the dynamics are any different, though, for relationships that are not based on heteronormative ideas of gender.

When I describe self-healing and health perspectives, I do realize that there are people born with health dis-abilities or challenges that seem unsolvable in our current age and time.

Although I have used many scientific sources to enrich my views, I have no intention of claiming any of my statements to be scientifically correct. It is not the purpose of this book to find one truth, only to find our own individual truths.

Acknowledgements

Writing this book has been one great adventure. Being a first-time writer, I had little idea where to start, how to structure and how important it was to trust my wisdom and personal process. I learned to discern what was not authentically mine and trust that what felt true to me was worth sharing.

Many people have inspired and supported me in this endeavour. Some shared just one word, that triggered a whole new perspective, others were consistent with their unconditional support in each phase, some at great distance, unseen and online only.

There are those who actively worked with me in various roles. First of all, my gratitude to Carolien Jongbloed, not only for our most precious friendship but also as a great sparring partner. Together we explored in-depth our own inner processes and human dynamics from a broader perspective. I always remember her supporting words: 'your book needs to be written and trust it will be out when the timing is right'. Together with our mutual friend, Magdalena Geysen, they held the unconditional space for my work to come into fruition.

My gratitude to those who were willing to give direct feedback on work written: Claire Askes, Ruud Scherrenburg, Bart van der Meij, James Pope and Gert Askes. Their insights and reflections have made my writing more to the point and objective. It has been a joy to work with my daughter, Claire, who helped me from the start with gaining clarity on the book's intention, reading through my first pieces and was always my first line of support for an English phrase.

My dear friend Anouk Jungslager shared her creative energy and came up with the great idea for the little symbols for each chapter.

I have been helped with having a few people edit my work. First by Danielle, who came up with the lovely idea to add personal experiences. James Pope was so kind and wise to introduce me to Mark Broad, my editor. Mark did an amazing job improving my English. He asked many clarifying questions and made sentences more concise.

Rosa-Maria Marquez was an unexpected gift who appeared in my online-life at the right moment. She made the beautiful, very special artwork with the personalized lightcode and helped me with the design for the cover.

My partner, Sergio, kept me grounded with his loving support and unconditional presence. The insights I gained from our relationship dynamics made me understand and release the emotional co-dependencies that disempower me. These insights have been invaluable for this book.

Last but not least, my children, Claire, Julian and Valerie. They saw me writing, day-in, day-out, for one-and-a-half years straight, at the same spot at our kitchen table. Their support has been priceless and each in their unique way enriched the content of my book with their clarity, motivated me to take necessary breaks and challenged my vision. They surprised me most with their accelerated growth in these unprecedented times, so empowered and emotionally aware at such a young age.

We don't see the world as it is, we see it as we are

Anon.

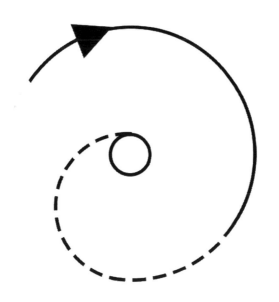

URGING

FROM OUTSIDE-IN WE LIVE,
WITH LITTLE AWARENESS

1. Urging

The time for a new paradigm is now

What a wonderful world that would be, where every child of every race, color, and creed on Earth could expect a shirt on his or her back, clean potable water to drink, nourishing food to eat, medical care as required, and sufficient free education to prepare for a useful and fulfilling life. We Earthlings have more than adequate resources to convert this dream into reality, including millions of young people looking for such a wonderful challenge. All we have to do to create the miracle is to change our priorities after a genuine change of heart.

Paul T. Hellyer

It is April 2020, and the world is captured by a pandemic. All economies are partially or completely shut down because of the threat of a virus, named COVID-19. It is a virus of the SARS family, which has been around in various mutations since early in the 21st century, but this one seems more dangerous. Within a month or two, since the first outbreak in China, the WHO declared the world in the state of a pandemic. What is happening is unprecedented.

The world is in chaos at all levels. Since day one, almost everyone has been overwhelmed by death statistics and hospital numbers like never before, while these numbers are only a fraction of the health challenges we normally choose to ignore. The fear lies in the contagiousness of something invisible that has a very low mortality risk for 99% of the world population, a little higher for those with compromised immune systems and the elderly. It was expected to be a lot more threatening at first, but after a couple of months it has turned out to be way lower. Nevertheless, the world stays paralyzed by the fear of death, disease, and loss of loved ones, and follows the somewhat inconsistent measures of our governments with little argument. Why would we doubt their strategy when it is their role to lead us?

Since we are led, for the most part, by governments that we have chosen in our democratic systems, we tend to follow their rules and policies without question. As such, we see no reason to open ourselves up to another perspective or way of thinking. Many of us trust the sources we read and see.

We have seen this before, in the event of 9/11. Since that day, the threat of terrorism has forced the world to take measures that limit our natural rights and freedoms. Options to move to or even visit another country became more difficult. War in the Middle East has caused millions to be homeless, sheltering in refugee camps for years. Up until this day, no government or organization has taken responsibility for solving this immense human disaster. After some years, it seems the western world lost interest and moved on. It was as if we had accepted the new measures for travelling and movement because of the threat of an invisible enemy, to be feared forever. Humans adjust easily, even when that means limits to their freedom.

This is how we have been programmed, continuously and unconsciously, perceiving a reality as normal and accepting it without question. Our systems and institutions have programmed us to believe that what our mainstream media says must be true and that what our government orders us to do must be followed. Regardless of the subject, whether it is starting a war in an area outside our country, whether it is a respiratory pathogen or an aeroplane flying into a building, the narrative and blind trust in the source has become more important than any counter fact. It is not that we don't debate at all, but we're not able see the broader picture to understand the human consequences. Open discussions have become more difficult, and in 2020 they have become nearly impossible. The fearful mind approves worldwide censorship of alternative viewpoints.

We have become divided, immensely, it even affects our inner social circles. Families, friendships and relationships are challenged or even torn apart because of different ideas about our current reality. One might expect that an event like a pandemic would bring people closer together, uniting against 'the danger', but the opposite is true. That, alone, should ring alarm bells as to the danger of this pandemic.

Current divisions on our planet have new parameters. It is no longer about right versus left, right versus wrong, west versus east, black versus white, or environment versus industrial wealth. Now it is love versus fear. It is not that both sides don't long for the same outcome. We all desire peace, balance, and a safe and healthy world where people can live freely. However, views on reality and possible solutions to our problems are sharply divided.

This is not a new human phenomenon: we have been behaving this way for ages. However, when this happens on a mass scale and billions of people trust one narrative blindly without critical thinking, the conclusion is apparent: we have lost the objective intellect, resilience, and inner wisdom that helps us thrive. We have lost our freedom.

As this book will show, we are experiencing a division between a low fear-based vibrational frequency with a narrow-minded attitude, versus a higher vibrational frequency where the perspective on reality is diverse and varied. The tricky thing is that one cannot jump easily into a higher frequency while being unaware of one's own state. It is like a catch-22: to shift one needs to become aware, as awareness is the shift itself.

Vibrational frequency

You are a living energy field. Your body is composed of energy-producing particles, each of which is in constant motion. So, like everything and everyone else in the universe, you are vibrating and radiating energy. Your energy field (your physical body) is not consistently the same in every moment, but moves up and down, depending on the information you pick up with your senses (and that is more than the generic five: seeing, hearing, smell, taste, touch). For example, when you hear music you love, your vibration rises. When you hear information that frightens you, your vibration lowers. When you enter a room with stressed people you feel their lower vibrational frequency and your body contracts in response.

Your vibrational frequency is related to your level of awareness, as in a bandwidth. People with a more expanded awareness can reach higher levels of vibrational frequency, stay there more consistently, and are less likely to receive information as threatening or fearful. Therefore they won't stay long in a lower vibrational frequency, as someone might with a less expanded awareness.

For centuries, the majority of the world's population has lived under constant pressure, to survive, earn money, pay off debt, find happiness and avoid illness, while living unhealthy lifestyles in packed and polluted cities. Most have been eating low-vibrational food, working long hours and living daily life with hardly any connection to nature. Perhaps this is not obvious to everyone, as we simply haven't known any better. In fact, we define this way of living as *comfortable*, especially if we are among those people who are reasonably wealthy, have nice social lives, can travel the world and pursue successful careers. Our focus is mainly on ourselves and our material comfort, which for the greater part defines our happiness – at least that is what we hope for.

Whether we live in wealth or in poverty, we are focused on the world outside ourselves to define our lives. The outer authority can be anything, a best friend, a belief system, a leader, a parent, a social media post. We constantly compare ourselves with others: we are better off than them (this feeds our confidence), or worse off (this feeds our victimhood) or equal (at ease). This costs most of our time and energy. We desire constant confirmation from our external environment, anything to acknowledge our existence, and we are not aware of how we influence the collective, how we affect the world around us. We don't see the world as it is, we see it as we are, and we turn a blind eye to whatever it is that we don't like to see.

The underlying cause of all of this is our low-vibrational frequency. Whether we are aware of it or not, we are in a constant state of fear which makes us uneasy. We use rational reasoning to find comfort outside of ourselves which only gives us false safety or temporary release. A human with a low frequency allows war, hatred and inequality to take place and his mind will always find a reason to make it another person's problem. We are stuck in the paradox of not being aware of that which we desire to be aware.

'Ignorance is bliss', they say. Safely abiding in one's bubble seems fair enough when you live in a country that provides comfort and a certain level of wealth. What if you are born less lucky? Is that just your fate, and should the rest of us not really care or feel responsible, or expect that some institute will solve it for us? As this book will show, we are not responsible for the situation itself, but we are responsible for not owning our role in the systems we give our support. Once we see that we can start looking at what causes inequality and find solutions together.

Are we truly unable to solve our world challenges?

*The concentration of extreme wealth at the top
is not a sign of a thriving economy, but a symptom
of a system that is failing the millions of hardworking people
on poverty wages who make our clothes and grow our food.*

Mark Goldring, Oxfam

We can take whatever statistics there are but the numbers show the same line overall: the rich become richer and the poorest half of the world population gains nothing and stays poor, living on less than $5.50/day (World Bank, 2017). In fact, fewer than 100 people own the same wealth as another 3.5 billion people together. Of the wealth gained in one year, 82% went only to one percent of the people, while half of the world gained nothing (Oxfam, 2018). In 2020, the year of the pandemic, the number of billionaires was exploding and together their wealth increased from $8 trillion to $13.1 trillion (Forbes, 2021). The number of children (under the age of five) dying of preventable disease and poverty-related causes, has been decreasing over the last three decades, but 5.1 million such deaths in 2019 (WHO) makes shrill contrast with the exorbitant increase in wealth of the relative few. Another painful number: at least one million children go missing each year and in 2020 there were 21.7 million reports registered relating to suspected child sexual exploitation – a 28% increase in one year (NCME).

We can solve poverty. No one would notice a decline in personal comfort when we redistribute global wealth and resources, according to new standards. War can become obsolete once we understand and let go of our need for power. Inequality can be diminished once we find compassion and understand that we fight against our own lack of self-worth. Discrimination and racism are unnatural, once we examine our belief systems and realize that we are programmed to buy into the 'divide and conquer-strategy' which has us play out the victim-versus-the-superior role.

Environmental issues are a result of our industrial paradigm, where greed has become more important than caring for nature and wildlife. The unimaginable scale at which child abuse and human trafficking takes place, could not continue if our law-and-order systems were entirely trustworthy. And our corrupt monetary system, where people and countries are kept in debt forever, needs a complete redesign. This will only happen if we are willing to stop consenting to power and control by the wealthy few.

In short: the world is out of balance and doesn't need to be at all.

The mess we have managed to get ourselves into, on a global scale, is way more complicated than the scope of this book. And yes, it can feel very overwhelming when the truth dawns on us. What is it that has caused us to ignore these issues? Why are we okay with the narrative that says: 'I cannot change this by myself, therefore I will just let it happen'? Why are we okay with blaming the current state of the world on its history, in order to explain the mess it has become? Are we so ignorant, thinking that so much evilness is only in the past and not happening under our watch?

What happens on a grand scale is happening in our individual lives as well. The same dynamic of blaming 'the other' is so common in our personal lives – we blame our upbringing, our ex, our past experiences, our boss, and we choose the role of the victim, over and over again. We expect that others ought to solve our problems, and it is this expectation that keeps dysfunctional mechanisms in place.

We are not victims of this situation, nor are we victims of our lives. Collectively, we created where we are today. This is a tough truth to swallow. Once we grasp this, we can immediately open up to the power

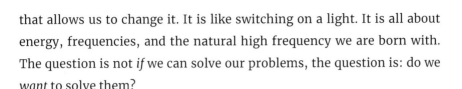

that allows us to change it. It is like switching on a light. It is all about energy, frequencies, and the natural high frequency we are born with. The question is not *if* we can solve our problems, the question is: do we *want* to solve them?

Our COVID pandemic, like any other world challenge, is not the issue but rather a symptom of an alarming situation. There will not be an almighty saviour that will solve this for us, and our governments will not make the positive shift happen either. Even if we invent new technology that solves all of our practical problems, it still won't solve the real challenges on our planet, in our country, or in our personal lives. We live in separation, disconnected from our heart, our natural gifts, and our inner wisdom. The answer lies within each one of us, as chapters ahead will show.

We live in unique times where we are invited or even pushed to observe the quality and effectiveness of our current systems and ask ourselves: on what values are our systems and its institutions based? Why do we approve of systems that are inhuman in many ways? Why are we aware of corruption and still allowing it to happen? Being a silent participant is to give consent to that system; this choice is not forced upon us.

All systems will have to crash and be redesigned from scratch. We are beyond repair, we need completely fresh solutions, based on new values. If we don't do this, being enslaved is our fate, as other people will decide on our lives for us. We are losing our freedom and seem okay with that – but are we really? Life on this planet has one base ground and that is free will. It is our human sovereignty, and we are all born with it. Whether we choose consciously or unconsciously, it is the same free will we use. Therefore, it is time to become aware of what we desire, for ourselves and for others. What is the life we want to live? What is the planet we desire for our children?

Once we open our eyes and raise our awareness, we will have to learn what trust actually is. Who can we trust if our government fails us? Who can we trust if it is no longer our newspaper we are loyal to? How does it even feel to trust someone by using our senses and not our collective beliefs? Do we trust ourselves? The latter is ultimately what is reflected in today's society. Our dishonesty and distrust of ourselves are ultimately our deepest pains.

We have learned to believe that solutions come from actions, such as starting an NGO to help third-world countries. This is good work, no doubt, but the solution to our planetary shift is more subtle, and has to be more profound if we want to make it sustainable for all. The solution is this: we need mankind to shift to a higher consciousness. We need an awakening of mankind. This book will prepare you for this shift, give you the tools you need to navigate it, and get you into your human driver's seat. The day you begin to raise your frequency consistently is the day you are contributing positively to this shift. Your actions will automatically be different: your communication, your perspective, your decisions, your choices, your ideas, your power – all of it. From a higher frequency we will own our planetary challenges. Finding solutions together from this higher frequency will unite us and we will finally find ourselves in a win-win situation.

It is the frequency where the shift is made. A person vibrating in a high frequency cannot hide from pain and cannot accept that humans purposefully hurt one another and other life forms. Being in a higher frequency gives an immediate sense of possibilities, options and solutions. More perspectives can be seen at once and it becomes natural to make choices that are win-win for all. Perhaps this sounds like a new language to you. However, we all experience glimpses of this state in our daily lives. When you feel energized and happy, you love to help others unselfishly. On the days you feel low, it is all about you or your suffering. Learning the subtle nuances of shifts in frequency is how we will raise our vibration collectively and consistently.

In what kind of world are we growing up?

For younger people out there it is almost unimaginable how chaotic and confusing this world must feel whilst growing up. Probably you'll follow the educational path that is generally available. You'll begin your career, fitting into a social life and finding a way into adulthood. In many, if not all aspects of your life, you most likely feel challenged. You are the first generation for whom at least 50% of the parents you know are divorced, where social media creates a constant pressure of FOMO (Fear of Missing Out) and comparing yourself with others. You most likely wonder why the school system is so outdated, and why you have to memorize trivial facts when every answer can be found with one click. There are times when you ask yourself: 'what can I do that makes any sense in this chaotic and uncertain world?'

When looking for a job you will most likely ask more questions about the purpose and culture of the company than the personal career possibilities Once you start working, you might wonder why all the processes are so complex, and why a non-transparent information culture is accepted, as this only blocks the flow of creation and adaptive market response. Perhaps you may even wonder about those in leadership positions and question their leadership capability.

At the same time you grow up in an era with seemingly unlimited technical solutions which can feel overwhelming and exciting as well. It stimulates the idea that anything is possible, and might make you forget your human nature.

Perhaps you feel lost and sense you don't belong. Life is intense, chaotic, heavy and often you feel depressed or down. You hide behind gaming and social media or spend hours by yourself. It is most likely quite difficult to express these feelings because emotionally you are numb. No one seems to understand you. Maybe you are labelled with ADHD, ADD, or any other non-mainstream way of thinking and acting, making you feel more an outcast than a human being valued for his or her talents.

When your heart is so open that the information from your mind is not in harmony with what you feel, you have a hard time trying to fit in. You might feel connected to other sources of information that are not widely recognized. But how do you share your wisdom and insights when you are considered not to know anything of value, because you haven't been 'properly' educated, according to the norm? If you don't have the right set of credentials the world will not listen to you.

It is painful to hear young people say that a planet of peace and freedom is a utopia and will never happen. What is it within us that prohibits our creating freedom for all? Have we already given up by the age of twenty-five? This is an age where one should be filled with the energy of invincibility and a long life ahead, where anything is possible. While you are finding your way, you are now faced with the most unique situation ever: a world in lockdown with the prospect of an economic and climate crisis. Now what? Although you are not responsible for the situation, it will be up to you and your generation, more than any other generation, to make a conscious decision about the future ahead.

We all have our role

If we look at the old meaning in Greek, the word 'chaos' means abyss or void. It is the emptiness that exists before things come into being, a formless void from which all things can be made. This feels truer than ever. Our hearts have no desire to go back to how it was, no matter how old you are, even though it might feel safe to the mind. There is a deep sense that a huge shift will emerge out of these times. How our future will look is entirely up to us!

In this stage of the phase that we're in, it is less important to define our dreams in detail. It is way more important to understand the essence of life and its frequency, its vibration. It is the vibration within us that creates our reality! This is simply the law of nature 'they' (upholders of the status quo) have forgotten to teach us.

Independent of our personal age, we all have a role in this huge shift, to create a humane outcome. It is up to the younger generations to create new systems, while older generations must let go of habitual beliefs, destructive patterns, and our collective and individual pains. We must let go of our attachments and our need to know best, based on past experience. This shift will create the necessary space for new ways and new systems to emerge.

Life is a play, but did we learn how to play? We have lost our childish curiosity. We feel hurt in our relationships as we cannot see the mirror effect of them, a gentle push for growth that we are often unable to recognize or understand. We spend 70% of our lives working, but many of us do not love what we do to pay the bills and wait for retirement to rid us of the burden. Is that how life is meant to be? Is that what we desire for generations to come?

What we will learn

This book is about exploring what makes one thrive. It is feeling into the deep essence of thriving. We will learn to unravel the paradox that it is not about us and yet we are the centre of it. We naturally seek connection from the moment we are born and have an innate desire to unlock our natural gifts and bring them to fruition so others will be served. We desire to live a meaningful life.

A thriving person is no longer compromising and suffering, but feels liberated and empowered. A thriving person knows his quality of being. He shows consciousness in action. He knows how to unlock and use his gifts to build his dreams, which always have the essence of being of service to the whole. A thriving person knows how to relate to others and take ownership of his emotions and actions. Most of all, a thriving person knows how to navigate through the waves of life, through the pain and the joy, with a resilience that feels effortless.

A thriving life for some means being impactful to many, while for others it is living a life in the simplest of ways. It is not about *what* we do, but *how* we do things. We each have our unique ways of being, and it is up to each of us in this lifetime to find those ways.

This is not a book that will describe what new systems are to be built. It will give the *prerequisites* for new systems to be designed, created, and adapted, based on human values. In short: this book will prepare you and give you the tools to empower yourself and step into your role, whatever that may be. By raising our awareness to a higher vibrating frequency, new systems will emerge and old ones become obsolete. This is the core of our shift, from outside-in to inside-out. The old and current way is reacting to outer impulses, for every action we take. In our new way, we reverse the process and will automatically sense our inner language and impulses. From there we will move, act and create.

Over the last two decades, many groups have been working on designing new systems. These frontrunners are ahead of the crowd, waiting for enough people to awaken so they may implement, adapt, and shape these new systems. Our current social platforms are a good example of a latent desire to connect globally, a desire for more information and a greater ability to share ourselves. That inner push makes it so that these platforms are massively adopted today. How we use them, if we let ourselves be controlled by them, is up to us.

Technological advancement is way ahead of our human evolution. There is no way back, and there shouldn't be. However, this also means that we need to speed up our conscious state so as not to allow ourselves to be controlled by technology.

This book is a straightforward call out to any heart who is touched by this but doesn't know where to start or how to contribute, no matter what age, background or family you were born into! This book calls out to anyone who has been on the journey of awakening for a while but who missed the guidelines on how to get into action. And to anyone who feels a bit lost but is eager to shift and make their life a thriving one.

All we need to do is connect within with our natural frequency, reconnect to the laws of nature and its wisdom, and detach from the fear-based programs that society pushes, by letting go our predicated beliefs, activating our self-healing system, and following the path that excites us. It may sound simple, but this really is the answer.

This book invites you to read beyond the words as theory and feel what the words do to your system, your body, your heart centre. This book invites you to open up to your senses and really feel. Learn to reflect, especially when you feel resistance. What is shared in these pages is not written as an absolute truth. There is no absolute truth, only perceptions and perspectives. Let these perspectives open, trigger, and inspire you to find your way.

As the core of our shift is to change our inner dynamic to inside-out, chapter 2 will start with our understanding of what *Being* is. We will get reacquainted with our inner world, how we grow up, are influenced and how we can deepen our empowerment.

In chapter 3, we will look at how we are influenced (and influence others) through *Connecting*, understanding the dynamics in all our relationships. This is where our inner work manifests in our daily life: who do we attract, interact with and what does it show us.

In chapter 4, *Living*, we zoom out and look at the dynamics in our world. Our lives beyond our social circles are highly influenced by our systems and institutions. Most of it we take for granted, but do we have the luxury to do so? And does it make sense to continue this way?

In order to make our fundamental shift from outside-in to inside-out, we need to *Release*. In chapter 5 we look at what no longer fits and all that holds us back. Although it might feel overwhelming at times, remember that the shift we are about to make on our planet is the most natural and positive change ever.

In chapter 6, *Thriving*, we will gain a broader understanding of how our new dynamic, inside-out, will look and feel, our fundament for improving life on earth. Last but not least, you will be invited to step into action. It is great to be in full alignment with yourself, but what next? How do you shift to a life in balance (within) and on our planet? How can we shift from outer pushed achievement to an inner driven path of excitement, integrate this in our daily life and make it happen?

Nothing will shift if we don't put into practice what we read. It all starts with a full 'yes' to yourself and to our future, an open mind, self-honesty and inner-reflection. A core practice and seven new basic skills are included in the book – make this your new way to live. Life is your playground, if you feel the drive to see it that way. Use this book to scribble, take notes and make it your own journal. Self-learning, self-coaching is the fastest way to grow. See your new way with the openness of a child exploring fresh perspectives, strengthen your inner senses and rewire yourself. Become the emotional grown-up with a childlike wonder. Share your new insights and questions with others – start the dialogue. Ask a close friend for reflection if you feel stuck. The ones who feel the inner drive for change will make a fundamental shift. For others there is the risk of staying stuck in the mind.

If there is anything to get out of this book, it's this: stop waiting for *the other* to improve your life and develop an understanding that you have all the natural power within yourself to make it happen. Be courageous, do the inner work, and write a new human story. History was *his-story* of our patriarchally dominated past, and certainly not *her-story*. Now it is time to make human-stories. As Plato said: those who tell the stories rule society. Let's write a new story, together, a human one that will guide our societies for generations to come.

BEING

THE SELF, RECONNECTING WITH YOUR ESSENCE

2. BEING

A thriving person is an awakened one

When my journey started, I was gifted an experience of the simplest form of healing, a clearing. I use the term 'simple', but it is perhaps the most difficult form there is for a healer; nevertheless simple in its essence. Mind you, I had no knowledge of any of this, back in 2012. I had read some books about ancient wisdoms and I was intrigued, but at the same time my mind told me that it was not something for me. Awakening is for the happy few, I told myself. I might have described myself as very sensitive, but what to do with that? It had brought me more stress than freedom in my life. Subconsciously, I was ready for a more drastic shift. I had hit the wall and was fed up with how I felt, conflicted in the way I showed up, stuck with my work, stuck with my social life that felt draining. 'When the student is ready, the teacher appears', they say. How true that is!

There he was, experienced in energy clearing, so I was told. Not a mystic type with long hair and sandals, on the contrary, he was well dressed, with incredible bright blue eyes. He felt familiar from the first second I set eyes on him.

I had booked the complete package: a house-plus-personal-clearing. I thought 'why not'? I had no idea what I had agreed to. I let him do his thing and later he confirmed where it felt uncomfortable in my house. The spaces felt so light after they were cleared. Then we sat down for a personal clearing. We sat next to each other and he placed his hand gently on my back. Whether I imagined it or not, his finger pressed very gently, barely noticeable, at various spots on my back and neck, but on the inside a whole world shifted.

When I 'woke up' after my first session, that day back in 2012, he said something like: 'it is all just energy'. Just energy? I had no idea what he was talking about. I had just been through my weirdest experience ever. I had felt like a large fish in a deep ocean, pushed to the dark bottom of the sea, hardly able to breathe or survive, alternating with moments of fresh air that felt so liberating. Energy? What energy? I was completely exhausted. I had no energy left at all, but weirdly enough, things were lifted and shifted as if something had been removed from my body, even from my memory. I felt different and I knew he was right, but my mind was racing. What the hell had just happened?

Was I awakened after that first session? No, I had frozen and stopped the session when it came too close. He asked if he could put his hand on my stomach, but I was not ready to go there. A second session happened some weeks later. The weeks in between were intense, my body felt ill, releasing in any way possible. I felt different, very different. I knew that something profound was underway.

The second session went a lot deeper, but in a different way. It was more emotional and definitely shifted my frequency to a higher state! When I opened my eyes, everything felt different, the light was super bright, the noises from the street were very intense, it was as if I was floating and I was unsure I would be able to walk out the door, back into normal life. The most profound feeling was the sense of my heart area, overflowing with love. Love for everything and every detail. I was in that state for months. The memory of many painful conflicts in my life had been erased. In fact, many of my feelings had changed. Life felt light and I was full of compassion for everyone and everything. For the first time in ages I felt energized again.

Was everything cleared, healed, and done after two sessions? Oh no, things had only just started!

The next several years, in short, became a journey of reading, learning, experimenting, exploring and integrating. My curiosity was insatiable. I wanted to know what had happened, what it meant and I had only one goal: to clear anything that was holding me back. I wanted to become completely transparent, where nothing sticks, nothing triggers and all experiences and encounters just flow through.

Well, after nine years, life has changed tremendously. Becoming transparent and frictionless is not the ultimate goal, I now know, but it *will be an inevitable result. There is nothing to reach for other than being fully present and resilient with life.*

I am ever grateful to him, for his amazing ability to hold space and be fully present. The experience awakened something in me that showed me my path towards freedom.

So what has happened? Awakening feels like a bubble has burst. Apparently there is something within us that drives us to live. It is more than just a survival instinct. In the worst and most threatening situations, we still connect to this life force. We find an inner power, to live through painful periods and stand up again. We are often not conscious of this inner driving force but it is perhaps best described as pure aliveness. When our inner life force unleashes its full power, it becomes a thriving overwhelming energy that moves mountains. Our limited self is out of the way, nothing can block us or hold us back. This power is the outer expression of who we are, without an ego-agenda. It merges with a gentle and pure compassion, to serve the Self and others in complete balance. That in turn positively affects our life energy and our personal health.

There are many ways to give words to that which Richard Rudd in the *Gene Keys* describes as: 'that cosmic part of each of us that transcends our mortal body'. When we awaken, we connect to that cosmic presence, that comes with many names: the Self, the Soul, I AM, Spirit, God.... It is an expression of consciousness, a state of being aware. It is this inner vibrational field we can connect with, that has no limits to its scale or in its knowing. But how and why would we want this? If this part of us is so evident and natural, why is it not a normal experience for everyone? Well, for one, most of us haven't been taught or shown that it is our natural state. We have been led to believe that this path to enlightenment, which is seen as the fully awakened state, is something mystical, only experienced by the select few. Others say your quest in life is determined by karma. And another perspective holds that this is part of our evolutionary growth. Or have we been programmed not to awaken, so that we remain enslaved to the systems on earth?

What if there is no magical button to awaken you,
but simply a matter of choice?

Well, you are here now, reading these words, so some curiosity has been *awakened* in you! Let's start here by taking away all mystery around terminologies like awakening and enlightenment. Awakening is simply *matter of choice:* to become fully aware of oneself, the way we interact with others and how we are connected to life. Perhaps this choice comes more easily and naturally to some, and remains unattainable for others. It is still a choice and available to all of us at any moment. In short, it is an inside job and requires consistent focus, no matter what your initiation to awakening has been.

Awakening is the path to freedom, inner freedom. It is a freedom to experience all possibilities, to have unlimited choices. Freedom is when you feel there is nothing to lose, nothing to achieve, an ultimate state of fearlessness, free from anything that holds you back. To experience all the beauty, which is felt in everything, in pain and in joy. It is the freedom to be alive, in the moment, open, curious, adventurous, to laugh, love and share unconditionally, to be infinitely curious, passionate to grow, explore and learn. These are all natural tendencies and part of our human nature. Then you live life in lightness, enlightened.

To awaken to ourselves is to awaken to the world we live in. When we all awaken, even just a little bit, we immediately make this world a better place. The only thing that is in the way is *us*. We are the problem and the solution.

Our problem is within our beliefs and patterns. We are completely programmed by them. That is a logical result of (ages of) repeating cycles and our natural instinct to adjust and copy the behaviours of others, to survive. As newborns we are dependent on our parents for our survival. Safety, care, and touch are the most important ingredients. Food is still necessary for growth, within the evolutionary phase our species is in. It is a direct result of the low vibrational state of our collective that our dense bodies need food. However, food is less important compared to other essentials: to feel safe, cared for, and connected.

To fit in with the new environment, a baby learns to eat, walk and talk in ways the environment shows them. This includes communication, emotional dynamics, manners, values, ideas and more. The baby explores, adjusts, copies, and disregards what is not relevant based on feelings of safety and the blueprint with which it was born. It is a combination of inherited DNA (and all its stored memory patterns) which is passed on through our biological lineage, and the energetic imprint we receive at the moment of birth from the planetary constellation in our cosmos. This blueprint defines your potential, it is up to you to choose in which frequency you will explore life, as this book will show you.

Looking into the eyes of a baby, you will see an endless depth and openness. There is little to no identity, in the sense of a persona; instead there is wonder. We are born fully aware with all our senses wide open. That is the natural way for a baby to go through the motions before another form of communication is developed. From the moment life is conceived it is undeniable that the environment and thus the energy field of the mother has a crucial influence on the foetus's biological, emotional and mental structures. It is a co-creation process, of the foetus and the mother.

A foetus develops itself in a world of frequencies of tones, colours, sounds, emotions, thoughts, physical reactions, and any other input from the environment. How the mother responds to all the outer and inner inputs will directly influence the foetus. A stress reaction is picked up by the foetus, and so is laughter, love, and joy. From our earliest moment when we start life, we receive imprints that define our initial reaction patterns.

Our DNA is still a mystery to us, however, it is not the only thing that has a big influence on our lives. To keep it simple, we are all born with a blueprint, a set of definitions, sensitivities, and an adaptable system. This adaptability is necessary for survival. We are part of a greater biosphere, in which we wouldn't survive if we were incapable of change. Resilience is vital for any organism. Currently accepted medical science leaves us often as disempowered victims of our genes. This could not be less true! A genetically inherited illness is not *by definition* an illness for the next generation. It's a heightened susceptibility to that illness, but not a predetermined outcome. The influence of environment, mind patterns, beliefs, memories, and most of all, our response to all of that, will define illness more than anything inherited.

Epigenetics, a young science, has shown us that our adaptability is the most important thing. To function, all cells in our body are equipped with receptors that scan the environment constantly. The information received triggers a reaction within the cell. When we feel stressed or frightened, the cells react accordingly so we can fight, take flight, or freeze. The cells don't know the difference between stress caused by a fearful thought or an actual life-threatening situation. The reaction is the same! We adjust ourselves to what we perceive, with a natural drive to stay healthy and alive. However, there is a limit to how far a body can adjust. The way we live our comfortable lives does not always strengthen our bodies.

We often take our bodies for granted. Now, it is time for us to appreciate and work with the only thing that keeps our human experience alive. Our genius system receives and responds 24/7 in ways we never realize.

How we respond to this broad set of information is complex. But it is in *our response* that we can make a huge change for ourselves. To awaken is to become aware of our inner and outer environment in any single moment in a new natural way. Only with awareness can we choose to change whatever feels out of alignment, that is why it is more than intellectual understanding of a spiritual message. Awakening is seeing through the veil that keeps us imprisoned. For that we need to embody the awakened state. Only then will we understand what true freedom means.

It is not what we experience, it is how we respond
to our experiences that makes all the difference in life.

Growing up

During our childhood, we perceive information and experiences in various ways. Something seemingly insignificant is felt (and stored) as very painful, while other events don't influence us at all. While growing up, we experience and absorb many different imprints, take on beliefs, learn skills, copy behaviour, and develop manners. For example, how we define healthy food is a belief, how we eat food is a skill, the way we do it is a manner, and how we apply it in a social context is a behaviour.

All these imprints are translated as little patterns and programs that we run, on autopilot, for the rest of our lives, at least for 95–99% of the time. Our unconscious mind 'tells' us what to do, how to do things, and what we believe to be true. There is little to no awareness of this process, which is constantly unfolding. The autopilot inside uses patterns to function optimally, which is a great solution for many things. Relearning how to walk each morning would make life quite impossible. So, let's say for 90% of our daily tasks we should be grateful to this amazing autopilot function within us. The refinement is in the last 10% which needs our awareness and self-reflection. Take the example of experiencing pain in the left knee. Soon our body adjusts itself, with a new pattern, to use the right leg more than the left, to compensate. If unconscious of that unbalanced adjustment, we can end up at the doctor complaining about our right knee, instead of the left, where it all started.

Another example is our eating patterns and the beliefs behind them. When we grow up with the belief that we need three meals a day, we develop a pattern accordingly. As an independent adult, you still get up in the morning believing you need breakfast, lunch, and dinner. This belief is not only a physical imprint (you do feel hungry at these three times of the day) but also a strong emotional and social connection. We might think this habit is unchangeable, or we question the need to change it as 'this is just the right way to feed our bodies'. This is an example of a belief becoming 'truth'. Once we do become more aware of our body's signs, we can learn to eat intuitively and follow the needs of our body. In the beginning, our body is still programmed to be 'hungry' at certain times. After a while, when we learn how to listen to our inner senses, we find that there are many influences around our food consumption: our physical state requires food (need for food), our emotional stress leads to cravings (food becomes a distraction), and our social circumstances (meet for a meal, or routine family dinners). We soon notice that we often eat out of habit, expectation, or emotional unbalance and less out of physical need. Intuitive eating will lead to a lighter, more balanced, and healthier system. When our ability to listen to our body becomes more refined, eventually we no longer have need of diets, we'll develop it naturally.

Our attachment to our beliefs

A belief is something we have taken on as a truth. How parents or those who raise us deal with emotions, what they believe to be true in their religion, economic vision, their norms and values around money, plus many other cultural and family ideas, all influence the persona of the child.

•

The same counts for input from social circles, television, movies, news information, political ideas, and education. Growing into adulthood, we keep reconfirming most of our beliefs and adding new ones over the years, due to life's new experiences.

There is a slight difference between dogma and belief. The first is more related to imposed group behaviour (religion, education, cultural, social) and the latter to family systems and personal experiences. However, the essence results in the same. When they limit you, they give the message: 'I am not good enough', or 'I need to adjust to belong to the group/family to receive the comfort and safety I need'.

Beliefs and dogmas trigger our fears at many levels and push us into inauthentic thinking and compromised behaviour constantly. When we look at areas of our lives where we feel insecure, hurt or limited, we exude a neediness either to be seen, to be heard, to be loved and/or to matter. Take time to feel into which of these four shows up more in your behaviour and how that expresses itself: are you more of a reactive (outward) or of a repressive nature (inward). The 'comedian' and the 'grey mouse' can be equally inauthentic and limited by a belief of 'not being good enough'.

The list of beliefs and dogmas is endless and personal to each one of us. Most run deep and feel fixed and unchangeable, but not one belief ever is! All they ever tell us is what we believe to be true about our persona, the world we live in and the limits of our lives. It is as if we need something to hold onto, to live. We need beliefs to confirm our existence, to make sense of our life on earth. Without an identity, we would feel lost and alienated. However, too much attachment is how we remain small, our lives a struggle and our relationships challenging.

The belief itself is less the issue, they are just ideas or perspectives. Being attached to our beliefs makes questioning them uncomfortable or even fearful. This is not the case with all the beliefs we hold, of course, but it is true with many of them. To be more precise, we have built our identity and persona around our beliefs. We have *become* our beliefs. So, to question a belief is to question ourselves. This makes us resistant to change. The triggered discomfort results in offensive and defensive behavioural patterns.

Nothing has meaning until you give it meaning.

In short, by the time a child becomes an adult, a mixture of copied behaviour, created patterns, DNA blueprint activation, dogma's and a wide range of beliefs including emotional and experimental imprints, combine into the persona. In simpler terms: we give meaning to anything we have experienced and adapted since the moment we were conceived, and we perceive it through the coloured lens of our DNA blueprint. Almost anything we believe to be true can be seen differently, by giving it another meaning.

The sentence 'nothing has meaning until I give it meaning' was a realization in my early youth and a game I played by myself. Somehow I was fascinated by the words we had chosen to name things. I could look at a tree and then tried to imagine how it would feel if the tree was called an airplane instead. Almost impossible to do. I also noticed that it made a difference if a new label was less of a big step. To name a tree 'a ladder' is easier to imagine than naming it an airplane. With an airplane there are so many automated associations that don't match the image of a tree.

It was only after 2012 that I learned about belief systems and how they accumulated into my idea of my persona. I struggled with the idea for a long time. Beliefs about myself I didn't like were quite easy to identify, but then what? First I tried to replace them with beliefs I did resonate with. It was almost as if I created a new me, but that felt weird and unachievable. Until, I suddenly understood the essential word: attachment. I didn't have to become a new me, a new character, a new personality. I needed to release my attachment to a belief that defines me. The difference is subtle but the effect huge. Soon I realized that I never would change into someone new, but the way I feel about myself and show up has a different nuance. By releasing the attachments, I accept the beliefs as a full part of me, but I gratefully let go of the role they once served. And that shift makes my personality softer, where it was too harsh, and shining, where it was a bit dull.

My experience in 2012 had not so much changed my beliefs nor my attachments to them, but it had erased some core emotional pains and with it parts of my memory of old stories. That in itself made me restore my natural weight in a couple of weeks, without any active focus. So yes, beliefs are stored in our cells as stuck energy.

Going through these beliefs is not a one-off thing you can do in a few weeks. It's a continuous process of unravelling layers of attachment. Sometimes it is related to skills and gifts, other times it is related to relationships, work, political views and so on. Each unveiled layer liberates me.

Life will show us our limiting beliefs in different versions until we are ready to release all attachment to it. Just a few sessions of therapy or some moments of self-reflection may reveal a theme to us, but just noticing them here and there isn't enough to release the core pain body. The game changer is the shift in our patterns!

The game changer is in our patterns

Our beliefs are so deeply ingrained in us that we relive them each day through the patterns we have acquired. What we are doing is repeating the life we lived the day before, without objectivity. Each morning we have the opportunity to make a fresh start. However, before we know it, we are completely unconscious of our daily routine taking over. We follow the same pattern and thus create the same events and experiences. We check our social media, read our newspaper, eat the same breakfast, check our to-do list based on yesterday's plan and continue our day in familiar ways.

We create the same day every day, with our behavioural and thinking patterns based on the past, beliefs and dogma's. Guess what, each day that we project our old ideas into the future, we will get the same results. In other words, we find it difficult to let go of our old routines and to create a fresh moment in each new second. Of course, there are moments where a new idea enters our mind, and we might take a little time to wonder how great it would be if... but soon we find reason to dismiss that and go back to our daily life, with its predefined chores and plans to secure our future.

Even when we are open to new ideas, for example at work, we often block change and opportunities by reacting from our past experience. 'We have tried that before', or 'people don't think like that', or 'that has never worked', and similar phrases, have not only killed many great new ideas but repeatedly block us from changing course.

A pattern is a mini series of steps related to how we think, how we reason with ourselves and others, how we act and react to information, and our emotional response. Most of our patterning is noticeable in our (re)actions – in other words, in our behaviour. To simplify: we pick up information in our environment (inside and outside our body) and that triggers reactive patterns, from amino acids to build proteins that create feelings, to thoughts that trigger behaviour. New neuroscience is one way to influence these subconscious patterns, but here we focus more on the essence of becoming fully self-aware.

The field of information is quite a new territory. We don't know for example where thoughts come from or who/what creates them. They are simply there, and if we want to actively create a thought, it seems nearly impossible. Just tell yourself: *I want to have another thought right now.*

You will notice that your mind may stay silent for quite a while until you are no longer focused on 'having thoughts', and then they appear again. They seem to lead a life of their own, as long as we are not present in the moment and unconscious of this process.

Given that our thoughts, beliefs, and subconscious mind are quite complex to us and hard to grasp, it is much more effective to become aware of ourselves in daily life. Observing ourselves, our actions, and our reactive patterns will soon bring us to the underlying beliefs and the pain related to them. For example, if you have been working on your pain body, around dealing with narcissistic family members, you are likely aware of the related limiting belief that has made you feel not good enough. However, you might not be aware of the related 'pleasing' pattern and the subtleties of this pattern in your daily life. This natural reaction, for you to want to please others, will show up in many other areas in your life. While you are happy that you have dealt with some of your childhood pain, you will continue to reactivate this pain in other areas – this is simply a different facet of the same diamond. Becoming aware of your pleasing pattern gives you not only something to work with, but it will shift your reaction to a conscious one. If you are no longer the pleaser, people won't tend to show egoistical or narcissistic behaviour around you. It is not so much that the narcissist is healed, rather it is that you are no longer triggering this behaviour in them as *your* behaviour changes. And even better, you will attract other people into your life who are more aligned with the renewed you.

Or, anything we react to with an emotional response that is defensive, offensive, dismissive, or superior, or anything that triggers emotions in us, is based on an underlying belief that is worth exploring (please note: it can be a positive or negative emotion!). Although a little more complex, most of our physical reactions, such as pain, itching, rash, infection, or another imbalance, hides a belief and often related old pain as well.

•

Our challenge, and opportunity to awaken, lies in becoming aware of all our patterns, in relation to others and to the events that unfold in our lives.

It took some years before I saw the big game changer for my automated patterning.

In the years after my awakening I felt this deep inner solidness growing. I no longer felt shy or uncomfortable in situations, but my pattern had stayed the same. While I felt more open, spontaneous, and liberated, I didn't understand why people still ignored me or didn't include me. I had to become very conscious how I entered a group, a meeting, or a party. I had to push myself sometimes as it felt so unnatural to ask for the attention of the group or to be spontaneous. Weirdly enough, while I did my best to change my behaviour, the ones very close to me often reacted with surprise and they could respond to my spontaneity with 'have you been drinking or something?'. It was super frustrating and to overcome this cost me some tears. Until I noticed that it was more subtle (oh, the mind is so cunning). When there was no forcing of new behaviour, but just naturally being me, those comments disappeared. Of course I still love to observe and give others more space, that is my natural way too.

To work with this for myself required observation, self-reflection, practice, and release. Each time I notice I go into defence mode or feel discomfort, I ask myself: 'what do I believe to be true here for myself and the situation?'. And of course, I don't always feel like doing this inner search, so sometimes I ignore the signs. But over the years I have found great benefit in doing the work!

For example, if I hear myself judging others, I know belief is linked there as well. Somehow I make myself superior to their situation and my reaction shows that 'I know better'. But why is that? What is it in me that I find not good enough or haven't received acknowledgement for from others? So it is an indirect way of saying: please confirm that I see (or do) things right, and at a deeper level, please affirm me for who I am. The pattern here is judging, the belief is I am not recognized for something. The attachment to that belief is that I need others to confirm my persona, as I am not grounded in my Self in that moment (more about that later).

After a while, recognizing the behaviour pattern is the easy part. Changing it, I found more challenging, until I experienced the important step of acknowledgement of the feelings that came up (the pain body that was triggered). That only requires a few conscious moments and sensing where in my body I felt the contraction, breathing into it, giving it space. I can do this anywhere, no one even notices, and with more presence continue my day. After some time I noticed I started to (re-) act differently.

Last but not least, inner confirmation of my progress is so important. It can be damn hard work to go through these patterns and beliefs (especially in relationships where the other is less aware), so let's be gentle and proud about any step we take.

Our life in vibrating frequencies

Our perception of our world is relative to the tools which we use to perceive the world.

Eric Dowsett

All is energy. Really? Growing up and living in a world where everything is perceived and accepted as fixed matter is perhaps the greatest deception of all. We are stuck in this idea that matter is fixed and unchangeable (apart from some new science or quantum physics findings, but they remain theories for most of us). It is perhaps the core reason why we fear change. We simply are not convinced we can. We get stuck in rational discussions of proof and facts about why something is not changeable – and consequently, as long as we're stuck in that belief, nothing really is.

Each object we see consists of little particles circling around their centre, at a slower or faster speed. The lower the speed the more dense the matter appears to us, like a stone versus a radio wave. Our body isn't any different, a vibrating field of energy.

When we translate quantum science, simplified, it shows us that everything we see in our daily reality only becomes a reality once we give it our attention. As soon as it is out of focus it becomes a wave again. Any object is a wave and a form at the same time. The observer's attention, mental state, and intention manifests the 'fixed' reality into his perception of how things are. Obviously, this constant creation of our own reality goes at such a speed that not many of us have the ability yet to see objects as moving waves before shifting into form again, but a few do. As we are all born and raised with so many collective beliefs, we are, collectively, constantly recreating the same world, again and again.

When we follow this line of thinking we might accept that a table is made up of little spinning subatomic particles while it still feels and looks solid to our eyes and touch. So are our bodies. We appear solid, fixed unchangeable matter, but we consist mainly of energy. We receive energy through our food, the sun and earth. The level of vibrating frequency rises or falls according to the density of what we consume. An hour in the morning sun helps our frequency level rise, whereas a heavy meal makes our body more dense. The same effect happens with our thoughts. Negative thoughts lower our frequency, while an exciting idea lifts us up.

This new field might feel very complex and difficult. Opening up to these ideas and allowing them some play creates more expansion, than getting bogged down in trying to understand every detail.

> *Everything is energy! I was thrilled by this new perspective I was finding in several books, workshops, and courses. It all made sense to me although I couldn't, and still can't, explain the technical details. It feels like a knowing, something so logical. Back in 2012, my inner social circle thought it was*

nonsense. Again and again I had to give solid scientific proof, which I couldn't do in such a way that they would get it. I let the matter rest and continued to explore for myself.

Up to this day, I don't see matter as waves in front of my eyes before they become solid matter. Either I don't have that ability or I am stuck within a belief that I am not able to perceive reality that way. I am even open to the possibility that it might be a false idea, not even correct in the way I am explaining it here. Does it matter, for the journey?

Oh yes it does! The concept that anything can change, can shift into a higher vibration, lifted me out of my state of victimhood! It gave me a boost: 'I am able to change my life in any way I like'. This brought a tremendous feeling of empowerment, of being in the driving seat of my life.

It makes sense to me that there is so much more to it than what we define as fixed reality. The scene from the Matrix (the movie) where Morpheus explains reality to Neo, while they were in a virtual-reality scene, is brilliant to ponder upon:

'What is real? How do you define real? If you are talking about what you can feel, smell, taste and see, then "real" is electrical signals interpreted by your brain.'

The idea that there is so much more to discover keeps motivating me to explore and develop my senses. For a while I looked into various healing practices (Clearing, Reiki, Psych-K), but don't see myself working as a healer in that sense.

I learned to let go of my stories as much as possible. I am, with more consistency, learning to notice when I drop in frequency (due to a trigger) and to shift in that moment. Not to push it, but to breathe deep and 'do nothing' – and then it shifts. How simple, and magical. I also learn to discern other's state of being from my own so it won't influence me as much anymore.

I now notice when I am fully present and at ease, life feels light, my intuition is 'on' and synchronicity works for me. Obviously, it is still challenging in the moments I am not consciously present. Before I know it, I fall for the 'trigger trap' and believe the lower frequency is mine. By then, of course, it has become mine. I personalized it and dropped in frequency myself. It is actually quite irrelevant whether it is due to my own belief, someone else's or the environment, the fact that I react to it is what matters and that's what I can work with.

Perhaps the most important thing to take away from this book is the idea of opening up to energy and frequencies, inside and outside of ourselves. Here's why.

Energy vibrates at various frequencies. We recognize the extreme opposites of our vibrating state, the highs and lows that we experience most vividly. A low state: we have less energy, feel less vibrant and other people respond to our low energy. We end up in little quarrels over nothing. A high state: the days we feel great, energized, relaxed, confident, our higher vibrating frequency empowers us to conquer anything. Those are the days when no one argues with you. Thus, equally true and valid are the more subtle signals we might sense from the levels in between.

Energy can only shift form, it can never be destroyed. Raising your awareness is expanding the bandwidth of your vibrating frequency into higher levels consistently by becoming it, fully embodied. Applying the practices and insights in this book gives you the choice and tools to shift out of a low frequency into a higher one. Out of fear, into love and beyond.

A healthy body with a strong immune system vibrates at a higher level than someone who is ill. Giving someone who is ill a solution that is also low in frequency doesn't support the healing process, although it may help temporarily. Chemical solutions are lower in frequency than natural remedies. Something that is alive is by definition of a higher frequency than something that is made from synthetics or chemicals.

Another factor to realize is movement. Energy in a low frequency moves slowly. When you feel down (low frequency) the best way to make a shift is movement: walk, dance, jump. It doesn't solve the root cause but it can shake things up inside you. Support this process with conscious breathing and you create space for the little particles to shift.

Opening up to perceiving our world as vibrating energies makes all the difference to our transformation, personally and collectively, as this book will show. Once we understand that we are responsible for the life we live and the world we collectively create, it will push us out of our victim role. Raising our vibrating frequency consistently can only happen if we change our behaviour and stop consenting to actions that don't feel humanly aligned and push us down. More about that in a later chapter.

First we need to understand more about the cause of our current vibrating state and how we are consistently influenced by our belief systems, collective assumptions, and the role of our mind.

The ripple effect

One of the biggest influences on a child's development is the inability of a parent to deal with their own pain from past experiences. It leads to various forms of projection onto the child, and the cycle will repeat itself. It is not that the child is too sensitive to take a comment lightly, rather it is the parent who is unaware of the effect their projection causes. Breaking through the cycle of unconscious parenting will create a huge leap forward in our consciousness.

What counts for parenting, counts for *any* adult, independent of position. We all need to grow up emotionally and own our personal and collective pain. *Owning it* is the first step to breaking through the cycle of projecting and expecting others to solve life for us. Humanity is living in a low vibrational frequency of fear, suffering, and ignorance. Ignorance is why this state of our human collective is often referred to as 'asleep' or 'unawakened'. As long as we keep vibrating within this narrow bandwidth, we remain trapped in today's world. And it will get worse because the power structures of today's world are operating from fear, insecurity, and control. We won't get out of this low frequency without effort and determination.

Our common sense, critical thinking, objective viewpoint, and openness are all directly related to our vibrating frequency. A low vibrational state limits our views, within beliefs we unconsciously hold onto out of fear. A low vibrational state uses control to override fear that we are not able to acknowledge or even feel. A low vibrational state needs outer input to act, so a person living in this state is constantly dependent on what is happening outside of his body, and he has little awareness of the signs his own system is sending him.

The moment we truly acknowledge our complete selves, and own our thoughts, feelings and actions, our pain and limitations release. In this process, we shine light on what was dark. Light dissolves darkness. When our system has less darkness inside, it becomes lighter. The frequency will rise. With a higher frequency we create space in our minds to see more perspectives. In fact, our system will shift from a survival state to a balanced state, and more oxygen will flow through us. With a higher frequency, we are more alive. We take issues less personally and we are eager to find solutions that are not at cost of others.

We always influence others and the collective with our state of vibrating frequency. Would we raise it only slightly higher than the current average, the world will change. Someone who vibrates at a higher frequency has an uplifting effect on others. At a higher frequency we project less onto others, so allowing them space to open up to the same process. We are all drawn to light. As a result, many higher vibrating 'ripples' will cause an exponential rise in frequency amongst many people. So yes, it starts with you, any of you. Each one of us has the power to change the reality to a more desirable one. All it takes is a conscious choice and a commitment to do the work. Shifting our unconscious way of living to a conscious one.

The path of awakening is often focussed on our pains and how to release ourselves from our shadows. And yes, we have immense traumas to heal. It makes complete sense that those who have been severely traumatized one day open up to self-realization and release themselves from this intense burden. Their brave work is healing family lineages, which is so important for our collective awakening.

However, we are not all deeply and personally traumatized. Many of us have had little youth traumas, mainly caused by the unconscious upbringing of their parents. It is difficult to 'rate' traumas on a scale of painful and impactful. A seemingly small trauma can haunt one person his whole life while a heavily abused child can make the transition as a young adult. What matters more than defining the intensity is what you do with it. Whatever it is we desire to release, losing ourselves in endless analyses to get to the core of our trauma (what, why, how), is something to be wary of. We risk being stuck in suffering (reactivating pain) which only perpetuates more self-sabotaging patterns. It keeps the seeker seeking, unaware he is still trapped in the role of victim.

That cannot be the purpose of life, nor does it help many of us. It is always a personal choice, how you deal with and heal your past. Stay aware of where you keep yourself trapped. This is where shifting to 'perceiving life in frequencies' really helps us all, by releasing the dense energy that once got stuck in your body (see the core practice at the end of this chapter). Release yourself from your story, accept your past and each time you drop in frequency, you know you believed an old story to be real today. How does it help, to hold on to the story? Is it still true today? Shift back to sensing, is there still dense energy to release? Release. Try to keep it as simple as possible. Shadow work, as in deeply unravelling all the ins and outs, can be helpful, but eventually the energy needs to shift to be healed.

The 80:20 rules always applies. When we focus 20% on the painful limiting traumas and 80% on unleashing our gifts, passion, purpose and dreams, we make the shift faster! These are all beliefs as well, but when they feel intrinsically great, when they excite our heart, when they are more in alignment with our unique expression, it is a huge step forwards. The journey is to liberate ourselves and feel free in living the life that gives energy, feels balanced, creates exciting experiences and is meaningful. That is not a life that dismisses pain and old trauma. The shift is in the focus and that shifts the energy, your vibrational frequency into an upward spiral consistently.

When you invent new patterns and actions based on your authentic expression (passion and gifts), you will be faced with discomfort when you courageously share yourself in new ways. That is the right moment to deal with old pains. You can immediately see how it benefits you to release it, so you will do the necessary inner work. To find your gifts you can use challenges of the past, as they have trained you. The pleaser is trained as a brilliant observer with empathic abilities. Ask yourself how you can use more of your abilities. The dominant one is great at getting things done. Ask yourself how you can support others with this quality.

How do you find your natural gifts? Follow the path of excitement. Anything that you love doing is something that comes naturally and in which you most likely excel. Of course that doesn't free you from learning new skills or knowledge. But your excitement opens up natural curiosity. If there is one fundamental issue with our current educational system, it is that we don't follow our natural flow of learning and exploring but are forced through a program. Not the subjects themselves, but the timing and way it is imposed blocks many children in their development.

Our operating system is run by our mind: outside-in

We are who we think we are and we see the world as we are.

Do you like what you see, in your life, in the world – all of it? Face your mirror. If you don't like something 'out there', look inside at what it reflects about yourself. The external and internal factors are not literally one and the same, but in *frequency* they are at the same level. Judging corruptive behaviour is the same frequency.

When we project less low vibrating actions and thoughts on the field, there is less low vibrating behaviour reflected back in return. The same counts for the higher vibrations. This is the shift we are making in an upward spiral. Our mind, primarily, is what keeps us in our status quo, as long as it is running our operating system without our awareness.

The mind can be seen as a translator of the outer field – our experiences, interaction, information – and the inner field, our thoughts. Mind scans the outer world to see the persona (who we think we are) confirmed. It scans the inner world, the thoughts, to find the same confirmation. That feels safe. If the mind receives a different reflection then, simultaneously, the brain signals the body (physical reaction) and our mind comes up with an interpretation. Depending on it feeling positive or negative, we act accordingly. However, even positive events can be translated negative. A thought creates the same response as a comment or an event.

•

When we operate from our mind *alone,* we are focussed on the world outside our-Self and react to what is happening as well as trying to influence what is happening. We like to control our expectations, our lives. Most of us are wired this way. And as we repeat the same cycle, again and again through our upbringing, our societies, our systems, we pass it on to the next generation. Until we see through the dynamic.

As long as our mind runs the show, we are stuck in an endless cycle of seeking to fit in, by finding confirmation of our beliefs, and the positive confirmation from the dopamine that our body releases (e.g. the thumbs up on a social media post). That is how we see the world as we are. We all prefer a good feeling over a bad one, so it makes sense that we avoid contraction and desire more of the dopamine. But more often than not we are used to ignoring what we feel and our mind is cunning in coming up with ways to express ourselves inauthentically.

As long as we don't see that our beliefs are based on copied behaviour, inherited belief systems and traumatized, unhealed past, we stay trapped in our mind, unaware of our inner sensory field. To deal with all this outer input, we keep enforcing the protective shield around our hearts, which only makes it more difficult to connect with the Self.

The Self

The heart is the only reality. The mind is only a transient phase.
To remain as one's Self is to enter the Heart.

Ramana Maharshi

As we grow up we only learn to identify with our physical body as something solid and mortal. Between those opposing elements, the limitless Self and the mortal body, the journey to awaken is challenging for all and avoided by many. To surrender to this inner connection, we will have many experiences that can be best described as 'you die before you die'. What dies are our beliefs, our false ego or anything that keeps us trapped.

It is quite a radical shift, from the familiarity of our mind to acknowledging that we are a consciousness, the Self, experiencing life in a human body. In this shift we experience the natural flow of life as a movement from inside-out, and no longer outside-in according to our beliefs-directed mind. Connecting with this consciousness, or being the Self consistently, requires practice. We have to rewire ourselves and refine our senses. That doesn't happen overnight. One can read endless books and teachings with in-depth explanations, but it won't bring you a step closer if you cannot perceive it and *be* it. The whole crux is that it is not something that needs to be found. It is always there, you are *it* already. However that leaves many of us powerless – the hunt for our true nature can take years, or even a lifetime. It keeps the seeker seeking and makes the teacher the almighty guru. But, it doesn't have to take long!

As words and language are so sensitive to labelling and given meaning by the mind, experience becomes key. The moment you are one with it, you simply know it is the 'it' you were looking for. Nevertheless, the mind is helped with some guidance, as humans find it easier to surrender to the 'unknown' the moment we have some understanding of it.

How did my shift occur? Practice. In the beginning it was a fight with my thoughts. I tried to connect, through meditation, to feel something inside. That's what everyone in the spiritual world was talking about. Go within ... where do I go? My mind took over, again and again. How does that feel, where to feel it? All I got was doubtful thoughts: is this it?

So I changed my approach. I let go of meditation practices. Instead, I kept repeating the same thing, as often as possible during the day: I focussed on sensing or exploring my chest on the inside, then a thought narrative took over, until I noticed I was distracted, back to sensing, thought, awareness of thought, back to sensing. Endlessly ... and suddenly I just knew, this is it. A short wave of awe came over me. But quickly it was gone: a thought had come, awareness of thought, sensing ... and so on.

Within three weeks, the inner field, mainly in my chest, became stronger, its presence easier to sense. This was some years ago, around 2017. Remember my journey started in 2012. Five years were spent on understanding and gaining knowledge. Daily meditations didn't make the shift. To me it felt I had to rewire myself with a simple repetitive practice. Nowadays, the Self, this inner field, feels so natural. I am still triggered out of it, of course I am, but I can clearly see where my mind becomes too dominant. In a second I am back 'in', aligned again with my Self. I know, the way in is my way to freedom in daily life.

Please note that for some of us this inner field, the Self, is always a very natural experience, especially for those who were never really caught by the mind.

Once we are more open to perceiving life as energy, it is easier to connect with our inner being, the Self, our vibrating field. Connecting with this inner field is perceiving your body as energy waves. Within this field you can have different sensations. The more you refine your senses the more nuances you will feel.

Later I discovered that the strong energy of my solar plexus, the field behind your navel, and your third eye (centre of your head just above your eyebrow). Focussing on these three inner areas, heart–navel–forehead simultaneously, aligns my whole being into presence in a single second.

Observe what you sense by connecting with the inner space in your chest, not searching for anything. At first it might feel very tense and contracted (the protective shield you have to dismantle). You may have the urge to stop and give up. Know that you are only prevented by a false mechanism. When you stay consistently present with this field, the tension will soften and suddenly you will feel an overwhelming wave of love, an energy wave. That is when you know you've connected with the Self, you become the Self. Exploring this inner field, enlarging it, amplifying through every little corner of your physical body, you will soon perceive your system as one vibrating field.

Within this energy field there are different densities, some areas feel more dense and others lighter. Our breath is a great guide to moving through the inner field. The moment you direct your breath it easily expands and creates space in a specific area.

> *A great one to use, when you are in meetings or with others and you feel some tension rising: breathe, connect within, focus on the three centres and you feel the powerful wave, presence! With some practice you can do it with open eyes and no one in the room will even notice. Well, they actually do, as they feel your embodied presence!*

The Self is not limited to the physical boundaries of your body. By expanding your field of awareness to the room you are now, reading this book, you can sense the physicality of a wall as the density of the field changes.

This might all sound a little abstract, however sensing energies is quite normal to most of us. We all have experienced in our life the dense low-vibrating energy of another person, or a shift in energy the moment you walked into a room. To perceive that shift, we use the same natural abilities. What often makes it challenging is to define what is 'ours' and what is the energy you feel from other people. For example, entering a room and sensing a headache is a sensation you feel in your own body. That is the only way you can interpret what you sense. The headache you observe doesn't have to be yours, you can pick it up from someone else who is in that room or from a person who you think of and who is on the other side of the planet. Sensing is not restricted by distance or time. Staying in the observer mode is quite challenging, as we get so easily distracted by our other five senses, and most of all by our mind, which needs attention and confirmation.

Accepting that we can sense energy, that we are energy, opens up a world of new dimensions to explore. Even without having direct experience of the vibrating field with all its densities, we can imagine how we are all connected with one another. If a person can sense the energy, thoughts, and feelings of another person, we influence one another. This gives a whole new perspective on how we relate.

This connectedness, at more than just the material plane, is the starting point for thriving. Knowing and becoming conscious that every little particle of energy you influence, influences others around you, makes you understand that one cannot thrive alone. We can only thrive when we all thrive, a win-win for all.

How our mind keeps us stuck

Our mind is a busy bee and costs us a lot of energy if we let it run the show all by itself. Let's have a look at three ways how it takes us out of our present moment and inner alignment.

Reasoning mind:
'knows best'

The reasoning mind is good at finding arguments, often very knowledgeable of facts, using memory and logic and being analytical. Reasoning mind can be very knowledgeable about emotions, pain, suffering as if they were his own, but doesn't sense them (in the body). While the reasoning mind is at play, he doesn't accept pain as part of the argument. Therefore emotions (of his own or of the other) are downplayed, ignored, gaslighted as non-existent, or ridiculed. Once emotions do take over (but are still not acknowledged), for example in a heated conversation, the mind becomes less effective in reasoning. Defensive or offensive actions take over, like anger or blame. The reasoning mind can be highly manipulative, as it will do its best to avoid any underlying discomfort. Cognitive dissonance is a reaction resulting from our strongly developed reasoning mind (see chapter 4). A reasoning mind has little or no access to genuine empathy, the moment it is running the show!

How do you break the spell of reasoning? Pause, breathe, and sense within. You can do this silently or you can ask for a break in the heated argument. With a pause you can open up to the perspective of the other. Not from reasoning, but from sensing. Remember it is your beliefs you are defending or arguing about. Staying in the argument doesn't help. Trying to find the belief underneath it, is what opens you up. It helps to name what your belief is and to change your language with sentences like: I feel, I believe, from my perspective, this is how I see it.

Rationalizing mind:
'doesn't want to know about thoughts and feelings that are inconvenient or uncomfortable – it's all good or I stick with what I believe!'

The mind uses rationale to confirm its interpretation of a situation: 'it is okay' or 'it is what it is' or 'it will be fine' or 'just stay positive'. It often uses generalizations to make a point and confirm the ideas of the ego. Rationalizing mind finds logical reasons for why behaviour or thinking is not selfish. Or the opposite, why we all have to be more social and understanding. The rationalizing mind avoids discussions or questions. It prefers to ignore rather than to reason. A rationalizing mind is not looking for solutions or causes, it likes to keep things as is. That is why the rationalizing mind is excellent at thinking in excuses, manipulative in convincing others of the same and stays stuck in dreaming.

Where the reasoning mind pretends pain doesn't exist, the rationalizing mind overrides emotions. A rationalizing mind can appear empathic but is more sympathetic. Often people with a rationalizing mind are highly sensitive but, as a surviving mechanism, have learned to shut down their feelings or 'laugh away' pain and sorrow.

How do you break through the spell of rationalizing? Ask questions, try to stop assuming or making interpretations. Become curious. What am I escaping from or avoiding? Can it be a conflict, a new insight, change. The rationalizing mind is just as active internally as externally. Start within, explore what it is you avoid.

Monkey mind:
'knowing? I just follow my thoughts'

This is a different one that is only active in our thoughts. It is our great inner storyteller. The mind that shares random thoughts or keeps us captured in a whole narrative. Highly imaginative, its stories can be very negative or unrealistically positive. Our mind always takes us out of the present moment, but this one is either in the past (regretting what has happened) or in the future (fearing or fantasizing what is to come). The monkey mind is very emotionally driven. The problem with the monkey mind is that it stays in fantasy land and has a hard time in switching to action.

How do you stop the monkey talking? Say out loud what your mind is telling you. Guess what, after a few words or sentences you stop talking. The monkey mind doesn't match with your reality in that moment. So it disappears as soon as you consciously take it into the present moment. As ever, taking a breath, pausing and sensing come first. When the pain is very vivid (something just happened) ask yourself: how does it help me to repeat the story in my mind and relive the pain? How true is the story I am telling myself? How can I be sure it is true? Can I sense and acknowledge the pain without repeating the story? Can I pause and trust time will tell? Towards future ideas, it helps to ask yourself: what is it that I fear in my imagined reality? Even when you daydream of great success, the question remains the same. What is it that I fear, why the success is not a reality yet? Or what is a first step, to get me closer? With practice you will see lightness in breaking through the trick of the monkey.

Whatever mind you are most captured by, there is always an underlying limiting belief that keeps you trapped. The fear you are not naturally genius and powerful.

Our overactive mind (can be any of the three mentioned) also takes control of our feelings. We follow our emotions through our thinking and we become alienated from sensing it neutrally. We don't hear the translation of our feelings through inner soft-spoken messages (insights) as our mind is too loud with its thoughts and ideas. The thoughts activate more of the same feelings and thus we keep circling in the same reality, having a hard time opening up to our inner senses to guide us. Any thought that captures our attention takes us out of the now moment, out of presence. Every time a narrative has taken you out of the present moment, take a deep breath and align again. This shift takes practice, dedication and commitment; gradually you rewire your system.

Whew! The mind, I know it so well. I am a thinker, or I have become one, and highly sensitive at the same time. Not an easy combination. Of the three minds, my monkey mind bothered me most and longest. It drained my energy when it told me stories. I used to allow myself to dream away in my fantasy of how things will happen that haven't happened yet, mostly in the context of my relationships. When my ex-husband travelled a lot, sometimes fear came over me that something might have happened to him. In my mind, I had lived through the funeral before his next phone call. Or when I had a conflict with one of my friends, I could replay endless scenarios of our next encounter. These vivid imaginary stories are especially active at night.

Later, I realized that my monkey mind is mostly related to themes of dishonesty within a relationship. When I feel there is something off (I do pick something up), my monkey mind takes over (creates the wrong story). That is probably the reason why it never happened around my children. My relationship with them is very transparent and full of trust. I never worry about them.

A few things really helped me. To question myself: does this help me right now? And if that didn't work, I'd get up, because movement helps. But the best one was speaking my thoughts out loud. I really had a great laugh at myself, how silly my stories sounded. Now, my monkey mind is pretty quiet. How amazing! That doesn't mean I don't have thoughts, but I am no longer captured by them.

How does the mind work?

The mind watches out for your best interest. It listens closely to your language as thoughts are expressed. If you tell yourself: 'I am scared to speak in public and fear my presentation next week', no doubt you will procrastinate over preparations, postponing the inevitable. As anxiety rises, you might even feel physically ill on the day the presentation is due.

The mind recoils from pain, avoiding it for as long as possible. That might sound strange, as our suffering happens in the mind, arising from the negative stories we tell ourselves. But what is meant here is: the mind avoids pain you once experienced. Or it has no access to the source of the pain memory. Adults who have been very traumatized in their youth cannot always remember what happened. The pain a woman endures during childbirth cannot be recalled and felt again. It makes sense that we should prevent reliving our pains, again and again. The mind only wants to serve your best interest. This also explains why analysing and talking about trauma alone doesn't help you get closer to the place in your body where pain is stored.

When we suffer through our thought narratives, the mind keeps us in that loop to prevent us from feeling and opening up to a deeper level. It prevents us from reliving a painful old memory. The mind is reactive, not proactive, and operates at a superficial level while we are unaware of its beauty. It reacts to what is given: a thought that is negative stays negative until you actively decide to cancel that narrative. At a superficial level you can distract yourself and push the thought away. However, with that reaction, you also avoid the message that has been given to you.

The mind loves what is familiar. It repeats the same ideas, narratives, and logic, as a diligent servant of your best interest. It can only open up to new insights that are max 10% different from what you belief to be true today. We activate thoughts on why we should avoid something new. The unfamiliar causes an uneasiness we don't like to feel. Instead of examining our response, we shut down and stay where we are, reinforcing the notion that our status quo is good enough. To defend ourselves and resist the unknown, we use frustration, drama, denial, or anger.

Even more important than words are the images we create. Our mind is super imaginative, serving our creative qualities. Children are still masters at this. They can imagine a cup of sand to be the best cake ever tasted, and to them it is real. Growing up, our creative imagination gets lost along the way. Our collective (belief) systems push us into rational and factual thinking – factual according to the beliefs it perpetuates. We do fantasize, but that is not the same as imagining. With fantasy we still don't believe it is real. What we don't realize is that our thoughts and mental images contribute to our daily reality. We see the world as *we* are. Whether these ideas and thoughts are helpful or not makes no difference to the mind, it cannot tell the difference. Remember, the mind simply watches out for your best interest!

Living in a world where most of us are operating only *from* the mind, we keep each other *in* that state-of-mind. We argue using facts and evidence but ignore underlying truths due to the limited perspectives we can receive. We are stuck in a mind battle. In the year 2020 it played out in an information battle, which only pushed us more into our mind. But nothing is new. We have been doing so for a long time. We often argue in ways that were proven in the past. When a person states an idea, they need to show proof within the belief system that is commonly accepted. This stifles growth and stagnates creativity, those things our world needs most. Imagine what could happen if we were able to cross-pollinate various experts and knowledge.

Currently our world is full of experts in individual sciences and systems. The problem is that they do not easily understand each other .... Once we bring together the understandings of multiple spheres, physics and economics, mysticism and psychology, music and politics, we will see the higher view, and we can design a world based on higher evolutionary patterns.

Richard Rudd

This is not to dismiss or downgrade the mind. Not at all, the mind is a brilliant instrument. It connects and translates our inner and outer world. Once we understand the role of mind, we can recognize (awaken) which beliefs we want to keep and stop the limiting ones from running our lives on autopilot. We are more than our mind. If we can open up to including our sensory input, we receive more valuable information and learn to discern what pushes our frequency down.

Happiness comes from within

We all say we desire happiness. We eagerly try to find it in more possessions, more money, a better job, a better relationship, an hour of meditation and so on. Nothing outside yourself, not even the most perfect partner of your dreams, will make you happy. Happiness comes from within. Meditation is a great start, but not if it's only an isolated exercise. Can you make life a living meditation? Can you imagine more of what you want to happen in your life by fully embodying this reality, even before it actually happens?

We all have an understanding that things or people cannot make us happy, but instead of shifting the dynamic or exploring more what we are *not* seeing, we have convinced ourselves that true happiness is an illusion. So we settle for less. That is our rationalizing mind telling us we shouldn't change a thing. Not because the mind doesn't want us to be happy, but because the mind is not wired to seek something that is unfamiliar. The mind repeats patterns or programs as the only thing it knows. You cannot ask a computer program to run a different program all by itself. What we need to do is plug in the right ones that work for us.

Triggers

We love to have life under control. That is why our mind works overtime to keep us safe and secure. It doesn't matter if you are an intellectual who knows it all or a sensitive empath, as long as our mind overrules other systems we have, we are not able to find the peace and ease we all long for.

Whether we like it or not, our life is mostly run by our emotions, due to the chemicals that get released in our system. To awaken ourselves is to grow our awareness of our emotional state in every single second and learn to navigate. Our inner system is so brilliant it even created an inner learning system to help us grow.

When we raise our awareness of ourselves, we raise our vibrational state, we are less sensitive to the turmoil of our emotions. We all experience this, though we are not all conscious of it. We have good days, where everything flows, feels good and ends with you feeling happy, relaxed and satisfied. The next day the opposite is your reality. Has anything changed in your beliefs? Most likely not. What did happen, you were triggered by something, consciously or unconsciously. It can be a dream, one word you read, a remark, a memory or a pain in your body, or anything else that you picked up in your environment. Something in your emotional centre was triggered and you let yourself drop in vibration.

As long as our operating system is reactive to impulses (triggers), we are sensitive to emotional shifts. It is not the shift that is the issue, it is the unawareness of the shift. And it is the lack of understanding of how we react unconsciously with old patterns. A trigger happens in a split second. It pushes a feeling of dis-ease and an automated reaction. And in return we receive a reaction from our environment, or translate the information negatively, which triggers again, and so on. The cycle repeats itself, but not in an upward spiral. Before you know it, you feel less relaxed. A person who is wired with a positive mindset does have a huge advantage in the world today, but that doesn't make the person more awake, it only helps temporarily but it is not the complete solution.

We live life in a fragmented way

We are not in the well of suffering all the time. We actually know how life works *for* us. We do it all the time. There are many areas in each of our lives where there are no issues, no trigger events to spoil it. These areas are almost unnoticeable to you as they feel so natural. Where life goes easily and smoothly, we don't have an attachment to a belief system that holds us back, no fear or no stories we are not good enough. There is simply no question. We deserve it, so we create it very naturally. In the same way we create what we don't like to happen. We can learn a lot about our beliefs if we examine where life is in flow naturally and where it still feels stuck. How can you take the same naturalness with you in other areas to create more flow? It is the same you, it only differs in beliefs about yourself.

It was 2011, I was stuck. I saw no way out of my little world that felt painful to me. I had a great life, blessed with beautiful children, a loving husband, comfortable in many ways, many friends, in good health, travelled the world. That well-known dilemma: you have it all but you are not happy. Well, I was more than not happy. It suffocated me. I called a dear family friend who I knew to be an excellent therapist and someone I trusted. We conducted an experiment, I believe it was the second session.

Two chairs were placed opposite each other. I had to sit on both, one after the other. On each chair I had to feel whatever was presented in my awareness represented me. Then, while I was sitting on one of the two chairs, she asked: 'connect with your heart, what do you see?' while pointing at the other chair. 'Did she ask me to connect with a chair that represents me and I can connect with, from my heart?', I questioned internally.

My mind wanted to deny the idea at first. But then I felt fear, as I couldn't connect with my heart. Then I felt shame. I, the perfectionist, who knows best, who could get any job, who is a loving mother, who is sweet and gentle. I realized in one devastating second: I had lost the connection with my heart. Worse, I couldn't even feel it. Worse still, I never really felt it. I had lived 43 years and in that moment, I knew I had missed something vital.

It took me quite a while to understand it was not my fault I missed it. I had never learned, or I unlearned it, growing up. And I knew I was not the only one! How painful this realization is. Of course I knew I was not a heartless person, but it was a weird and an unreal idea that sensitivity, love, kindness are all there, without a conscious awareness of being connected with my heart-centre. Understanding that a connection was going to make all the difference was not the same as being consciously connected with my heart. This took quite a while, as my mind was so strong and active. However, this was the first time I realized how unconsciously we live life. These therapy sessions were so immensely valuable. I knew there was more to life. I knew that embodiment at a deeper level was necessary for me. It led to my instinctive push to invite the right guide to clear my house, in 2012.

When our mind is dominating our lives, we approach everything in a fragmented way. That is how it works for the mind. We have a body, with body parts, organs, five senses, etc. We have emotions. We know love, but that is more related to feelings, experiences and relationships. We have a brain that supports us with logic and analyses. We have a mind that confirms to us what to do. Perhaps that's oversimplified, but in general, we approach all parts separately and take most of them for granted. For example, when we have flu, we don't explore our emotional state, our beliefs, fears or environment, to find what brought our system out of balance. Instead, we blame it on the weather or someone else who spread flu around. Our societal systems are designed in the same way. All separate entities, separate subjects, separate problems, separate solutions (more in Chapter 4).

As long as our mind defines our life, we will not feel the need to explore the depth of other elements and connect the dots! We will stay reactive to outer impulses and avoid inner discomfort. We keep confirming our beliefs and repeating the patterns on autopilot.

To shift from a dominating mind-driven system to an embodied operating system requires understanding and practice. That is why awakening is a conscious choice. With anything we like to change, whether it is becoming more fit, losing weight, a loving connection with our partner, we need an inner desire to make the change irreversible. Often we need pain to activate this desire for change. And we have what we asked for, collectively and individually, in 2020, the start of the pandemic.

Our fear has come to the surface

In decades past many of us realized, more and more, that something had to change. We opened up to the field of personal development, behavioural science, deepened our leadership skills, embraced meditation and mindfulness, applied new healing methodologies, enriched ourselves with ancient spiritual teachings and so much more. We are moving and growing.

Until 2020, we did this in a very relaxed way. We chose from what was offered, depending on our own path and mostly in areas that felt comfortable or needed attention. Then came 2020 and the world was stopped. Independent of what you explored before or whether you didn't open up at all, we were all faced with our deepest fears.

The virus showed up in many ways, affecting each one of us differently. It let us experience where our immune system is unstable, weak, denied or ignored, but it went way beyond our physical immune system. Our resilience, our frequency, our awareness, our physical condition, our trust in life, in our ourselves and in our systems, our relationships, our family issues and many more areas, were all challenged and tested. Each one of us faced deep pains, even if you didn't feel them or did your best to ignore them. We all lost something or someone and our lives were turned upside down – or is it better to say inside out?

What was shown as well is that our planet doesn't need us at all. With a world in lockdown, nature thrived. What does that tell us about our manmade, controlled and superior way of living? What is it that will make us thrive? Have we been missing something?

Although we don't agree at all about beliefs, ideas and solutions, we all have felt in 2020 that we will not go back to how it was. Even for those who cannot describe why, there is a subtle knowing that something has to change. Unconsciously we know that our values and beliefs will have to yield and transform. With that, our systems will give way and become obsolete, as they will no longer serve our new values.

We will all die, but not necessarily the death we think or fear. Many resist the big change, not willingly, but fear has made them numb, unable to open up. Anxiously grasping for facts, to believe the story that's been told, no matter what side you were on. We all have our own path and our own free will. For some that path might lead to a physical death, for others it will be a huge breakthrough and life-changing times. That is for all time – any great change or shift comes with loss as well as growth.

Whatever our path is, the theme is fear in its broadest sense. We are ending an era where fear has run our lives. It is unavoidable and at the same it is unknown. The moment we see through it, whatever it is that each of us needs to see through, we are instantly released from the first layer and will shift in frequency. Fear is just fear, a frequency, that lives in the mind and keeps our system stuck because we have put fear into words, stories, beliefs, into 'something we fear'. Our fragmented approach prevents us from seeing what is happening, as we cannot rise to a state of observation and neutrality.

We will personally and collectively go through a process of letting go of any attachments that limit us in feeling free. It is like shedding all the layers we have felt protected by. Our *attachment* to eons of programmed patterns and beliefs will have to die collectively. This purifying process will go through each one us.

It goes way beyond personal beliefs. All attachments have to be released, to embrace life again, to unite. But at first it feels as if we failed ourselves, life failed us, we failed each other, our systems failed us. They all did – and didn't at all, a painful but beautiful paradox. When we feel we have nothing to grab, nothing to hold onto, and that no one will catch us, we connect with our deepest fear: our fear of having to surrender and trust our-Self. When we surrender, with each layer, something in us dies – but only to awaken us to a much greater and empowered Self. Awakening is to die before you die.

Deepen the inner connection

Rewiring ourselves in being one with the Self is where we define the difference between personal development and self-realization. Within personal development we stay within the persona, we do our work within the boundaries of our mind. With personality tests we can understand and work on our unconscious patterns and behavioural reactions. However, it doesn't matter how much insight we gain and change within the persona, we can never gain the complete depth that is required to liberate and empower ourselves. In fact, we risk deluding ourselves by creating a false safety again. As we have seen earlier, our mind will always protect us from feeling our deepest pain.

It makes sense why it doesn't work, for two reasons: one is that the persona, that is made up of beliefs, created the limitation in the first place! Secondly, when you are brave enough to let go of many limiting feelings within your persona, what is left at the end of the road? Nothing! Then you become no-one, at least, that is what you fear. That is too scary, so we build in some boundaries, not to surrender ourselves too far. You will hold on to those beliefs, avoiding what could open-up deep pains. It makes sense but doesn't help us when we wish to be freed from those pains. We enter the repetitive cycle again, keeping in place the belief that holds us back most.

Trauma work is always part of the path of self-realization,
yet not all trauma work leads to the same liberation.
Ultimately, only the sense of Self matters, all the rest
is an inevitable result and part of the process.

As we cannot solve our lives with the mind that created the problem, we have to go deeper to find the root cause, the core of our wound. The solidness and knowingness it brings, that your true nature – the Self – is who you are, beyond your mortal body, enables you to conquer anything. Only then can you truly surrender and see the root pain of your challenges. When you find this root cause, it is released in a second. This moment of epiphany, suddenly seeing through your own veil of beliefs, is when you feel the shift happening in your body, bringing a deep sense of release and heals pain you felt for so long.

As our mind is so strong, our beliefs so real to us and our patterns so automated, we very possibly need several iterations of these inner processes, to locate core woundings in areas that hold us back most. Self-honesty and self-reflecting abilities are undoubtedly needed, but lacking in many of us today.

Opening up to the path of self-realization and liberation, we will use many different solutions to support our journey. All these different solutions, including this book, are temporary permission slips to guide us. Our mind needs an outside perspective, a practice, a teaching, to answer questions. Who am I, why am I here, what is my purpose? What are my gifts and what is holding me back? Is it my brain that causes all this? Under what star constellation am I born and what does that tell me? How does my blueprint look? What are my personality traits? What is enlightenment? Am I awakened? How do I know my path? Can I heal myself, and how? Why is that one thing I desire so much not happening? Who are my angels, my guides? Am I connected to a Galactic family? Is there anything out there in space?

The list is long and diverse! Permission slips such as these are needed right now to support our collective human awakening.

But! Stay honest with yourself and watch out for when a method, a guidance, a teacher, or anything you use, becomes just another belief system and no longer works for you! The moment you proclaim these insights to another person as an absolute truth, you know it has become your dogma! Dogma limits your expansiveness and your growth. Everything we experience or see is only a perspective. A perspective that is only a reality in *that* particular state of being, in that vibrating frequency.

When we are able to feel consistently more connected with the Self and fully present and active in our daily lives, we are entering a new paradigm, a new way of living. No longer will we perceive others as separate, as we know that we are all interconnected. From that state we can feel our own empowerment and alignment. We start to reverse our dynamic, from inside-out we will move. Even though this is a process and the inner alignment is not always constant, we can start exploring. Knowing that we have touched something that is golden to us. That part that is immortal and gives us the fearlessness needed to let go of anything that restricts us and keeps us small.

Integrated embodied Self

Our mind is not the problem in all this. We need our mind, to make things happen, to live, to direct ourselves, to set intention, to be committed. These are all qualities of the ego part of our mind. However, we must not get lost in our mind or be misled by it. Observation is key. Observation gives us the quality of neutrality. The neutral zone is the essence for manifestation, as we will see later. First we will have to ease our emotional turmoil. That can only be achieved by a fully integrated approach.

When we live in and from the mind, we have little to no awareness of the body. We only notice the obvious things: hunger, pain, itches, tiredness, perhaps tension or nervousness, joy or lightness, and so on. But only when these sensations are so present that we cannot ignore them. Most of the time we don't even notice or automatically dismiss the signs. A lot of these patterns are inherited and reconfirmed again in our youth. 'Don't cry, it's okay', 'don't be so sensitive, it will soon be over', 'it's not time to eat, you will have to wait', 'don't be nervous, you will be fine', and many more. It is not that the advice was wrong per se, but we were repeatedly directed away from the signals our body gave us. Or they were ridiculed and not taken seriously.

When we live in and from the mind, we have little access to real empathy. We are so busy with ourselves, thinking that we listen or care, but we don't. It is quite a challenge to be *fully present*, without any agenda of our own.

My son, 15, got drunk one night and did something stupid; it was very innocent but it felt like a huge mistake to him, sincere as he is. He couldn't forgive himself, struggled with life and was on the edge. His father and I had just separated a few months before. He felt so lost and let down by the ones he loves most! He sank into an intense depression. A few weeks later, he woke me up. Again, in complete despair, his eyes were filled with fear and panic.

A calmness came over me and I sat at the end of his bed, in pure presence. I knew that I should not save him, that he should make the decision for himself. I knew him so well, his strong inner power was perhaps disconnected, but it was still there. It was up to him to choose.

63

I told him that I love him, either way, whatever he chooses to do. It was silent for a long time. Slowly he came back, his eyes told me more than any words could have done. He made a very conscious choice to live, there was no doubt.

Steadily he took his steps, all by himself, with the great support and patience of his siblings, his father, a therapist and me. About a year-and-a-half later he said to me: I am okay again. His eyes are ever shining, he's grown so much in his emotional awareness and is happy to be alive. A great life is in store for him and no doubt it will be impactful. I am so proud of him!

Presence is the embodied Self! Presence is the unconditional space where pure life is felt. Presence is the only state where we can objectively observe what is happening without any expectation. There is no doing in presence, only being. It is unconditional love. It is the space that heals, where we can surrender that which is stuck to a higher frequency field that presence offers.

When we are unaware of our present moment, we are not present in the only reality there is. That seems kind of weird, as we feel alive while being unaware, so where are we then? Our body with its consciousness, the Self, is always present in the NOW. Our mind is either in the past or in the future, thinking of something that is not a reality in that moment. Even if we are not aware of our senses every nano second, it doesn't mean we're not picking up information, we are just too busy to perceive it.

To understand the struggle between presence and our mind, the analogy of the video game is a good one. A video game has three levels: you are the character in the game, you are the gamer, or you are the programmer who designed the game.

*Being one with the **game-character** is the same as being one with your persona. That's what we all are most of the time. From that perspective you use your skills, experiences, your five senses, knowledge, defence weapons (mechanism) to survive in the game, just as we do constantly in life.*

Something happens outside of us and we react. When the game character is caught up in his thoughts, it weakens his position. As a character you are unaware of the Self (the gamer is the Self), but you have glimpses of where you feel something else in your game-life is leading you as well. The other characters in the game are just as busy with themselves as you are. And together you try to control the events, hope you are winning the game. Some are more competitive than others and need to win, some feel others always win. Luckily, in a video game, you have more than one life. Which, by the way, is not so far from our reality; remember, we 'die before we die'.

*Being **the gamer** is like being the Self of your game-character. You are well aware of your physical traits and weak spots, you have a better overview of the whole playing field (zooming out) to navigate through the game. The gamer needs to be very present (presence!) or the game loses its momentum. Too much distraction from thoughts will risk losing the game. To play well, the gamer uses many sources of information he picks up in the (game) field to make decisions. Intuition is key, synchronicity follows naturally. The gamer knows he is not in control of other game-characters, he cannot change them and knows that flow and resilience brings more to the game then losing energy on (useless) fights with others.*

*Now we are **the programmer** of the game. We zoom out even more. Here we can observe all levels, even the Self (the gamer) and of course the whole playing field, from various perspectives. What is the game we like to play? What game is being played that is designed by life? Do we like all the characters or what role do they play for the Self? What can the Self learn or experience? Do we like to redesign our game and create a new one? Being the programmer is being the creator in life, of course within limits of the natural technology (universal laws) and our inner purpose of the Self.*

Each moment is a seed from where a future is born and can grow into a completely different game. Each activity starts with a seed, planted in a single moment. Something as little as a thought that makes you move to get groceries, gives you input for new seeds. In that single point in time, you could have followed many other thoughts or hints, which would have brought you other experiences. Being present means not interfering with what is happening, only to observe and respond. For so long we have tried to interfere constantly with life. We plan, we expect, we direct. There is a constant pressure on us to make it all happen, which not only costs a huge amount of energy, but most of that energy is completely wasted on thoughts alone, with little action.

When we sense the field while in presence, we will hear our intuitive ideas. We will open up to other sources of information, the wisdom of our higher Self, of our collective consciousness. The exceptional cases, where little children become concert pianists, is not just talent; the child is linked to information from the field and is able to translate and put it into use. In our current reality that is an exception. Once we collectively move to higher frequencies, it will become more commonplace. What if you can work with more sources of information than just the knowledge your education and life experiences have taught you? You will not only step into the role of gamer, but you will also become the programmer. You will become conscious of your role as the programmer of your life. How does your life look, in your design?

Staying in this ultimate now moment, being fully present, is challenging. Perhaps less so during a dedicated meditation, but can you stay present while doing your normal chores, while being in a conversation with others, while being in a heated argument, while being ill? As soon as we are connected to things happening outside of us, we lose our present awareness, our presence. The chatter in our mind and being busy controlling life is just as distracting as watching a thriller movie, where you can get completely caught up.

Without feeling connected with the Self, without living from our inner centres, we will never give up our controlling mind. Without this deep inner connection, we will feel lost and can only rely on our mind.

Connecting with the Self is like rewiring and changing your operating system. That requires some time and focus, until the inner connection becomes your new normal. Then you will operate with one eye looking to the inside and one eye toward the outer world, having a constant inner alignment while being very active with all that happens in your daily life. It takes practice, but we didn't learn to walk in a day. Remember the proud face of a toddler when he takes his first steps – soon he's using every minute to practice. You will have the same smile on your face when you feel the overwhelming wave of love washing over you. Home again.

Stages of the embodied Self

When we learn to ride a bike, we don't start on a mountain bike. First we use one with trainer-wheels that give us support. The same goes for deepening the described process of inner change. Resistance is a funny thing. It is a result of our deep victim programming of self-sabotage. We choose pain over pleasure and suffering over freedom. Only by acknowledging this human trait can we make our path lighter. More importantly, the first layer of resistance will dissolve with it.

The second step is: learn to sense, in its broadest definition. We are all different, but we all prefer an easy path. Do the opposite, start exploring the road that shows resistance. Where do you feel tension, where do you let yourself be distracted? These are the moments you hit on something.

The third step is to experience a release of what feels stuck, physically or mentally. This process of letting go, releasing, purging, clearing, is essentially about something you want to get rid of. It can even have a physical expression, like vomiting, as if you felt choked and needed to get it out of your system. And don't be surprised if you start to burp regularly.

The fourth step is realizing it all needs to be generated through your system, through the physical body. It is a reverse movement from the third step, subtle, but nevertheless a reversal. It is the knowing that we are the human experience. The only thing that makes us human is the genius body with which we are born. It is designed to be alive and stay alive. It is the fractal of the whole, a copy of all elements and dynamics, in your personal version. It knows how to integrate all our human experiences and heal itself. The deepest layer of our healing process is taking it all in, what we wish to let go, and it all will be dissolved and transformed, inside of ourselves. That is deep cleansing of our DNA. We take it all in, we take full responsibility for any aspect we don't want, any human trait that doesn't feel humanly right. We swallow what we don't want anymore and give full trust to our body to heal it all.

Changing our operating system: inside-out

Now we have more understanding or even an embodied experience of what the Self is, we can open ourselves to rewiring our operating system, that drives our behaviour. Those more familiar with spiritual teachings probably hear 'shift from mind to heart'; to shift from 'the mind runs the show' to 'the Self (or heart) runs the show'. Well, it doesn't seem to be so clear cut and hardly ever is. Meeting in the middle seems a better way. What will be shifting is where we start from and what is leading in any moment. To feel where we operate from, we can best look at the way we make a decision. From our mind we follow a linear sequence, from the Self we follow an instantaneous thought.

Here is an example:

you go out to meet a friend. The linear way would be: check your keys, your phone. Then the thought of taking an umbrella comes up, but as it is a sunny day you leave the house without it. On your way home you get soaked by an unexpected change in the weather.

●

Alternatively: while you leave the house and notice the sun is shining, the thought comes up to bring an umbrella. You follow up on the (intuitive) idea and on the way back you were happy you did.

Note here that the thought in both operating systems is the same. When our mind is leading we translate it with logic and the information we consider in that moment (the sun is shining). When our Self is leading, we take the information as neutral and valid.

From a controlling point of view, one might not be able to see the benefit of a more Self-based operating system. However, the mind operating system knows only what the mind (and brain) knows. That means we are completely dependent on memory, analytics, and logical abilities. Intuition is known to all of us, but not considered reliable. Would one use intuitive knowing within a business meeting, to make a fundamental decision? We'd have to support it with 'facts' before we act upon it. In today's world we define facts as something measurable and proven by science, experts, authorities or our own five senses. That is all in the linear sequencing of the mind. For us to make a shift into trusting other, extra senses is a huge step to take. The first thing we automatically say to ourselves (or others), 'prove it'. And that is precisely what blocks the intuitive abilities!

We all have psychic abilities but they are often suppressed by our system and its dominating beliefs. Psychic abilities are seeing, feeling, hearing, or sensing beyond the boundaries of our currently perceived physical world. We may already use them without our knowing, picking-up information from the collective field through what we perceive as our thought. We don't know where our thoughts are from and whether they come from an area within our brain. We don't even know where our mind is 'located', yet we use it all the time. An intuitive hint, a knowing, an epiphany – they all appear as thoughts. Our mind is, as said, a perfect translator, analyser and can follow logic, as long as it stays objective, uninfluenced by a belief.

Young children show psychic capabilities but often are ridiculed for it. If we would let them explore life in their own flow and support these abilities, our educational system would have to shift radically. Home schooled children guided by conscious parents, for example, learn to read within days once they find inner motivation and purpose. They can share wisdom on a topic they've never encountered before or they start their own business at the age of 12 simply because they feel inspired.

If our mind operating system uses information from our outer world alone, we translate information based on comparison, judgement, achievement, linear patterns, and our belief systems. If this one is leading, outside-in, we keep being more reactive than proactive. When we shift to inside-out, from an embodied Self, we will perceive a more complete view of what is happening. From within we can sense what drives us, what blocks us, what we feel, what excites us, what we are compelled to do. Now we can be more proactive than reactive. Does that make our mind redundant? On the contrary, our mind will become super clear in translating what we sense into practical ideas and actions. That is where the three, mind-body-Self, meet in the middle.

When we take our first steps in shifting the operating system to a more embodied, Self-centred one, a world of synchronicities opens up. Following our inner excitement and alignment will make us move in a non-linear way (according to the logical mind) but once consistent with it, it soon makes sense of why we direct our energy a certain way. Best of all, it costs way less energy than the controlling and linear thinking patterns of the mind, like doubting, hesitating, planning, checking, finding facts.

Activate Self-healing

When I felt sick as a child, my mother often quoted her father (a hospital nurse): 'if you don't do anything it takes 14 days, if you take a pill it takes two weeks.'

That I experienced the benefit of rest, instead of automatically taking a pill, certainly helped me to have a different outlook on health. Nevertheless, I had my fair share of illnesses and chronic headaches over the years.

I am not at all opposed to our western medical solutions, but the fragmented and single-minded approach doesn't seem the only and not always the best way.

Since 2012, I own my actions and choices. I honour my body's genius abilities to heal dis-ease. I know when I ignored my inner signs for too long. This shift feels very empowering, energizing and has resulted in no illnesses or infections at all. Do I know and heal everything? No, the environment we live in is complex and supporting care for my body is still needed at times.

To me, it is of no use to hang on to fears and beliefs around health and aging. I reversed the process, from outside-in to inside-out and so far it really works for me.

There is so much we don't know! There is so much we are not supposed to know. We live in systems where others dictate what is good for us and what we're expected to learn, eat, or see as the best solution. We live in societies where science defines what health is. Our lives are rooted in fear, we even fear our own body. Fear, as in: we don't trust it, we don't collaborate with it, we don't perceive it as beautiful, we don't worship it, we don't celebrate it. We simply take it for granted. This leads to challenges in many areas of our life: our sexual intimacy, our struggle with weight and looks, our self-esteem, our health, our self-worth.

Our social norms define our ideal weight, not our natural weight. Some people can feel highly energized with a body that is according to our norm 'heavier', while a skinny person can feel constantly drained and is considered 'healthy'. Feeling energized, active, fit, with a clear mind that feels inspired, creative and open, is a healthy system, whatever the weight or shape it comes in.

Our body has a natural ability to heal itself, it shows in so many ways. It can heal a cut, a broken bone, rid itself of flu or an infection. Why is it in essence different when we are confronted with more severe illnesses? Could it be that we have missed some signs? Have we overlooked something indirectly related, like stress, emotional burden, grief, a bad habit, change in environment or toxins in our food, that might have led to this disease? Could we just be okay in not knowing and shift to trusting and activating our self-healing abilities, in the same way as when we heal a broken bone? We might live longer on average but that is more a result of wealth and improved living circumstances than of healthy living habits. We eat less healthily and too much, struggle with stress and emotional dis-eases; we move less, disconnected from nature and we love the easy remedy of a chemical pill.

The secret behind any healing modality is a higher vibrating frequency and holistic view. Whether that frequency field is offered by someone else or by yourself, it is still up to you to allow healing to happen. A higher vibrating energy releases what was stuck in a lower frequency. Healing can happen instantly, it shifts the vibrating frequency. Become aware of the frequency of the support you welcome. Make a conscious choice. Short term chemicals might be useful to release the system of severe pain or infection, but what is your long-term solution?

Reflecting on your own limiting beliefs around this subject, becoming aware of the rationalizing (or reasoning) arguments of your mind that prevent you from exploring new ideas, is a start to healing your relationship with your body. Listen to your body. Its language is loud and clear. This topic is linked to many other belief systems. For example, we know we need some rest as we have been working too hard, but we feel we need to show up, to avoid comments, not lose our job and to maintain our place socially. The opposite is also true: we hide behind our illness, dwelling in our sorrow as we don't own our life and our body. We judge others as much as we judge ourselves on this topic.

This is not an easy topic for many of us. We all have lost someone to illness. We need proof before we trust that we can heal ourselves of any disease. If someone does recover from a severe illness, we call it a miracle. A miracle from where, from who? Again we attribute it to something external. And as the next person dies, it reconfirms our earlier beliefs.

We will not see proof the first instant we give it a try. We won't heal everything at once, in the same way we don't get all illnesses at once. But are we willing to make a start?

Immunity is decided by your frequency, not by exposure.
Jacqueline Hobbs

Our physical system is challenged by unhealthy environments, and we (silently) support the actions of corporations and our governments who have priorities other than our health. Like chemical solutions spread on our lands and in the air we breathe. High frequency networks are rolled out to provide us with 'the internet of things' and we have little idea of the consequence. The exposure to environmental change doesn't make you ill by definition, your own frequency defines your vulnerability. Again, we have to reverse the process: from outside-in to inside-out.

The moment we activate our self-healing mechanism, we will open up to a new view on aging, health, and food. We will discover the power of our breath and immune system (the Wim Hof Method, for example). We will eat intuitively. And so much more. It is time to stop taking our amazing vehicle for granted and start honouring its abilities. A holistic approach is required to open up all our energy centres and awaken to a higher frequency.

Consciously choose your frequency and develop your inner compass

To navigate through life in an embodied way, it is is not enough to meditate in the morning and forget this inner alignment the rest of the day, thinking you are awakened. It helps to start your day with an inner alignment practice, but staying with it through your day is where life really shifts!

We have a genius system within ourselves to guide us. But, our overstimulating, stressful world numbs the senses in many ways, that is why we can't read the genius communication from our inner world. As long as our sensory connection is lacking, everything in life remains a struggle and our excitement feels weak and unstable. We need our inner senses; we cannot ignore this step. The inner compass is a determiner for life.

Everything is energy and as humans we are part of the collective energy field on our planet like all organisms. We readily pick up and resonate with the frequencies around us. Nevertheless, it is our free will to choose and realize the vibrating state of being, in any given moment. That is what defines how we feel, not the other way around. It is also our responsibility to own who we are and what we do. We cannot blame the outer world for how we feel or for what is done to us! Whatever we pick up in our environment, influences our vibrating field. Depending on our reaction, it lowers or raises our field. That is to say, it influences us but it doesn't need to. How we react is our choice. Do we believe what we feel and react accordingly, or do we decide: 'no, this lowers my vibration, I won't allow that to happen – back into my core alignment and stay in my present moment'. But, be sure you are not avoiding anything, be self-honest and reflective at all times.

Keeping our vibrational field high, embodied and consistent, is where life feels light and empowered. That is the freedom we all desire. That doesn't mean that life is always blissful and joyous. It is our awareness and attitude to *how* we stay present when we deal with painful events. Seeing the insight, or allowing the loss to go through us, releases whatever needs to be released. This is how we show deep respect and compassion to ourselves and those involved. When we go through this process consciously, we will shift back into higher frequencies quite easily and naturally.

Emotional waves are inevitable, but when we are unaware we get sucked into a vortex where our vibrational field is pulled lower. From that state of low vibration it is difficult to be objective. It is not so much the emotion that blinds us, it is our low vibrating field that narrows our perspective. From that narrow perspective we can see only one story, one solution. We blame others for our situation.

In that narrow perspective it is hard to see what the experience shows us. The more we fight ourselves, the longer we stay in this low vibrating field, until we own our state of being. The moment you admit that your perspective might not be beneficial, the moment you can see through beliefs that limit you, the moment you surrender to receiving the painful experience as a gentle gift for growth, that is when you shift and release. These dark painful places can feel super intense, as our mind keeps repeating narratives that keep us low. Were we able to turn off our thoughts, it would only be a physically painful experience which makes it easier to surrender to.

It requires a delicate balance to go through these deep vortexes in an empowered way. The mind could rush you into a fake 'higher vibration'. You push the pain away and force yourself into a better mood, which is not the same as a higher vibration. Dwelling too long in the pain might make you subject to the role of the victim. Over time you will get out of it again but no healing has taken place. Staying very present with what is happening is the only way to surrender and release the pain. Anything that triggers you pulls you into the emotional vortex and is always an opportunity for growth and inner releasing. With practice and awareness these waves become your best teacher. (See core practice at the end of this chapter.)

There are many ways to delve into this matter and neuroscientists, like Andrew Huberman, are uncovering the geniality of our system. It works with many little neuro modulators, designed to pick up signals from our inner and outer world and express them in chemicals that influence our state of being. Another approach, as a guide to raising awareness, is to define our emotional state as our vibrating frequency. Dr David Hawkins is perhaps best known for his Map of Consciousness, explaining all 17 stages, from shame to enlightenment.

These are both amazing insights, worth exploring, but can we simplify it to work with in the moment?

If we wish to raise our awareness and elevate our vibrating frequency consistently, we need a guide that tells us whether our present moment is in resonance or not. Independent of what caused the state we are in, all we need to know is: do we feel it supports us or does it bring us down. No stories, no past experiences, not even beliefs, nothing need be taken into consideration, it is a *sensory* exploration, in or out of alignment.

This requires practice, not be deceived by the mind and old patterns of denial.

•

Never forget, release what feels stuck (conscious breath) in the moment. Sometimes, this stuckness needs more attention, but take these as objective and neutral as possible, don't fall back for too long.

Become more conscious of your six senses – sight, hearing, touch, smell, taste, and intuition – and connect them to your inner reaction. For example, what happens when you hear music you like? How does that feel and where do you feel it within you? And what happens when you hear something that is, for you, out of tune or in tune? Can you notice the moment just prior to that which you recognize as 'sound'? Play with all your senses.

The inner connection with the Self is your true inner compass. The more you learn about your inner sensory world, the easier it will be to sense your Self, the inner field. When we are more aligned with our natural higher frequency, there will be fewer triggers and we become more resilient, as if we ride with the waves of life.

If you don't own your vision, someone else will define it for you.

The beauty is, life always works for you if you let it happen in alignment with who you are. Anything in between an inner clear 'yes' and 'no' is our old pattern of being, a puppet on a string reacting to outer events. When we show up more authentically, aligned, healthy and vibrant and we gain more clarity in our sense of purpose and direction. Simply start by doing more of the things that you love doing, in return, life will show you more opportunities that feel in alignment with you. Your circle of influence will equally benefit and be inspired by it. That creates the ripple effect.

•

Mirror effect: how we move through life

Let's put our years of practice, to look *outside* ourselves, into good use. Observe what you see reflected and then look within, until you can reverse the process naturally. By having an honest and objective look at your own life, you can feel where your movement starts: outside or inside. When we look at our (re-) actions, we can recognize our automated patterns and narratives. The latter brings us back to where we feel attached, the core of all our issues. We have to reverse the process to make progress.

Or, follow a more badass approach. Drop all stories and learn to sense in frequencies. Each time you feel something shifting, pause and be present. It requires radical self-honesty and total ownership over every aspect in your life, your body. It is a process in solitude while you are living your normal life. It is the most simple and pure way. Or use a mixture of both methods. Either way, you have started the shift.

This chapter has touched upon the essence of our being, our natural form. In the next two chapters we will see more of our human *being*, but in the context of interacting with others and how we live together on our planet. It will show us the mirror-effect of life: we learn most if we see the meaning of the reflection. Let's first dive a little deeper and see how we are connected, who we attract and how we interact.

CORE PRACTICE

Presence is the core of all practices

Presence is the physical embodiment of the Now moment, the only experience of reality. Anytime we are not present, we are either in the past, in the future, or distracted by something outside ourselves. Then we play a role in the movie we are not consciously directing ourselves.

The practice:

Sit (or lie down) and become conscious of feeling your body touching the surface.

Then focus on your breath and follow it for a while.

Connect with your inner field, starting at the centre of your chest. Just sense what you feel inside you. Try not to name it or question it.

When you notice you were distracted, take a breath, and focus again on your inner field.

If your chest has a lot of tension (and feels uncomfortable at first), wander around in your body: feel your inner feet, your inner hands, your inner throat, your inner belly, behind your navel.

Repeat this practice as often as you can during the day. It is more helpful to repeat it often, than to sit for a long time just once a day.

You will know when you have connected with the Self, this energy field that has its core in your body but is unlimited in its expansion. Don't give up or get frustrated if you don't feel it yet. Remember, connecting with the Self is the most natural way for us, only we have not been taught.

After a while, when your inner field feels more present, you can practice 'one eye on the inside, on eye to the outside'. Be present 'inside', while you are doing something else: walking, watching a screen, having a conversation, a meeting, reading a book. Play with it.

*Make **presence** your living meditation.*

Release

Sense where you feel tension in your body and bring your attention to that area so your breath will follow. Breathe more consciously and with your breath create more space in that area. Acknowledge anything that comes up but don't dive into a story or an explanation. Insights are useful, but they come by themselves, they appear 'out of nowhere', not through created logic and reasoning.

When you get distracted by thoughts, bring yourself back.

Continue as long as possible until you feel the tension is reduced or released completely.

You can do this for as long as you like, or in the moment while you are being triggered by something.

*If you are new to this, focus more on this practice than **presence** alone. See this practice to reconnect with your body by activating your sensory system. When you have been used to ignoring your inner body, you might feel a lot of tension at first. Don't let this discourage you, it has been your normal way for a long time – now it is time to shift it. That takes some practice and focus.*

Also be aware that you might feel more tension, more emotions, darker moments in the first phase. Old pain is energy that is stuck. When it gets your attention, you might feel it for the first time consciously. Weirdly enough it is easier for us to handle a headache than to be consciously present with the energy in that area. The cause connected to your physical pain is what makes you uncomfortable.

Feel the empowerment getting stronger each time you consciously say yes to yourself. Own your life, your body. Now it is you who is directing your life.

Both release and presence is your base ground, from which to move consistently in an upward spiral, into a higher vibrating frequency.

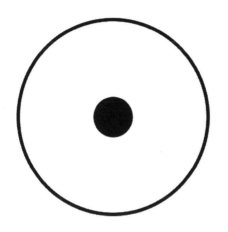

CONNECTING

OUR RELATIONSHIPS,
THEY REFLECT US

3. Connecting

We hardly notice how much impact
we have on each other, the moment we do, everything will shift

Humans are complicated creatures. We love to belong, to be social, to find our intimate partners, yet our relationships reveal so many challenges. Though often unaware of it, we feel the pain of separation in the connection we seek. In other words, it is the disconnection with our Self that is reflected in our relationships. That is the pain we feel, the void we live with. As long as we have no or little sense of Self, more often than not we show up inauthentically and out of alignment. We compensate for this unsettling feeling, either by becoming too egoistic or too compromising, often a mix of both, depending on the relationship. This counts for any relationship we are in. To put it simply, anything that is not healed within ourselves and any gift that is not unleashed, is mirrored by the persons we meet. It is as if we need others to know more about ourselves and our natural alignment with the Self.

A whole new branch of relationship coaches, therapists, tantra experts, communication specialists and mediators has grown rapidly in the past decade. Apparently we are ready to evolve our relationships to another level. Understanding what is happening, the dynamics of relationships, combined with a willingness to own our own challenges, will accelerate this evolution. It is quite a challenge to stay open to these deep processes when not everyone around you is ready to open up at the same time. However, in our journey we need the interaction, the mirror and deep understanding of how we influence each other.

It is relatively easy to feel amazing and liberated on your meditation pillow. Or to stay within the safety of your newly found community with like-minded people. Or live the life in the safe comfort of your bubble. But then you walk into your partner, you call your mother or read a social media post or receive a disappointing message, and something hits (triggers) you. We often don't see the gentle invitation to look inside, rather we use various tactics to avoid inner discomfort. Blaming, anger, agitation, advising, knowing best, falling silent, pleasing, being bossy, ignoring, gaslighting ... the list is long. All ways to project it outwardly, in what feels like a temporary release. Meanwhile, we are not aware that we have dropped in our vibrating frequency. In that lower vibration, we fall back into old patterns of avoidance of our inner Self. If we would fully own the source of our projection, our pain, we would never project anything negative on anyone else. Instead we keep recreating our drama, our victim role, as it is our comfort space, where we don't feel we need to own anything. But it is a false safety. We all desire to be seen for who we are! We fail to see that our best teachers are all around us.

Souls learn from other souls, not from books or lectures.

Rumi

All trauma is ours to feel and to heal. The relationship, the other, offers a space to go through that process, by ourselves, and not to drag the other into our pain. But, the same counts for the other side, right? We all desire the same, to liberate ourselves and explore our gifts and natural expression. Even for those who are completely unaware of themselves. As we don't always travel together on this journey, it really helps to approach it with openness, lightness and some humour, to see through our own drama or ego play. Don't wait for the other to change.

'You complete me' is what we will leave behind and we will shift into: I complete myself and thank you for showing me and being my teacher. We are always the teacher and the student at the same time, as in a dance. What will shift is our emotional co-dependency. Any behaviour that shows some form of dishonesty is avoidance of inner pain or the lack of our authentic expression. To take full ownership, we need to grow up emotionally. That is the current phase of the awakening in our evolutionary journey as mankind.

When we move towards a higher vibrational field, the dynamic in a relationship cannot be other than different. We will explore new levels, in more depth, move faster through cycles together and live more in the present moment to experience the beauty life offers. We will learn to be more unique in our individuality, while we move to a new level of connectedness through learning what intimacy actually is, keeping our heart open, no matter what. It is scarier than being physically intimate with someone you fall in love with. Only through a deep understanding of our relationships we will truly experience what thriving is, as we all will thrive.

'Which is more important', asked Big Panda, 'the journey or the destination?'
'The company', said Tiny Dragon.

James Norbury

This chapter will get to the core of the dynamics within our relationships. This is a crucial element in understanding how life works. You will realize that all the people you attracted in your life played, and often still play, a role. And without doubt, you do (or did) the same for them.

> *Three times in my life I have been confronted with an unexpected outburst of a close friend who, out of the blue, ended the friendship. I know I am not a perfect friend and I do have my flaws, even more so when I was less aware of my own role, but I have never been mean to anyone. Needless to say, it has hurt me immensely.*
>
> *What and how it all happened is less relevant than what it showed me. I seem to radiate something that triggers another person at a deeper point than the regular level of friendship. I have a strong sensitivity for dishonesty. When something feels out of tune I sense it immediately. This dishonesty gives me an immediate discomfort which shows (non-verbally)*

in my facial expression and posture before I am even aware of it. The dishonesty can be within me or with the other, that is not always clear. But my reaction has its effect on the interaction. It is often impossible to point out the dishonesty but once it has come to the surface, it lingers between me and the other. Next to all that, when I do speak up or address anything that is a little more sensitive, my emotions show up strongly and can be overpowering.

The three break ups didn't leave me in resentment. I guess I am not so susceptible to resentment. But I am to injustice. For a while after each break up, I felt powerless as I was suddenly rejected without any opportunity to talk or counteract. Each of them simply disappeared from my life.

Well, one friend came back, after ten years. I felt no need to go through the old events. I could feel that we both had done our inner work. At the time, she had shown me that I needed to show more of myself, step into my own power, own my life. Our breakup was one of the major events that led to my awakening in 2012.

Who do we attract in life?

The people we meet reflect the answers we seek.

Anon.

Understanding how we attract people in our lives gives a whole new perspective on our relationships. As we act on autopilot for at least 95% of the time, one can only imagine how little we are aware of our field of attraction, in the broadest sense. It is our vibrating field, sending signals to the world, messages of our inner beliefs, fears, and gifts we desire to unlock. We are little conscious of this process at all its levels.

You attract people in your field that respond to the frequency you exude, and you attract people that can show you lessons or insights your inner self wants to learn. The people you draw into your life respond to that field, either as they share the same beliefs and similar fears or they show you the opposite, the opportunity to unlock your gifts, and often a combination of both.

You also attract people you cannot accept with the understanding of your mind. They might enter your life for a beautiful ride but your inner fear makes you push that person away, opportunity missed! Those who hope to find their new partner are often unaware that their signals are the opposite of what they desire. A vibration of 'I am afraid to commit' or 'I am not worth being loved', might not be present in your mind but can still be present in the energy of your system. The mind has its role to protect you, so it will come up with reasons to dismiss people who don't fit the criteria. By exploring our attraction field in more intuitive ways, we can surpass our mind, which has little idea of who is the perfect person to meet (partner, new friend, new business partner etc).

The repetitive cycle of abusive relationships might not apply to you, but that doesn't mean you're not affected by the dynamic of repeating patterns. We keep repeating a pattern until we see through it. Not just with our partners, also with friends, colleagues, workplaces, and at its deepest level with our family. All people you attract offer you a field of information by which to unlock yourself and reconnect with the Self. Embracing this perspective will make you value your relationships more and you will be able to choose more consciously to leave some behind, as those relationships no longer serve you. It is impossible to give a definition of when a relationship no longer serves you, you can only decide that for yourself.

The people you meet are either reflections of a repeated cycle or guides towards a new start. Notice the difference.

Anon.

Meeting the right people at the right time happens in various ways. Some people cross our paths without us even being aware. A connection can be a short interaction in a park that gives you the clarity you have been seeking. Others we meet without understanding but there is a deep recognition that it is right.

What if we really just trust that the people we meet reflect the answers we seek? That means trusting our unconscious, the Self. What if we would trust that life always creates a positive outcome? Who would we meet? Can we let go of time and expectation? Can we let go of our desire to control the outcome, which is always based on the limited thinking of our mind? Can we trust that the partner we meet, because we feel attracted at a deep level, might not fit our expected checklist, but could well be the perfect partner for us at this moment in time? What if that person shows you a side of yourself you were not yet aware of? This might mean a radical shift (from outside-in to inside-out) and it might cause some bumps in the road, but if we follow our journey naturally, it will be in an upward spiral.

In our current societies we use persona characteristics to open up to other people. Elements like background, social class, religion, political preference, level of education, are at the forefront of saying yes to new friends, a work environment, or a new partner. This makes a lot of sense. The same counts for personality traits, similar interests and humour. The likeable factors appear most readily with people who are more alike. But when does it become too comfortable? When are you avoiding the ones who challenge you? When we stick to the persona characteristics alone we miss out on many beautiful and insightful connections. And we might remain in comfortable relationships, uninspired.

Attracting people into our lives doesn't mean we have to keep them forever. When relationships cost too much and give little in return, it is a good moment to reflect. Finding your balance is not to dismiss the other, it is to become aware of your patterns, you inner response and your own blind spots. If it is consistently out of balance and you're unable to shift the dynamic, it might be time to move on.

Becoming aware of resonance or dissonance will be very helpful on the journey of raising our awareness. The shift and new insights you are gaining can make you feel lonely in the beginning. You see things differently and others see a change in you they cannot define, which stirs both curiosity and discomfort.

Forcing friendship is of no use if it has lost its mutual resonance. But before jumping to conclusions, be courageous in sharing what you experience on your journey. You might be surprised how many realize they're interested in taking the same new direction. As long as we don't share, no one knows what our inner world looks like. But be wary, stay open to any viewpoints and reflections you receive, it will only accelerate your growth.

Family matters

When you think you are enlightened, spend a few days with your family.

Anon.

Do you recognize this? Let's say you are the youngest in the family you grew up in. As soon as you enter a family meet up, you act like the little one again. You step into your old role, blindly and so do your family members – even at the age of fifty! No doubt you do the same with them. Its shows how strong and interconnected our patterns are. Not just with ourselves, but with each family member. As long as there is emotional pain, the old pattern gets activated, and that counts for anyone, your family members included.

If you have little awareness of the dynamics within your current relationships, have a look at the family dynamics you grew up in. It is the best place to discover your pains and patterns, as that is where most of it started, the pain of our inner child. Often we look for the why: why did we attract our family or why did we endure our pains. That's understandable, but less helpful. Try questions like: how can I shift this experience? How does it show up in my current relationships?

The healing process of your youth experiences is a lonely one. We love to work with our family members, but more often than not it is hard to find support in this process, in the way you desire. The energetic family cords run deep and are complicated, involving information over generations. And while you go through your process, you activate something for other members as well. You rock the boat, as they say, but how they react is unpredictable. It can be ignored, create distance (conflict) or you are misunderstood.

While you are doing your best to work on your inner self and do your part to heal your family lineage, you seem to be least appreciated by those who are close. Let it not discourage you. Once you have cleared these cords, you are no longer in need of reward, you have transcended it.

What is it, anyway, that makes us so sensitive to sharing ourselves more vulnerably in this familiar and supposedly safe and loving environment? Why don't we have more honest, reflective dialogues? Not owning our own pains is one thing, but the cultural family belief system and all the indoctrination and expectation to respect that system, creates another challenge in the healing process. Healing only takes place through complete surrender to any outcome. However, we have learned to accept that family bonds are to be respected. It is this pressure on these relationships that makes it challenging to fully surrender to any outcome.

Instead we choose to compromise, hold our breath and give in to our old family patterns. What we fail to see is that no relationship is ever really broken. Yes, we might go separate ways for a while, in mutual respect, but that allows greater chance of healing, reuniting, and moving the relationship to another level of an emotionally grown-up family. Any child would dream of that outcome – and so does our inner child!

A client, only 23 years old, was struggling with procrastination. He tried mind-set programs, tried to discipline himself, but he kept falling back. His sleep patterns were irregular, especially troubled falling asleep and social distractions were full-on. Yet, he loved his job. We delved into his family history. He'd had a rough childhood, enduring daily beatings from his stepfather. The process of forgiveness, toward his stepfather, his biological father, and his mother, felt very challenging, but after a while he took the time and went through it with resolve. He felt blown away by the result, which he described as an awakening experience.

However, his sleep patterns didn't change much and he still had traits of procrastination. So we went back into his childhood. It turned out he'd learned to lie absolutely still during the mandatory afternoon rest, to avoid another slap. Falling asleep wasn't a comfortable space for him, to say the least. Soon, he had a painful but very insightful dream, where he knew he had to break free from feeling responsible for what had happened to him and knowing that he couldn't carry the pain of his mother. Throughout all this he remained compassionate toward everyone, he cleared the energetic cords. Within two months he broke free from his old pains and procrastinating patterns. What a brave young man.

The case above shows that the parents weren't involved in the healing process of the young man. At least not in his current reality. That doesn't mean that nothing happened on their side during this process. Healing work is always happening on an energetic level, in the field and directly in the energetic cords between the people involved (see the beautiful work of Bert Hellinger). Remember it is all energy. Stories and memories are only there to ease the mind into understanding what happened. What we want to shift is the frequency of the stuck, dense energy.

In 2020, the year of the Covid pandemic, families became more divided than ever. Choosing 'a side' was almost inevitable and everyone was confronted with their own reaction. It is as if the virus infected family dynamics, activating the family immune system. How this process will unfold, only time will tell.

Your family is also a great source for reconnecting with your gifts. They are the ones who remember you as a child. They have seen the first signs of your gifts, natural talents, and ways you behaved and reacted. Were you the thinker, the problem solver, the peacemaker, the activist, the observer, the creative, the joker or the social one?

There are so many gems to be found in our youth, seeds that were planted. Feeling back into your childhood memories, what you loved to do, what you were passionate about, how your friends reacted to you, what it was that you brought into the play, yields many beautiful insights about your natural gifts. It is a mixture of gaining insights in your pains and your gifts, as each shadow has a gift related to it. Keep remembering that and flip the coin.

Emotional co-dependency

Our relationships are entangled in an emotional co-dependency, as long as we fail to grow up emotionally and own our life completely. We keep shifting between the roles of the child and the parent and never become the adult, independent of our age. As long as we are not conscious of our inner emotional state at any given moment, we will be influenced or influence the other with a neediness. We fail to see the gift in the reflection another person offers us. It is where we experience that we are not complete, and sense the incompleteness of the other. It's not always easy to tell the difference.

What makes it co-dependent is that we don't own our pain or situation or we feel responsible for the pain or situation of others. Using the three labels indicates the emotional awareness of one's position in that moment.

When we become the 'child', we want the other to take care of us, solve or organize things for us. When we become the 'parent' we love to take care of things, give advice, find solutions, or reject help as we believe we can manage on our own. In the role of the parent we know what is best for others. In the role of the 'adult', we are not blinded by our emotions or old patterns nor do we feel responsible for others' behaviour, situation, or emotions. We have more of an overview of each role in the triangle and act with full respect and support to all parties involved, including our own. In the role of the adult, we are emotionally neutral. That doesn't mean we don't share our emotion, but we are not blinded by it.

This triangle role play of child-parent-adult, our emotional unawareness and behaviour that comes with it, shows up in any relationship, including the organizations we work in, the government running our country or any other relationship on which we feel dependent. The more dependent we feel, or the less responsible we are, the more we stay stuck in this co-dependency.

How often do we give unsolicited advice when someone shares a dilemma? How often do we follow the proposals of our government, feeling they need to solve our issues or organize our lives? How often do we follow the leader without owning our role and taking responsibility?

If we really disentangle co-dependent relationships, we realize how flawed is the whole idea of leadership. How often we hide behind our fear and refrain from our responsibility. How intense the role of a leader must feel, pushed into being responsible for others. No wonder our leaders need to divert to other ways of control, perhaps even compromising their integrity, when no one accepts their own responsibility.

In relationships, the more intimate ones, we love to bathe in the safety of the commitment. With our loved ones, we feel we can neglect our role, our responsibility as an individual, because we expect forgiveness. Like a teenager who pushes the boundaries, knowing the unconditional love and forgiveness of his parents. In order to release the complex layers of emotional entanglement, we have to cut the umbilical cord again, the symbiotic connection we needed while growing up. As long we haven't released this cord as an adult, we are trying to find a new cord in our relationships to nurture us and keep us safe.

It is unrelated to what role you play in the relationship. Both the egoist and the empath, show their struggles in becoming emotionally grown up. You either ignore emotions or you are bypassing your own individuality.

Our co-dependency patterns are often not such a 'big thing'. And that is exactly where the beautiful opportunities lie, to shine light on our inner processes and prevent getting into unnecessary relationship challenges of blame, irritation, or finally, separation. It is about creating awareness of where you compromise yourself, where you are manipulating the other, or become too selfish.

The term manipulation might sound extreme, but it is what is happening and it really helps to see it this way, to open our eyes. Forcing the other to react in a way that you desire is a form of manipulation, by using inauthentic behaviour, controlling acts, convincing, playing the victim, advising, gaslighting and many more ways of defence and offense. Perhaps you are not conscious of your inner motivations to force the other, so it feels there is no premeditation, but unconsciously there is, when we are hiding our fears (false ego) and feel the other needs to adjust for our comfort.

What we often fail to see is that we are never responsible for the feelings and actions of the other. We are only responsible for our own. That is already enough to deal with. However, it helps the relationship a great deal to acknowledge the other for his story, pain or struggle; sincerely and not to be patronizing. At the same time, leave it there and focus on your own challenges and patterns.

Whatever you don't like about the other is theirs to explore. Guess what, what you don't like about the other is somehow a version of what you don't like about yourself or feel missing. There is always something to shine light on. Cherish and be grateful for the relationship and do your inner work.

Become bluntly honest with yourself
and embrace the reflection your receive.

Shifting into our adult role more consciously doesn't mean the healing work within our relationships and family is done instantly. Some of the deep-rooted patterns need a lot of awareness to clear. Where we limit ourselves is rooted in our past and only through living life, diving into new relations, new experiences, do we create awareness of these limits.

The collective would be served by more parents being conscious of their adult role. It starts with being aware that no one *owns* the life of another, which means no one can decide what is best for a child to experience – not even a parent! All we can give our children is love and a safe space to develop themselves. Of course, this is not to be confused with giving guidance on learning how to live life in a sensible way. But how many parents project their own expectations on their children's journey and have a hard time accepting opposite choices or ideas? And yes, it is challenging to see your children struggling when you feel you know better. Try to shift from giving advice to asking questions and show your deep interest in what moves them. Learn to be present with them instead of endless conversations where you project your ideas. Observe where they mirror your shortcomings and work with that for yourself. It is about the intention with which you direct your energy, more than any words you say.

Thomas Gordon showed us great insights on how relational communication can support relationships to grow with graciousness. Don't think that relational communication is only soft and sweet. It can be very direct and passionate. Clearing our energies through expressing ourselves in a pure way is very healing for the personal and interpersonal dynamic. In our adult role, we listen actively, as we are genuinely curious to hear what the other has to share. We don't take their message personally, but hold space for the other to express what needs expressing. When we need to acknowledge a painful memory, we can still do this with full respect to ourselves and others. Communicating that you take that position is so helpful, for the other to support you. Sentences like 'I know I am acting out of the hurt child right now but this memory sparks an anger in me that needs to be seen'. Or ' I feel you need more space for yourself, yet I'd also like to acknowledge my need for you to be more present in my life'.

Communicating honestly and authentically without any projection is needed to work through our emotions and only to own our own. It definitely requires practice and attention to develop this way of communicating.

It is not so much a mystery when life shows us our time to deal with our wounds, it is a mystery why we don't see the signs.

While most of us are unaware of our inner wounding, we step into the grown-up world to connect and find our tribe, our intimate relationships and become participants in the systems of our society. It is only logical, due to this unawareness, that we project our childhood pains onto the people we meet. And it is only logical that our systems reflect our emotional immaturity! More about that in chapter 4.

Do we realize that we fall in love to liberate ourselves?

You must love in such a way that the person you love feels free.

Thich Nhat Hanh

That intimate relationships are special is known since early childhood, when we discover the special feeling of having a crush on someone. Our heart races, the butterflies make our stomach tingle and we love to be closer to that special one. This feeling is new to us and very different from the feelings we have for our parents and the siblings we grow up with.

With our intimate partners we add an extra level of attraction which distinguish these relationships from any other. The physical and chemical attraction has its roots in our inability to be honest with ourselves, as Richard Rudd explains in the *Gene Keys*. We need to hide something for the other in order to attract the other. If that deep sense of tension wasn't there, we would be intimate with everyone and wouldn't have developed our cultural differences, country nations and so on. We attract those who can unlock our honesty.

We seek connection and intimacy to fill the void in our sense of Self. We are at a crossroads, with our primal instinctive drive to reproduce, versus our consciousness pushing to liberate itself, to become whole. Evolution pushes us to new ways of relating with others but most of all with ourselves. Our naked self-honesty will unlock our natural life force and will open up all chakra centres. Finally life will rush through us in full transparency.

We can already see this shift happening. We are exploring different styles of intimate relationships and even our gender definitions are questioned. In general we are moving away from marrying, for reasons economic, religious, or social. We desire freedom and yet the more individualized our societies become, the more we seek belonging and connecting. As our lonely path of self-focus through our ego driven mind is ending, we are starting to realize that it disconnected us. A deeply painful realization, that asks for forgiveness of mankind before we can shift.

Our intimate relationships offer the sacred space to go through these deep processes of forgiveness and to release what no longer serves us. Only when we value this space, while each of the partners owns his process, will we heal in an accelerated way. In the sacred connection anything comes to the surface, as nothing can hide. When both partners own their darkness, light is able to shine through. It will shift our relationship dynamic towards new higher vibrational frequencies.

Our intimate relationships show the biggest paradox for our soul. We hide behind the safety of being in a relationship and it is the relationship that pushes us to surrender and face all our fears. Our unconscious knows what it needs to become conscious. The partners we meet in our life, the persons we attract, the ones who touch us in some shape or form, are the ones who show us our path. Not all the way, but at least for a while, to discover more about ourselves. Every partner is the perfect partner in that moment of our lives. Even the ones who treated you badly.

It is no surprise, now the awareness of mankind is rising and we enter a new phase in our human evolution, that our intimate relationships are shaking and changing. Emancipation, sexual revolution, gender quests, open relationships and the increase in divorce rates definitely show the shift. Our belief systems around marriage and divorce are changing. We were taught that divorce is a sin, an act of weakness, forbidden by belief systems or simply not done. Now we are counter reacting and divorce has become a normal thing. While going through this phase of experimenting, we will acknowledge the deeper essence of our intimate relationships, guiding us in our emotional growth and preparing us for our new paradigm.

Whatever it is we need to see, no one is going to rescue us from our deepest pains, all freedom lies within. All wisdom, all knowledge to heal, all questions to answer... everything is within ourselves. There is no solution outside of us. That is the ultimate freedom we all seek, freedom from our suffering.

The reflection and entanglement of energies

When we fall in love we feel on top of the world. The correct expression should be we *rise* in love. We open our heart and experience its high vibrating frequency. Or, do we indeed fall in the void that our intimate relationship shows us?

In the first period of being in love, our sensed perception of our persona often only shows its best side. Not because we want to appear in a better light, but because in our lifted frequency, our shadow side disappears into the background. When we are truly in the frequency of love, we are unconditional and forgiving to others. Does that mean that our shadow side has vanished? Most likely not. To experience our shadow side, our pains and woundings, we need to be in a low frequency. In a state of love you cannot even feel your pain. Of course you can remember the painful events of your past, but if you are truly in this loving frequency, those memories don't hurt.

Unfortunately, for most of us, this phase of 'falling in love' doesn't last forever. After a while, we drop into the frequency bandwidth we had before we fell in love. This bandwidth is for most of us lower than the love frequency. The same happens for our partner.

It is therefore no surprise that the dynamic of the relationship shifts after the 'honeymoon period', when we let our unconscious patterns run our daily lives again. We become less unconditional towards the relationship. Little demands and expectations slip in, of how things should go. Having no high demands of the relationships and being the easy-going one, can and will cause tensions as well.

Whatever the examples, under the surface you are perceiving a reflection of yourself through the interaction with your partner. It is not a clear mirror image, it is way more subtle and therefore more difficult to read. The fact that you have fallen in love and experienced this state of unity, if only briefly, has opened you up. It made you vulnerable. We immediately know we have something valuable to lose and we risk the possibility of being rejected. And at an unconscious level, we opened our heart and emotional centres in our system, where disbalances are stored. We long to heal yet it is so challenging to become vulnerable and risk that it won't work out. So we compromise, ignore, avoid, please, dominate. Of course, it is not all that bad, the majority of the time our relationships are fun, loving, caring, and inspiring.

Somehow, the longer the relationship lasts, the more we tend to focus on our partner's shortcomings rather than the gifts we initially fell for and felt blossoming within ourselves. We are helped more by unleashing and stimulating each other's gifts and deal from there with the old pains that show up. Remember the 80:20 focus.

Keeping a relationship healthy, with enough growth is an art. Not everyone is willing to dig a little deeper. Being vulnerable is new to us. We are only gradually getting used to expressing our emotions, so this will take a while. Those not willing to go through personal work are not less triggered by the dynamics of the relationship than those prepared to explore.

Whether you go deep and explore the inner work or go for the emotional status quo, the levels of stress, concern, irritation, external distractions, illness and lack of sexual intimacy will be more or less the same. There is no ripple-free relationship and all challenges of any intimate relationship have the same root cause: our childhood pains and our lost connection with our sense of Self. Knowing that root cause will prevent you getting all tangled up in endless dialogue only focussed on the symptoms, or ending the relationship for the wrong reasons. Having said that, the other side bears a risk as well. Those who are aware of the root cause can analyse any ripple that comes to the surface through beautiful dialogue but might miss out on all the fun and lightness the relationship offers. The choice is always yours – what you do with the signs you are willing to see.

Seeing through the 10 main dynamics will shift all our relationships

It is not the purpose of this book to explore all our intimate relationship challenges and solutions in depth, that would deserve a book in itself. More, we would serve ourselves if we looked at *all* our relationships and not just the one with our intimate (or potential) partner.

No matter what relationship we look at, whether it is with ourself, our partner, our friends, our family, our children, our government or boss, similar dynamics happen everywhere. Once we see through that lens, it is a lot easier to untangle ourselves from the story (the judgement labels) and start making a change. Then there'll be change in all relationships!

The flow of change is always: recognize, acknowledge, commit to change and do the work.

Our basic tools to help you in that process are:

- *radical self-honesty through self-reflection and observation;*
- *own your role (thoughts, feelings, actions, inactions) and responsibility for the energy you exude – pure emotions are valid, hidden agendas not;*
- *become resilient, we learn and explore;*
- *live life in frequencies, feel, sense where it shifts, gets triggered or elevated;*
- *realign with your natural high vibrating frequency by making it a conscious choice each time: do I let it influence my frequency? Breathe, release, hold space;*
- *make conscious choices, not ego- or fear-driven ones;*
- *become transparent, with a clear mind and emotionally neutral;*
- *a trigger is always an invitation to look within: 'If it sticks it clicks';*
- *any dynamic or pain you want to shift, start by changing the pattern.*

(see also: seven new skills at the end of this chapter)

1. Shift from 'I love you' to 'I see you'

Technically we cannot love the other person. Love is a frequency, a state of being, not an active verb or an emotion. When we are 'in love', we are experiencing that frequency. What is more accurate when someone expresses his love for you, is that he sees you for who you are, the Self. It is the soul connection we feel and would like to express. When we emphasize 'I see you', we become more aware of the essence of the other. Whether it is your partner, your child, or a best friend. Seeing the essence and connecting with the essence, is supporting the empowerment of the other. To heal our relationships we have to start focussing and supporting the gifts of others instead of criticizing their shortcomings.

2. You cannot change the other and change is a given

Most of us know this one, but we have a hard time embracing and surrendering to its simple truth. That we cannot change the other is frustrating in any relationship, just as much as being too rigid to think nothing needs changing. The challenge with change is that we desire it and we resist it, as change is always about gaining something new and letting go of something old.

In a relationship the idea of change is scarier, as we don't know what we might lose or gain. So we love the other to change according to our expectation (=control) so we won't be disappointed. Or we love to keep things as they are. We could say that women tend to focus on changing the other and men tend to avoid (personal) growth. Both, men and women, often lack the self-reflective skills to see through this dynamic so no-one really makes a constructive effort. We project so we don't have to change ourselves.

We cannot live the life of another person. We cannot expect our partner (government, boss, friend, parent) to become who we'd like them to be. Neither can we expect the relationship to go well without investing any effort. In the dynamic we act and react. Both need equal attention and we can only own our role. Often, we have become so busy with our focus on the imperfection of our others, that it takes us away from our own journey and intentions. Find balance. Respect and giving the other the space you love to give yourself, keeps any relationship healthy. Growth comes from within and change is inevitable.

3. Know that the other always knows, we are resonating beings

You cannot hide anything, it always comes out. The dishonesty is what we feel but we don't know how to deal with it. We feel it within ourselves and with others. That is the unsettling feeling, which is often expressed in gaslighting, emotional pressure, jealousy, distrust, or suspicion. Within intimate commitments, your partner knows when something is off for you and vice versa. It can be getting too caught-up in a hobby, too much work, stress, a flirtation, being hung up on social media, infidelity, a distrust in yourself or just being unhappy. We don't need to know precisely which, to sense this subtle shift in energy. With other relationships it isn't any different. We simply know when someone is bending the truth or pretends to be someone they are not. What we feel is inauthenticity, being out of tune. The frequency has dropped or is not in harmony. Or we have dropped and are out of tune. We disconnect (we withdraw) *or* we compromise out of fear to lose the connection. As we are often unable to give words to this unsettling feeling, we get triggered into a whole set of reactions which only makes it worse.

4. You have free will and relationships come with commitment: learn to balance

Practically all adult relationships arise out of free will. No one forced you into it. You can end it anytime as well, no one forces you to stay in it. That is the easy part. Where we get confused is in our false expectations, labels, beliefs, projections. Often out of fear we compromise our free will and we suffer. It is okay to suffer and compromise for a little while, as we love to stretch the boundaries. However, being in a relationship and self-sabotaging your life is not serving anyone, least of all your children. Free will is also choosing to stay in the relationship and own your role that comes with the commitment. It can feel easier to walk away – repeat the same cycle in a new relationship – than face your inner process. Free will is also owning your gifts and exploring them, expanding them. More often than not, we tend to adjust ourselves and lose our freedom. Are we adjusting out of free will, or are we compromising?

5. Male and female dynamics

Instinctively, men tend to connect through sexual attraction and estimate the availability of a woman from that viewpoint. They are, at first, not emotionally committed. Women look first for reliability and safety and connect emotionally. If a man doesn't become emotionally available, a woman will finally close her heart and lose interest. This is one of the essential differences between the feminine and masculine energy and less related to gender, and even independent of the type of relationship! In a work environment, for example, a person who has more feminine energy, tends to seek first reliability and values connection more than one with more dominant masculin energy. Embracing our different instincts on both sides, in this time of our evolution, helps us shift to a new paradigm. To put it in black and white and generalised: women (more dominant feminine energy) need to find their empowerment (self-reliance) and men (more masculine) need to open up to emotional connection (vulnerability).

6. Stop the win-lose dynamics

We are often trapped in a love-fear dynamic, which gets reflected in our frequency. We fight with our inner fears, we become arrogant, we know better, we create conflicts, we feel the need to convince, we feel the need to hurt the other as we feel hurt by the other. Our arguments can be so intense and painful, because we need to win or fear to lose. In this low vibrating frequency we cannot see our way out, we cannot open up to a space of empathy or self-reflection. To stop this dynamic, a pause is needed. We need a breathing space in the conflict, to release the tension. The tension is not personal, but we take it personally. Arguments and heated conflicts can be valuable, but only for a short time.

We use 'projected statements' (you do this, they do this) instead of 'I statements' (I feel, I need, I think). In the win-lose dynamic no one really ever wins, especially between partners. Approaching any relationship with a focus on win-win makes all the difference to our growth.

7. Shift from expect to respect and from conditional to acknowledging

The emotional co-dependency is the underlying reason why our relationships are highly conditional. We are too often led by our emotional challenges and childhood traumas, forgetting that our relationships are best served by respect and acknowledgement.

Because of our inability to own our lives, we expect a lot from others: to organize life for us (institutions, systems, and technology), to make us feel safe (all relationships), to feel loved (family systems, personal relationships), to live healthily (food, fresh air, nature). What do we give in return? Where do we show respect, and how?

We often take things, life, or persons for granted and without acknowledgement. Our expectations make the relationships conditional: 'I expect you to do this for me, so I don't need to take ownership of the issue you are solving'. That is our current outside-in movement. To change it, we need to move from within. This starts with respect to ourselves, honouring our lives, acknowledging our challenges. Only then is it easier to acknowledge other people for who they are, why they behave the way they do, and show respect for their journey. That doesn't mean you have to agree with everyone or accept immoral/abusive behaviour.

It is in the entanglement of our emotions, where we keep each other captured in a low vibrating frequency. Bringing release in this entanglement is where we liberate any relationship from immoral, abusive, or conditional behaviour.

8. Ask, or trust in not knowing

We love to assume that we know what is happening or what is meant in a conversation. We are not used to verifying our assumptions. Becoming aware of the 'assumption effect' is a great eye opener. Often we don't realize that with making an assumption we open a timeline with its consequences. Life always reflects back our energy, including the frequency of assumptions we make. When you assume your partner did something you don't like, your whole attitude responds to that line of thinking. We hear, see, and read everything in an emotionally coloured way because we look for confirmation. Which we will always find! The assumptions become a truth for you, a timeline, a chosen path.

A little assumption becomes a belief over time which we fiercely need to defend. In our intimate relationship, this behaviour can lead to a lot of miscommunication of repeated assumptions and by the time you end up at relationship counselling or a divorce, both of you have no idea where it all started. The same happens in our societies. It is equally full of assumptions. It is the basis for stigmatizing, labelling people. To break free from assumptions, we can simply ask, become curious and open.

The feeling might be right when something feels off, the assumption (translation of the feeling) might be wrong. Stick with the feeling and stay open. Trust that sooner or later life will show you the answer you need and that matches your frequency in an upward spiral.

9. Relearning to express ourselves

Maybe it is because of the end of the patriarchal times or because it is the end of all times, but we are breaking free from many old dynamics that no longer serve us. What we are moving towards no one knows yet, but we sense it will be different. While we are moving through this transition period, authentic expression is so important, to establish new balance in relationships. Just inner work alone is not enough.

For centuries we haven't been able to express ourselves authentically, as we feared rejection, ridicule or worse. If we want to leave the blame game behind us, we need to find a new voice, or at least a new tone.

Our throat chakra, which is the channel between the mind and the heart, plays an important role here. Sharing our truth, expressing anger, finding our authentic expression, are all related to this area. As this area has been undermined for so long, we will struggle with it, at first, and our expression will sound harsh and perhaps even painful for the other. Even though our heart begins to open up, our mind is still very dominant. Where the expression is coming from, the mind or the heart, can be felt in the tone of voice, the flow of speaking and the vibration. Over time it will soften until we don't need to express ourselves so much anymore. The role of language will change eventually and we will use other senses to communicate.

10. Learn to play, stop resisting

We attract people in our lives to enjoy life, share beautiful experiences together and live freely. Let's play instead of resisting what comes up. Remember you choose out of free will. Treat that as curiosity towards yourself, your partner, your government, your boss and even your parents. The relationship dynamics feel a lot lighter if you are playfully curious, even when it hurts. Playing is not being superficial or accepting all actions. Playing is choosing to see the experience in the pain, instead of letting yourself fall in the downward spiral, because then you have taken it too personally and have become the victim. To discover our own sovereignty we often hear the advice: set your boundaries. This is a tricky one as it can easily become another form of defence or resistance. Instead of setting a boundary, which is more like creating a fence, you can shift to stating a boundary, but make it an embodied one, not a hollow phrase. Setting a boundary sounds like: I need, I want, I desire, often followed by what you expect of the other. A stated boundary sounds like: I expect that you will treat me with the same respect you like to be treated with, while I am exploring my own purpose, and I love you to do the same. A subtle but important difference. It supports freedom. No fence is needed as an aligned stated boundary is the expression of an embodied value.

Betrayal will show us the way to intimacy and transparency

A truth can walk naked ... but a lie always needs to be dressed ...

Khalil Gibran

We all have felt betrayed in our lives. We can only experience this with those we have given our trust, including ourselves, our systems, and institutions, even life itself. That is why betrayal feels intense, heavy, and deeply painful. If we are able to look at the dynamic more objectively, we can see any form of betrayal as a glitch in the field of trust. Trust is the most natural form to relate to life. Our essence, the Self, doesn't know distrust, it just is a consciousness, aware of itself. But from the moment we're born (and arguably even since we are conceived) we translate experiences as painful and joyful, that is part of being human. And soon, early in life, we lost trust in ourselves, 'that part of our persona that is not good enough'. It leads to more experiences that confirm our distrust. And that triggers a whole series of struggles, pains, and out-of-balance behaviours. But worse, we accept that distrust is more familiar than trust. Therefore we find it okay that we are non-transparent with each other. Our systems and institutions are (openly) full of this behaviour: political fraud, marketing lies, religious dogma based on false history and so on.

Instead of looking for change, we rest in acceptance, hoping it is less bad than it is or that it doesn't hurt the other so much (rationalization). This is where we are stuck: the never-ending cycle of distrust-betrayal-acceptance-betrayal-distrust. We are betrayed and we betray the other.

Distrust is based in fear. A fully aligned high-vibrating person will never feel betrayed and won't be betrayed. If we could only trust this to be true...

Betrayal, like any other subject, is a matter of frequency. Each frequency level has its form of betrayal. Very low vibrating people use various forms of force and manipulation, a mid-level vibrating person is perhaps less intentional in their betrayal but they are rationalizing their less trustworthy behaviour (a little lie). For those with consistently high vibration, betrayal will not be part of their behaviour, transparency becomes key.

Betrayal hurts! Of course it does. But, we only break through the cycle of betrayal once we stop being a victim and feeling powerless.

> *You perhaps betray the people that you love most because*
> *you know that you have the expectation of forgiveness.*
> Let Them All Talk (movie)

What a beautiful line on which to pause and feel within how true this is.

In our intimate relationships, betrayal comes in various ways, from flirtations to infidelity. But it includes all our actions where we are too caught up with distractions, at the cost of the relationship and its commitment. Whether something is really innocent or not is known to us. In other words, what defines betrayal is where we knowingly compromise the relationship. Would it be really innocent, we would be transparent, right? So another way of assessing your whereabouts is feeling how honest you are about it.

Infidelity doesn't happen by itself, it is a conscious choice. We know when we cross the line, but we rationalize our actions or dismiss the hurt feelings of our partner to cover up the discomfort we feel. We seek attention, to have ourselves confirmed by others. We all know this need for attention. Let's start by being honest with ourselves and admit it, just to ourselves, silently. That would soon release a lot of tension around the subject! Secondly, let's admit and acknowledge that we know it hurts our partner when we cross the line. We wouldn't like it the other way round, would we? So what is it that makes this subject such a tough one to release?

First of all, there are so many beliefs and stigmas around the infidelity theme. Our media, movies and social media platforms play a huge role in this, by feeding and reinforcing it until we believe our only reality to be that we cannot trust each other. The stories we share keep the patterns and dynamics alive. We love the gossip, but all it does is add to the underlying fear of separation, distrust, and commitment. From our early years we are confronted with these themes, even before we are ready for a serious commitment. Weirdly enough, there is even a stigma in gender: the young man who has affairs is macho, and the women a slut. Just imagine the imprint of that, at a young age, on the safety of relationships.

Secondly, we distract ourselves not so much because we feel less for our partner or very unhappy in the relationship, but more because we are not willing to see the imbalance within ourselves. At least not in the moment it comes to the surface. Then we drop in our frequency and become unconscious of the Self. That is the dishonesty, unfaithfulness we feel. Our relationship only mirrors that. By the way, we do the same when we are single, we just don't recognize it as being unfaithful to our Self.

Instead of being honest with ourselves by acknowledging the emptiness we feel, we do the opposite. We disconnect, energetically, and compromise the commitment (if only for a little while). That is what our partner picks up. As long as we are unaware of what happens, we continue. We hide the discomfort and seek the confirmation outside ourselves, outside our relationship. We need these little moments to feel seen and it can be as innocent as a brief flirty chat with someone. In this lower vibrating frequency we *might be* unconscious of our actions but we consciously choose to ignore feelings that come up. That is why it evokes secretiveness and feelings of guilt. We even feel more guilt towards ourselves than towards our partner. We cannot face our own shame so we keep it a secret. And from one little secret we go to the next one...

Whatever it is we are seeking outside, we apparently cannot fill that void within ourselves and don't feel that the relationship gives the sacred safe space to open up. Only in a lower vibrating state are we able to hurt another person or ourselves. In a high vibrating state there is no desire to be distracted at all, you are fully present. You have no desire to flirt as you don't need any confirmation. When you fell in love (higher frequency) you didn't feel that desire either, remember? Infidelity doesn't happen because the relationship gets boring, it happens because we have dropped. If the relationship would truly be over, there is no need to betray either as you will simply leave and move on. In other words, if you still feel the relationship is worth your energy (for whatever reason) then get to work and stop hiding. If not, leave and stop hurting your partner.

> In different periods of my life, I have been in all three roles: the victim (I was betrayed), the perpetrator (I was unfaithful) and the third party (I interfered in another commitment knowingly). All three experiences were seemingly 'innocent' and extremely short. Nevertheless, there is no excuse, nothing to be proud of.

I knew the feeling of rage and despair when I discovered the betrayal, I knew the feeling of shame when I couldn't be honest, I knew the feeling of denial when I overstepped a line. Each role hurts.

I also experienced that each event doesn't need to damage the relationship for ever, but it does require a serious effort to heal the commitment again. It simply hurts to feel dishonest and disconnected. I needed to heal and forgive myself (and the other) for all my roles, including the victim.

Not everything needs to be out in the open, but if actions and behaviour don't change, trust is not restored. In my experience, lack of acknowledgement and continuation of denial, while the truth is out, is worse than the transgression itself. Denial (or dishonesty) gives me a feeling of being denied in my existence.

When either one of you feels off, there is something to explore in the theme of trust and dependency. Don't disregard or dismiss this sign, things will only get worse and will influence the foundation of the commitment. As it is always felt on both sides, we get easily tangled up in a lot of confusion. In this confusion we get angry at each other, suspicious, irritated, or worse and we do things we actually don't want to do. What hurts is the non-transparency and dishonesty. Knowing something is off, but the other leaves you hanging, makes the relationship more unsafe. It provokes jealousy and suspicion which leads to arguments and more lies. That is how we often end up in a downward spiral:

we cross the line innocently » we keep it a secret » more unsafety » more distraction outside, less innocent » less connection » less intimacy » cross more lines, more destructive » more distraction » we never get to heal ourselves ....

Finally we separate and most likely repeat the same pattern and dynamic in a new relationship.

How to break, or better, prevent the downward spiral? We need to learn to be radically honest with ourselves, to own our pains, our discomfort, our incompleteness. We need to raise our awareness of ourselves. We don't have to bother our partner with our feelings the moment we feel the desire to seek attention outside or when we feel attracted to another person. However, we do owe it to our commitment, to reflect within *before* our actions become less innocent, repetitive, and worse, destructive.

When the distraction is something like an addiction, to gambling, alcohol, drugs, porn, or work, the imbalance is felt as well. It is the same disconnection of energy. These distractions are more often out in the open and might feel less threatening at first, but can be just as harmful to the commitment.

Infidelity is not possible when the third party, who knowingly gets involved, chooses not to play the role anymore, not even for flirty chats, sexting or secret meetings. Simply stop making excuses, pretending that it is okay, because it never is. What would happen, if we refuse to interfere with monogamous relationships? What a great gift to the world. We, the third party, won't have to fear infidelity either, when we engage in new monogamous relationships ourselves. Can you see how we keep this painful cycle in place? Collectively we would heal way faster, as our relationships could provide the safe space we all long for, with the absence of external threat. Let's never be that external threat.

However, we are not there yet. The third party is still available. As with anything it comes down to us, by saying no to temptation and observing what we feel. There is nothing wrong with feeling attracted to someone else. What if we share that feeling with our partner? It might shine light on something that is missing in the relationship. Scary and uncomfortable no doubt, but now there is something to work with.

For some couples it might work to shift to an open relationship, with consent of all parties involved. But is it really open at all levels? Is it really with the conscious full consent of all parties? Is that really the solution? Or are we again walking away from ourselves and have we come up with new ways to conceal our inner discomfort? Remember, our mind always comes up with great reasoning, to avoid our deep inner pains.

Whatever the imbalance that led to any form of infidelity, we have to step out of ourselves to see the bigger picture. In its broadest definition, 'betrayal = distrust' is a theme for us all. A great steppingstone toward exploring what gets mirrored. Perhaps it is our chance to step up, into our own empowerment. Perhaps it is our role to heal our partners' pain around this theme. We attracted our partner for good reasons even if we don't yet know our themes.

Dealing with infidelity is a very intimate matter, staying vulnerably open to ourselves and giving the other the space and trust to do the same. We all fear rejection, being left behind.

Isn't it weird that we are able to be unfaithful, risking a whole relationship, but that we are afraid to be honest? Isn't it weird that we blame, criticize or lie, but that we cannot be transparent about what really bothers us? For that we need to be nakedly intimate with one another, by being fully clear about our insecurities, our pains, our desires and even our gifts.

That is the intimacy we fear. We have immense layers of trauma stacked in our DNA, more even than all our own direct experiences. What to do with all that? Our cultural layers, memories from our ancestors, our belief systems: all are deeply tied into the theme of trust. Sexual intimacy has a double role in this. We use it either to hide ourselves more, or to experience moments of deep release and connection that we desire so much. You are the only one who knows whether you are hiding from yourself or connecting deeply with yourself and your partner, at any given moment. That deep connection is what we long for, to let another, your loved one, go through your heart, unconditionally. That is pure freedom.

Closely related to the theme of distrust are our old, distorted patterns and roles of the false egoist and the false empath.

Egoist, narcissist and empath

False ego is dominating our planet right now. We are so narrow and self-focussed that we are not able to communicate well. Communication is needed for connection, harmony, and balance. That goes beyond using words and language. We've lost healthy communication between organisms, at all levels. Our cells don't communicate efficiently, so we become ill. We can't understand each other, so we feel lost and separated. And worse, we lose our communication with nature and disconnect from the most important organism, our planet.

We live in service-to-self societies. Service to self is more accurately defined as service to our identity, persona. We are focussed on making sure we feel safe, whatever that safety means. Most decisions, choices or actions are made to confirm our identity, our own thinking and beliefs. That behaviour has a price, the price of destruction. As long as we are so narrowly focussed on ourselves, we must admit that we have lost the connection to life. That is our false ego at play.

There is nothing wrong with our ego when our behaviour (communication) is coming from a full sense of awareness (in a high vibrating frequency). Imagine we all were 100% aware of the Self, emotionally balanced, fully complete, then our ego will show its real purpose. We will know our natural power and no longer seek any confirmation outside. From this balanced state, we would never make a decision at the cost of another, ourselves or nature. The other would not allow it anyway, as everyone would be acting in the same aligned way. Paradoxically, there wouldn't even be any neediness to get something for ourselves. If we all would be balanced and fully aligned, egoism becomes a healthy sense of ego. In that state our ego will be driven by our heart and not our mind alone. We finally will understand what 'consciousness in action' means. Our actions would by definition come with a focus on a win-win for all involved.

We are not there yet.

The empath is on the other side of this spectrum right now, but often quite unbalanced as this quality is pretty new to us. Empathy is the ability to sense and understand another person's state of being, without your own perspective interfering. An empath automatically picks up the information, switches to (active) listening, giving and holding space, often endlessly. When the egoist is unable to see the empath in a healthy way, the empaths receives nothing in return, feels drained and falls back (drop in frequency) in the same or similar lower vibrating frequency of the false egoist.

This disbalance is draining, but is the empath able to give enough focus to the Self? Having empathic abilities doesn't automatically mean you have a high awareness of the Self, your inner alignment and your inner woundings. The unhealed empath expects the other to fill their inner void, which is just as egoistic in that moment as the automated behaviour of an unhealed egoist. Both the empath and the egoist become needy, which makes the interaction conditional – they only express it in completely opposite ways. Where the egoist becomes too selfish, the empath becomes too social, too caring or the victim. Where the egoist is an absolute master in taking care of his own needs, the empath is a master in feeling what the other needs. Both are out of balance, as long as we are unhealed.

If there was no empath or caring energy on this planet, humanity would destroy itself, as the egoist would have no mirror to heal the pain that is hidden underneath their selfish behaviour. The other version is true as well: if there were no selfish egoist, the unhealed empath would have no mirror to heal either. The empath would have no mirror to come into their healthy empowerment and experience the balance of a healthy sense of Self versus a healthy care for others. It is an absolute painful dynamic that hurts many and creates a lot of destruction. So far, it only seems to get worse first. To heal this dynamic, humanity experiences extreme versions of the unhealthy egoist, the ruthless behaviour of the narcissist, the lowest vibrating frequency.

The narcissist has no sense of Self at all, they are here to gain everything for themselves at the cost of the other. With a total lack of any inner heart connection, they abuse others without feeling an ounce of remorse. They vibrate at such a low level, the level of apathy, that they use manipulation to relate to others. They unconsciously feed off the energy of fear in others, as that is what makes them feel powerful. They use power and control through manipulation, not to feel their own fear. They are disconnected with the Self and have lost any ability to sense. If they would allow feelings to come in, they risk feeling their own fear. A true narcissist has lost humanness and it is highly questionable whether this pathologic pattern can be healed in a lifetime. It is often a result of strong repetitive dynamics in family lines, passed on to the next generation through intense abusive traumas inflicted on the young child and destroying all feelings of connection, since the day they were born or even conceived.

Even though they appear (almost) soulless, they might still feel very aligned with their purpose in this lifetime. That is why many narcissists are very successful, well known and fully accepted and even admired by many. Those who admire them for their successes are not aware of their highly narcissistic behaviour. Of course they aren't, as a narcissist knows well how to play their role.

Without the extreme actions of the narcissist, mankind wouldn't be pushed into their empowerment and develop a healthy sense of empathy and egoism.

One of the biggest reasons why we cannot see through these dynamics yet, is our own low vibrating state. In that state, we use strategies of the egoist and sometimes even of the narcissist ourselves, but that is not an easy one to admit.

To put it in numbers might help, scale 1-1000:

- *a narcissist and someone highly victimised, operate on average at a frequency of 55, apathy;*
- *our collective vibrates at an average scale of 200-230 a position of neutrality but as soon as we are under stress we drop to lower vibrations;*
- *an aligned person is on average at 500 (our natural love frequency);*
- *an enlightened person is at 700 or higher;*
- *any moment we vibrate lower than 200, we are operating from a contracted, restricted system that searches for safety for itself first (fear driven). In this state we either become obedient, ignorant, or highly dominant.*

(inspired by David R. Hawkins and Bruce D. Schneider)

These numbers are given to illustrate the gap more than to dive into the scientific proof of these measurements. Before we can shift any vibration within ourselves, we have to become aware of our state in any moment and eventually in all moments. Acknowledging to ourselves that we have dropped and shown our egoistic self is where can make a choice to change our behaviour. A different behaviour will change the frequency, as it is a choice to stop projecting our egoistic behaviour onto others or stop being overly empathic.

It is important to realize that we vibrate on average within a certain bandwidth and, as long as we are unbalanced, we can vibrate higher in some areas of our life and a lot lower in other areas. As narcissism has become an often-used term these days, it doesn't mean that each person showing some signs of narcissistic behaviour is in low vibration in all areas of his life. Right now, humanity shows a variety of narcissistic, egoistic and empathic behaviours.

As long as we collectively vibrate at a lower consciousness than our natural state, we will see the result of our egoistic programming in our relationships. The egoist archetype mirrors the insecurity and lack of self-esteem and empowerment. We don't like this reflection at all, so we use our defences to attack the egoist or even blame the person for being a narcissist. It is not that we are wrong in those observations. The problem is that it often reduces our own empowerment in that same moment. This subtle low vibrating energy (blaming) evokes a neediness that the other needs to change. It is for the empath to learn a healthy sense of Self, embrace their empowerment, ask for their desires to be met and express themselves authentically. In that way they can tap into their healthy egoism. That will shift the egoist in the position that they need to develop their empathic abilities. The naturally aligned empath won't buy into their self-centred energy anymore. That is why our relationships are so valuable, to break through these old and painful dynamics.

How to move into balance

We know it by now: it is all about our own work, our inner pains, our inner connection. Yes it is, and we can be of great help to each other. One of the biggest challenges in the journey of awakening, the path of self-realization, is balancing the act of self-love and love for others. 'I create my own reality' is where the tension lies. If we follow that line and create our own reality, how are our realities related and influencing each other? How do I decide what is in the best interest of the relationship and for myself, simultaneously? By owning our own life, our actions, the air we breathe is where we simultaneously need to become aware how we influence others with it. Where do we shift, from self-care into love for others? It is not the same as thinking that you know what the other person needs, a good intent doesn't always make a right action. A good intent with an unpleasant result for the other is still an intent driven by the ego.

As said before, we cannot live in a world full egoistic traits. Our world shows the results: it destroys our humanness, we destroy each other through our manipulative force and victimhood, we destroy nature through our carelessness. Neither can we live in a world full of empaths only. Nothing will get done, we will lose our sense of direction and intent. We will lose our natural drive as creative ideas require a manifesting energy, balancing a receptive and creative force.

We are coming out of paradigms where the egoist had the dominant position and there was little space for the empath (our capitalistic and socialistic thinking). Those systems promote the egoist, and take advantage of the empath. However, that is the mind driven egoist, not the pure one with a healthy sense of Self! The pure empath has no place in our system yet, as the energy of giving and receiving is not supported. The energy of the empath is too fragile at a collective level. We easily shift into our false sense of empathy, by sacrificing ourselves for the other as a result of our belief systems. We have been led to believe that we are responsible for the other and that we have to consider everyone which is highly abused by our narcissistic driven systems of power and control.

It makes sense that in our shift to a new paradigm, the sensitive ones are the first to open up to this deep inner journey that initiates the shift. They start doing the inner work, feel drawn to spiritual, mystic teachings and healing practices. They are pushing for the so-needed change. Any system out of balance will have a counter reaction first. The empath movement represents this counter reaction. It is reflected in personal relationships, in our systems and at global level, but it hasn't embraced its full power yet.

Separation is always in form, never in love

Quite a journey, isn't it?

I have often been asked: 'why do you dive so deep and never get tired of it?' Well, there is no way back. I can't unsee what I see. Once I had peeked through the veil, even if only for a second, I had to move forward. Not driven from the outer world but from inside, an inner drive that makes me curious. Of course, we all do it differently, I can see that with others. My focus and passion is dynamics. The inner dynamics, in my relations and those of our systems. I zoom in and out, always.

In my life I know well the pain of letting go of people. Friends who suddenly 'broke up with me', partners I lovingly let go and there is sadly a list of people close to me who died way too young.

Letting go of my ex-partners has always taken me quite a while. With my ex-husband, the whole period lasted five years, well, with hindsight that is. We were married for 14 years, three beautiful children, when something shifted in 2012. That 'something that shifted' happened within me. I changed my view on being related, I wanted to grow together and clear unhealed issues. I desired to explore in depth. There was no wish to leave, on the contrary, a desire to move to another level.

Well, that is easier said than done. I became quite absorbed with my journey and new fields of interest. And my husband was confronted with this change in me and did his best to stay open and move alongside. Of course, this is the short version, but we both did our best to make it work. Until, in 2017, we decided to release our commitment.

With loss comes grief, for all involved, and especially for our innocent children, who were left with the consequences of something they had no responsibility for.

What I am most grateful for is the openness and compassion with which we went through the divorce. That required a conscious choice from both of us. It felt so important to release what was no longer a reality, instead of lingering in the past with resentment and grief.

Until I was in it myself, I never understood why divorcing is such a lonely process, but it is. No one can advise you. Anyone who talks about his relationship challenges with others is not ready to separate yet! I know now that there is this defining moment that shows the right answer. Then it is time to release. Honestly, until that defining moment, I was convinced we would stay together. But after that moment, I never doubted my decision, for which I am forever grateful. Divorcing is most difficult when children are involved, so I needed to be 100% sure. No resentment left, no regret, only gratefulness for the time we had.

Sometimes we need to step out of a dynamic: the marriage ends, the friendship cools down, a conflict is too big, the parenting has been too suffocating, the boss is too bossy. Sometimes we leave too soon: we find an escape, we can't deal with our own stuff, we blame, we project, we break up. There is no right or wrong here, nor 'a one defined process for all break-ups', however we are burdening each other with the stigma. The stigma of the good and the bad, the shame and the guilt, the winner and the looser, the perpetrator and the victim. Often the people around us, fuel this stigma even more with their ideas, opinions, and their own fears.

The stigma is a result of our attachments to our beliefs, our persona, our fears. Even when our partner chooses to leave the relationship out of escapism, unable to face his own stuff, we still have a choice to stay stuck in resentment, grief and anger or we can open up to a new way forward in life. Sometimes, things get decided for us and we don't always know why. Can we trust the silver lining? Can we also refrain from forming opinions about other people who are separating? How does our judgement help them, or the pain underneath?

As it is futile to resist change, why is separating so hard to embrace? Why is it so difficult to accept that it is sometimes necessary to break free from something? Why is it so difficult to make that choice for ourselves? Why is it challenging, when the choice is made for us? Separation is the outer form of our inner release, to detach – chapter five is dedicated to this. It has many layers and at the same time it is simple. All we need to know is *who* makes the choice or feels left behind: our persona with all its beliefs and fears *or* the Self with an inner knowing? The first gets fed by input (outside ideas), whereas the Self often speaks a new language we feel challenged to trust. So we struggle, we doubt or it gets decided for us. Neither of these feelings are comforting, but the real breakthrough is shifting the movement, from outside-in to inside-out. Only then, you will know what your relationship needs.

Unfortunately, many relationships end in conflict, fights, or endless discussion on how to separate. Finances, possessions, and the children become the three main points of the conflict instead of the pain underneath. We need law, lawyers and mediators, to reach an agreement. What once started as a loving connection ends in conflict. The unacknowledged and unresolved pain, the projection and the inability to communicate, is why things end in a painful way. When we feel hurt by the other, we find it so difficult to look at our own role. We are never responsible for the other person's attitude or action, but we are always part of the dynamic and responsible for our own role and the choices we made. Perhaps we even made a wrong choice initially, to say yes to a full commitment while we knew intuitively that there was something to be wary of. We ignored the signs. All these elements fuel the conflict. Our inner struggle with accepting it didn't work out, feeling rejected and of course the resistance to being alone again. Taking that all in for ourselves, without any projection on our (ex) partner, requires inner work.

Why is it that we are so resentful? We struggle, being honest with ourselves. We cannot own our pain and choose to self-sabotage our lives by staying the victim of this pain. Any relationship that ends with feelings of resentment is not ended. The energetic cord is still attached and connected. Choosing not to see a friend, an ex-partner or even a family member, out of resentment, is only a temporarily solution. The burden is not released when a person is out of sight. Resentment is one of our most damaging pains. We hold onto it out of anger, but we only hurt ourselves. It eats us up and diminishes our health. The sad thing is: resentment doesn't solve anything. Resentment is what keeps the pain alive, maintains the connection and leaves you stuck in the past. It doesn't matter whether it is your mother, your ex-partner, your ex-best friend, the attachment to resentment keeps the relationship alive, in a painful way. This pain blocks you from moving forward. In fact, you take this pain with you into your next relationship and it affects that too.

As we are still learning to make this shift, to trust our Self, we might separate or be separated for 'wrong' reasons. That doesn't release us from our responsibility to separate in positive ways.

We celebrate weddings but we hardly ever honour endings.

A relationship (the formal aspect of it) is truly over when nothing sticks anymore, no resentment, no blaming, no judgement, and no fear about moving forward. Love and respect is what is always there, only the form has changed.

Before you move on, heal 'what is still sticking'. Clear all cords before you get entangled in new ones. Feeling deeply into the dynamics (mentioned earlier in this chapter) is where you can explore your shortcomings and your desires.

Be grateful for what the relationship gave you or still gives you. Be grateful to yourself when you honour your honesty, time to complete yourself.

We don't experience new pain, we relive old ones.

Separating with compassion and gratitude is healing for anyone involved. It is choosing self-love, with respect to what was. This can be true of separation in all its forms, including the death of a partner.

Forgiveness

Next to gratefulness comes a deeper layer, forgiveness – all part of the releasing process. Such a loaded word that can spark resistance: why should I forgive the other who has hurt me? Why do I need to forgive myself when I was the victim? I was only a child, how can I forgive? We feel so hurt, how can we forgive? Is it an option to ignore our pain and hope that time will heal wounds? What if time doesn't heal wounds and only puts them in the box of forgetfulness? Who are we serving if we wait?

Instead of answering these questions, we often end up devoting time and energy to sharing our stories of how painful it was. Hoping that helps to release us from this pain, as we so much desire to be seen, to be loved, to be heard and to matter.

As a child we had every right to be loved by our adults and siblings. When that was not happening, we were hurt. Resentment and hatred makes sense, as it is difficult to understand why you were hurt as an innocent child. But it is the adult mind that keeps the resentment alive. When we stay stuck in revenge we can become the parents we hated as a child.

Underneath, this runs a deep programmed belief. We somehow have been taught that people cannot improve or change, 'once a perpetrator always a perpetrator'. That fixed judgement is why we feel that punishment is needed. It keeps us stuck in the low vibrating field, fighting pain with hatred, but that's not how to shift energy that's stuck.

So we repeat the cycle, not in the same way, but we keep hurting each other and ourselves. That is a fact of life, as long as we live it unconsciously. Opening up to forgiveness is the greatest gift to our collective progress and we need it now more than ever. Even the most narcissistic person must be forgiven, for our own liberation. It is the mind that defines hate and resentment, not the heart.

Forgiveness requires an open, compassionate attitude towards all that has happened. It requires courage to embrace your hurt ego, your hurt little child, your angry self, anything that is in the way. It is a conscious choice to choose for yourself, pure self-love. That is what forgiveness is all about.

It is so much less about the other than we might have believed. We were taught that forgiveness is to step over our own boundaries and be compassionate to others' actions, but there is no self-love in that process. Real and deep forgiveness is to release oneself from the burden by letting the other be released as well. It is a win-win! Yet, it is a process we can only do by ourselves.

The process of forgiveness requires us to feel into the energetic connection first. Before we can start, we have to open ourselves up to a higher frequency, the frequency of love. It is of no use to stay stuck in a lower vibration, it won't release anything. As we are integral parts of this field, we include ourselves in this process of forgiving. Forgiveness therefore often asks for some time and inner preparation.

Ho'oponopono is a beautiful process for forgiveness:

I am sorry
I forgive you
I thank you
I love you

This mantra combines the different elements of honest regret, love, gratefulness and forgiveness. All elements are equally important. To use this mantra effectively, a meditative state is needed. Visualizing the person you want to forgive, connect by heart and repeat the mantra many times, while you stay fully focussed on the person – which can be anyone including yourself or inner child. Stay open to all pain that comes up, no resistance. That is all it needs. To know if the forgiveness process is completed, feel back into the connection. If there is any hiccough, tension, remorse or resentment, the process is not completed. Just repeat it, again and again, until it is healed.

Forgiving will awaken your Self and shift you into this higher frequency more consistently. We will feel elevated, enriched, emotionally grown-up and empowered. We will realize that no one is to blame but our ancient dynamic of dishonesty and non-transparency. It is always a play of frequencies and it starts within. Soon new doors will open, new roads to travel and new experiences to explore.

The game we play

Once we realize we cannot change the other or control life, we become humble and self-reflective. Much of the transformation takes place in the silent connectedness between you and others. Trust that you attract(ed) the right people in your life for the right reasons. The game we play is to experience, explore and grow, knowing that change is inevitable. It is a choice to shift in our frequency more consciously and consistently with the insight we gain.

Each relationship, friendship, family line, colleague shows an opportunity for growth. That doesn't mean we have to accept everything. It is like a dance of expressing, reflecting, and releasing, with a constant openness of your heart. That is pure Tantra. The process asks for so much softness and gentleness towards oneself. Kindness is not the same as feeling sorry for oneself, as we gently say goodbye to our role as the victim. The kindest thing to do for ourselves is to let no other close our heart!

Self Love is often misunderstood. It is such an easy phrase and such a challenge to *be*. It is who we are, the core of our being, yet it can only be fully experienced in relationship with others! Finding our balance, our presence, in this interaction is where we will feel less and less triggered.

The game we play is to learn to move through all these waves with resilience and curiosity. That is freedom. We are not here only to heal our pains, we are here to unleash our potential, our gifts, express our uniqueness (80:20 focus).

The game we play is played in a bigger field, beyond our relationships and the people we know in person, by name or face. In order to organize ourselves we created systems, a structure of various institutions, leading entities, ideologies, laws and regulations. A highly complex entirety, yet inseparably integrated with our daily lives, our relationships, and our being. We have already seen how we are influenced since birth by belief systems, programs, and patterns. We have learned how our awareness can support us in breaking free from those that limit our expansion. We know that our relationships are bringing our pains and gifts to the surface. Yet, we need to zoom out, connect the dots, to see how our systems deeply influence our being! Only then are we able to consciously choose to release what no longer supports our life.

NEW SKILLS

Seven new skills to develop for a thriving life

1. Observation
Learn to zoom out, to take things less personally. Look at the situation as an outsider, to see what is happening. Become the gamer or even the programmer of the game and look at your life as a playing field, where you are one of the characters. You can do this at any moment, about anything that occurs. Do you feel triggered? If it sticks it clicks, so explore.

Zoom out: what was said, what happened, why am I triggered? What is the story of the other? Perhaps it was not about me, I only felt the discomfort of the other person and made it my own story.

Zoom out and feel into dynamics in the field, look at the bigger picture. Stop ignoring or dismissing information upfront, do the research, learn and explore. Look at cause and effect, or cause and symptom. Learn to discern. Then feel where you stand, and how you act.

*Becoming the observer is a great skill to learn, to navigate in this shift. Don't be afraid that it might make you distant or aloof – on the contrary, combining this skill with the other six, you will soon find that you only become **more** engaged and involved.*

2. Self-reflection
Self-reflection is being the observer of your persona, in more detail, to understand how you operate today and decide if you need to make some changes. While the observer looks at you, the persona, and the other (outer world), self-reflection takes it deeper within. Questions like: 'What am I proud of and would love to see more of?' 'What are my amazing skills and gifts? Can I fully own these?' 'Why do I react this way?' 'What do I believe to be true here and is it still true?' 'What makes me uncomfortable and where do I sense it?' 'Why do I act this way and do I like my actions?' 'Do I like my life and the role I take?' 'What is my passion and have I created enough space to show it to the world or am I held back and why?' 'What do I fear in life?'

Self-reflection is to look in your own mirror. Standing in front of the mirror and talking out loud to yourself is a great way to affirm yourself. Even if your life looks different today, embodying now who you'll love to be tomorrow is where your life shifts.

3. Honesty
Honesty is the way to become authentic. Honesty needs little explanation but requires a lot of courage! It is even more challenging to be self-honest while your environment is hardly self-aware. Nevertheless, once you are working with the observer and self-reflection, you cannot escape self-honesty. Any discomfort you feel is where you are not honest with yourself, and most likely not honest with your environment. We are all perfect imperfections. An honest person is vibrant, attractive, radiant, calm and self-assured.

4. Ownership
Own every breath, thought, feeling and action. Own your role. It is the opposite of projecting, judging, blaming or stigmatizing. Stop hiding behind a good intention once you see it is not received well. Stop being selfish in little things convenient to you, while you criticize others of doing the same. Stop being the victim, or feeling powerless. Step up, ask for help, walk your talk. Own the life you have been given. Make it a meaningful one, in every second.

5. Conscious choice
Free will is the basic law that creates and sustains life. Honour your free will and the free will of others. We are all entitled to make our own choices, but make it conscious – not forced by others, not by being manipulated by others, not driven by fear. Make a conscious choice to make a change for yourself when current situations no longer resonate for you, or when old habits no longer align with the 'new you'. Say goodbye to the role of the victim, the resentful, the frustrated one, the pessimist, the ignorant, the selfish, the arrogant. Choose your vibrating frequency in each 'now' moment.

6. Consistency

To unlearn what no longer fits, to create the life we desire, to attract the right people and synchronicities in life, we need to be consistent in our thoughts, feelings, and actions.

Re-pattern, re-align and re-lease. Be resilient and adaptable. Live your life with others and their quests. Learn to balance giving and receiving. If we desire new action, new experiences, to bring our gifts and passion into fruition, we need to be consistent and do the work. We cannot expect to change with just one attempt.

7. Empathy

Empathy is never about you. Not your ideas, interpretation, feelings, advice or help you like to offer. It is purely observing what you sense is occurring with the other – active listening to what the other has to say. Take the information you receive consciously and react with a selfless action that supports the other, again, without your personal interpretation. Check, if needed, to confirm that the action is right for the other. Most often empathy is an act in silence, showing up in full presence.

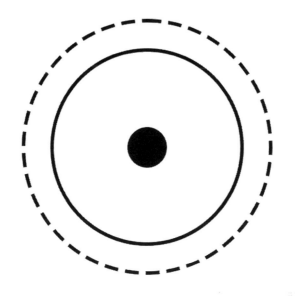

LIVING

OUR ROLE AND RESPONSIBILITY

4. Living

Learn to connect the dots

Since I was very young I often wondered why there is so much violence and war. History books, movies, news, bible stories, all shared varieties of conflict. I wasn't much of a philosopher so I didn't go into depth, it was just an observation. I avoided violent movies and couldn't understand how people watched them to relax. I didn't feel drawn to becoming a freedom fighter either. In general, I avoided conflicts and was highly sensitive to tensions with other people.

The events of 9/11 and years following marked my first major awakening to how our systems work, or rather, do not work. I remember being furious that many governments supported the invasion in Iraq. Everything felt wrong: the reason, the motive, the rationalization. If there was a threat of terrorism than this was not the answer. I remember being so surprised later, when more critics confirmed that President Bush had lied about the threat of 'weapons of mass destruction' to justify invading Iraq, the world wasn't really shocked. He just got away with it and up to this day the region is fractured and unstable.

I became more vested in the dynamics of our world. Piece by piece, I connected things and weirdly, once you see through the main dynamics, everything appears in a different light. Perhaps that is why I am more interested in dynamics and know little about facts and proof. It doesn't help that I have a bad memory for names and data. In fact it often frustrated me that, when I did start a discussion around a sensitive subject, I would be cornered for not having enough proof. But I feel so deeply that it doesn't really matter. For me that would be more a trap. There are thousands of specialists out there for each subject. I look at the big picture, dynamics, events, people in power, how these things affect us and, most of all, how we react.

Ultimately it is about me, my reaction and actions. Anything out there that hits or hurts me tells me something more about me. So I zoom in and out all the time. Of course I make misjudgements, or I am too aggressive in needing to get my point across. Oh, I have learned so much and I'm still learning. Especially the nuance between being aggressive (out of frustration) and being angry (from passion) in my words or energy. With frustration energy I push people away or don't spark any interest. The needed shift seems so obvious to me that I find it frustrating, why people can't feel the urge to explore.

Another weird thing I noticed is that I can't feel hatred to a person or group. I can dislike a person, especially when his actions are inhuman to me and even more when someone is lying and gets away with it. I can hate behaviour but I can't hate people. Perhaps my years of training in observation, and feeling where something or someone is out of tune, is what makes me more objective but not less passionate.

For the first time in my life, writing this book, I had to sense my own view and describe it authentically, through my lens. And at the same time, keep it open and inviting. That process really showed me, at deep cell level, that facts are never absolute but always coloured by perspective. I knew this as a theory but since 2020 it became my best practical lesson. I learned to trust my senses more. Does it make sense to me (zoom in) and does it make sense for all (zoom out) and if not, what is there to learn, what pattern to unravel, what dynamic of egoism is deeply rooted in our DNA and how does it show up in my daily life?

We live together on a beautiful planet, with endless possibilities and probabilities. Our creative energy is limitless and we always know how to advance and grow, through our innate desire to seek answers and explore. We are colourful in many ways, not just in skin or hair colour, but in a huge variety of talents, gifts, and intellect. We are excellent in bringing forth traditions that build foundations for our cultures, another way to express our special characteristics. Tradition also bonds us, gives us the safety of belonging and deepens our inner being. Not just shamanic, religious or spiritual traditions, but also the traditions we grow up with in the family, school, social groups and so on.

In our colourful way, we play out different roles. There is no right or wrong, although we tend to use judgment to define people as good or bad. Yes, there is a deep shadow inside us, we can call that bad – and it certainly can show up in harmful ways – but it also has its purpose. Our shadow side pushes us and others into the light. Some people play-out the shadow role in their lives. Wherever they come into positions of influence they hurt others badly. However, they are unconscious of their hurtful role as for them it feels aligned with their purpose (which is not the same as a high vibrating frequency alignment!).

There is a strong, long-standing, destructive power on earth. It causes wars, destruction, death and suffering. It is an accumulation of shadow sides that strengthen each other and meet with little counter force, which is light. The dark side is overpowering our natural light. As long as this force is strong, our light is dimmed, again and again, as we don't have enough inner groundedness to keep it shining.

That is the core problem in our world: our average frequency is so low that we keep getting pulled down into our shadows. Not climate change, fights, wars, disputes, or whatever else. These are all consequences of the real cause. We need to see this dark side within us, that has been ruling our planet for ages. Ruling in the sense of being the dominating force in our actions. As long as we don't see it or we deny it is there, it will live within us and in subtle ways be present in our actions. It will pass on through generations until we break the cycle. As we have seen, repeating bad habits (unconsciously) can be addictive. It is false security, and we keep doing it. We all have some of this darkness in us, but not all to the same degree, nor are we all in the same position of influence.

It is important to understand that a low vibrating person can be highly creative, intelligent, and talented. Frequency is related to emotions, a state of being or a level of awareness, not to talent or gifts. Lower vibrations use force (in various forms) to bring forth intentions. High vibrations use natural power to manifest. But it is our average low human vibrating frequency, or our level of awareness, that allows a destructive force to be played out.

This chapter will give words to this dark force. Therefore it is perhaps not a light and cheerful chapter. 'No pain, no change' means that pain is unavoidable. You are invited (perhaps even challenged) to stay open and reflect on what you read. Through questions you are guided, to feel within and hopefully find relief. Acknowledging that there is pain, and that we do have a problem collectively, is the release we need to support our paradigm shift. Denial is our worst enemy and keeps us stuck.

The purpose of this chapter is to show predominately the downside of our systems – the way we live together and the dynamics that prevail. We must force ourselves to see, with unflinching gaze, the collective pain that causes daily suffering for so many people on earth. This is not to dismiss or ignore all the good and amazing things that are happening on the planet. This is to show where we have a hard time acknowledging what is happening, right under our nose.

More importantly we have to acknowledge our own role, as we are integral to all of it. Only then will we collectively be able to unleash our potential. We will discover soon that we only thrive when we all thrive. And to understand what thriving really means, we have to understand all the dynamics in our field. Only then can we tell if we truly thrive or if we only created a comfortable life for ourselves, to satisfy false ego.

> *When we consider the needs of the group more important*
> *than that of the individual no one is thriving.*
>
> Foster Gamble

We need to break free from our social programmed spell. A spell that lacks compassion and shifts our human nature in the pressure to conform. That is why it is necessary to have this double awakening. Alongside our inner process to awaken to the Self, is the expansion of our awareness of our system, how we live together. They are intertwined. When we dive into the process of expanding our awareness, we cannot stop at our personal lives and our inner journey. Yes, that is where we experience all of it, that is from where we will make the shift, but it will only happen when we truly understand how we play a role in the bigger scheme. We have already seen how we are programmed through various belief systems, from an early age. We have recognized how they influence our adult lives, until we are able to see through them. If we understand that dynamic, then next is a logical consequence: our level of awareness of our personal belief systems defines our belief system for our collective and hence the future of our children. We won't change all beliefs at once but we can make a start with seeing through them. Only then we can make a conscious choice.

What is meant by systems and dynamics?

We are used to the fact that we need to be highly organized to live on this planet with billions of people. We created many systems to make this happen and all of them are based on beliefs, patterns, and dynamics: education, health, earth resources (energy, water, minerals etc), monetary and tax, food and agriculture, science, information, security, law and justice, economic (stock market), country and global leadership, and religion. For most of us, these systems are a given, things we grow up with and don't question much. Nor are we aware of how dependent we have become on those systems. Perhaps we vote very consciously for our next government, believing we have influence through our democracy, but for most of us that is about as far as our interference goes. Willingly we give up some of our freedom, believing it is necessary for, or a consequence of, being organized together.

In the previous chapters we have looked at inner freedom (Being) and the freedom to stay our authentic self within our relationships (Connecting). Aware of it or not, we all have an innate desire to be free in all areas of life. Yet most of us feel free only as long as we have enough money to live the life we desire. Making money comes from hard work, maybe some good luck or being born into wealth, at least that is what we believe to be true. However within our current systems that is not possible for the large majority, neither are the systems empowering us to become independent and free. Most of us struggle to make a living, work long days and save for a half-decent pension. Many more can't live without hunger or the struggle of not having enough food the next day. Those who live a comfortable life have become numb to what happens elsewhere. A new war, another year of famine in a faraway country, a natural disaster, they are all just news lines for a couple of days and soon forgotten. Why is that? Don't we care?

Looking at the challenges in our world today, is it safe to conclude that our current systems have resulted in a planet that is destroying itself? Some questions to ponder:

- are our systems designed to optimize the potential of everyone?
- have our systems managed to create peace and safety for everyone?
- how is it possible that our technological progress is growing exponentially, but the happiness of life on earth seems to be in a downward spiral?
- how come our systems teach us little about our natural self-healing abilities, instead stimulating us to disconnect from nature, and allowing economics that make money of our health?
- is it possible that we are in denial of these issues because they feel too complex for us at an individual level, and we feel we lack the power to make any difference?

- when large numbers of people are organized through systems that tend to become global, how big is the risk that we lose our independence and become docile followers?

- do we know what drives our global leaders, those in charge of solving our collective challenges?

So, what is happening? What is it that makes our world so out of balance? Shouldn't we all be thriving? Are we not thriving because those in power do not mean us to thrive? And are the 'needs of the group' used to keep us in pain and suffering? If striving for the needs of the group keeps the individual in struggle, who is served? No-one, or a small group at the top? Now we hear that the planet is overpopulated. Can we only thrive when there are fewer of us? We have to see and more importantly *sense* for ourselves what is causing it, to know if we want it to continue.

The pandemic of 2020 caught us all by surprise, for different reasons. For many, the leaders are heroes, taking the right action to prevent the spread of a virus. For others, the leaders are evil, taking extreme and unnecessary measures that rob the people of their rights and freedoms. And for yet others, these are just the necessary steps we must go through, and they willingly follow the measures. The world has never been more divided. But it is clear to everyone that we won't go back to how things were – something has changed, we all feel it. How our new lives will look like is entirely up to us, all of us. The collective reaction and its possible consequences are used in this chapter only to illustrate the dynamics: how do we, humans, react to our environment in general and our systems in particular.

What is different from any other time is that the pandemic of 2020 has rapidly restricted our freedom, in all areas of our life. Are we moving towards more top-down control or is it just temporary? There is no human being, *not* in a position of power, who voluntarily says 'yes' to top-down control, as that might quickly become totalitarianism. So how can that even be an outcome?

Well, history has shown us, again and again, that those who have lived through the rise of oppressive governments seldom realized the perilous situation they were in until it was too late. However, history also shows us that those intentions were always hidden in plain sight and that adversity creates change. 'No pain, no change' expresses itself at all levels, from inner change, to revolutions and natural extinction. When our lives stay in the status quo, we feel no urge to evolve. When we zoom out and look at our biological evolution, any moment in time when a species (organism) is threatened with extinction due to a change in their environment, adaptive behaviour and evolutionary change are required. It is up to us to find out if we are in an existential crisis, where we need to redefine ourselves, or if this is just a temporary set-back, soon to resume life as it was.

To sense if our organizing systems influence our evolution in a positive or negative way, we have to gain a greater understanding of what is happening. By looking at the dynamics and tactics that run our systems, industrial sectors, and politics, we can ensure we don't get lost in facts and data. Just be aware of what's driving your understanding: the mind based in opinion, or the heart based in curiosity.

This chapter is not meant to convince you of one truth. Its purpose is to open you up by sharing (other) perspectives and questions. Remember that when we are stuck in our mind, we can only perceive small amounts of new information outside our current beliefs. Each of us defines reality from his weakest point, where we can't admit other perspectives. This belief is the one that we defend (or hide) the longest and will colour our perspective more than any other. What is more important is to sense the dynamics and tactics and feel whether they make sense, feel morally right, are empowering to you and if you would wish them for future generations.

Also be aware when you feel resistance or denial toward new information. You might, for example, dismiss a line that mentions 'those in fear' as it feels not applicable to you. The problem is, we don't recognize that most of us are in a subtle state of fear, constantly. Resistance and denial always come from a source of fear. Keep observing your reactions, instead of formulating opinions, and search with an open mind. There is so much information out there. Our technology, the internet, books, courses, all invite us to explore. To reach a broader overview it is paramount to see a variety of sources. No source is completely objective. The writer, the institution behind the writer, the organization that broadcasts, the platform that designs the algorithm, the corporation that wants profit... all of them colour information (see the documentary *Social Dilemma* for a little peek at how our online world predefines our reality). Although there are a few major online sources and platforms, new ones are emerging to enrich us in our exploration.

What really supports our curiosity is to escape the mindset 'that is just how it is' or 'there is no other solution' or 'there is nothing I can do'. Those positions don't drive progress, but are only defensive and trigger our impotence.

To solve any problem begins with recognizing there is one.

Only when we recognize that there is some force working against us will we be able to break free from it, as we will no longer give it our consent.

Please note: when we talk about systems and tactics, it includes both sides of the spectrum. The aim here is to gain more understanding of our own dynamic and reverse it. From outside-in to inside-out, from unconscious reacting to conscious inner sensing and then responding, to break the spell of dynamics that don't serve us in any way.

Forces and dynamics that characterize our system: the power pyramid

Let's have a look at common power structures. The current model running in most of our organizations and institutions is the power structure of a pyramid. The pyramid works according to one rule: those at the top decide and they are a small minority, compared to the number of people over whom they have power. Some believe this is practical, even necessary, in leading large numbers of people. Perhaps it is practical, but it's no necessity – there are other proven ways to organize ourselves. But more importantly, for a pyramid system to work for the benefit of all there must be trust, transparency, and a good working objective. And that is not the case in our hierarchal *power-driven* structures.

Anyone who has worked at top level in large corporations knows where and when they had to adjust their ethics or rationalize their actions, to play along with the game and meet their financial targets instead of being a good human leader. The pressure to comply is strong for those concerned with position and power in the hierarchal ladder. New organizational models are introduced but, in reality, the dynamics of power shift only slightly.

At a geopolitical and economic level, we see the same pyramid structure. We, the people, are almost at the lowest level, below us are animals and nature. It is safe to say that we know little of what happens at higher levels. The question is: do we need to know, or can we trust it blindly?

We have been led to believe that the leaders of all countries run their own independent show within their own state and sovereignty, but less is true.

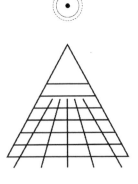

*The power pyramid: horizontally the layers of power and vertical
the industry segments, all compartmentalized*

From the bottom up, a simplified version of the pyramid looks like this:

· animal life on land, water, air, and nature;

· inhabitants, we the people;

· governments of all countries including their national institutions
(except for leaders of the most dominant countries, they are a little
higher up);

· big corporations dominating economic systems (large commercial
businesses, big tech, pharma, chemicals giants, oil and gas
corporations, investment groups, insurance companies, news
corporations, top universities, science and health institutions,
organized crime) – they influence how we live our lives;

· institutions like UN, WHO, WTO, NATO and IMF intended to guide
global stability and growth;

· international banks, central banks and Federal Reserve (all privately
owned);

· at the top (if it is actually the very top) are the dynasts, the
extremely wealthy families of long-standing, the magnates, the
royals and landed aristocrats – in short, names that keep coming
back through history and seem, over time, to have the greatest
visible influence. Together, they are linked to our industries,
institutions, and important political leaders.

*There is no other agency of government that
can overrule actions that we take.*

Alan Greenspan, Federal Reserve

Although this book is described from a western point of view, China
and Russia are equally playing dominant roles in the highest echelons.
Perhaps one could say: at the top of this pyramid is a pyramid within,
where the different parties are in another power structure and battle,
over the course of centuries. That triggers another question: who is our
enemy really and for what reasons?

To make it more complex, there are wealthy foundations (NGOs)
presenting themselves as philanthropists and influencing the world
dynamic with their agendas and money. There are global (closed)
networks, from Ivy league clubs to Freemasonry, Club of Rome, WEF
and Bilderberg. There is the Vatican. There are two large investment
groups at the top (Vanguard, BlackRock) with a dominant share in
every industry.

How these foundations, the top of these networks and investment
groups are exactly positioned in the pyramid is less relevant than the
fact that they are financing and circulating globally at *top* level, higher
than our governments, and popping up in every major sector and
institution. They have money and omnipresence.

In rough terms, we could say less than 1% rules over 99%, we the
people. The 1% have influence in every area of our lives, including
our democratically chosen governments without having been elected
themselves. This brings us to the next question.

Dare we admit that we lost our democracy?

The complex dynamics of past centuries and industrial revolutions are beyond the scope of this book. But we can see that corporations have become stronger, more powerful than our country's chosen leadership. For example, governmental responsibilities, like healthcare, utilities, education, public transport, become industrial enterprises (or directly influence them). Corporations, to optimize production and market expansion, become global players and create new levels of competition. Governments are in the game as well, offering favourable terms for corporations to settle their headquarters (with tax optimization and flexibility on environmental impact). All of this is considered a logical consequence of meeting the needs and demands of growing populations.

Of course, the industrial revolution has brought many benefits (jobs, wealth, education, personal growth, improved living standards) as well as raising our needs and driving our greed in mass consumption. We play an important role in giving corporations their power. Without consumers there is no market. We support tech giants by becoming addicted to their solutions. Consequently they gain undue influence over our societies.

During the latter part of the twentieth century, wealth was more equally distributed in western societies, allowing less developed countries opportunities to grow. But since the beginning of this century economic benefits are no longer equally distributed. The gap between the very few ultra-rich and the general population is growing and growing. In other words, the industrial and tech revolution has led to a system in which corporations, NGOs and global institutions have major influence on national governments and therefore weaken our democracies.

National governments are supposed to define the laws that determine how we live, but they seem relatively low in the power structure. Are they free to define their own strategy, how much do they know, how transparent is it, up at the top? How are they influenced by the geopolitical forces? And when the top level of the pyramid controls every layer below, leading all segments (largest stakeholders in all the leading corporations), we have forces in control that are not chosen democratically.

Should we even be bothered about all this? Many might say: those with money have power, that has always been the case. Or, maybe they are doing their best for us, with good intentions. But supposing they decide our freedoms and future in ways we don't like? Is there any democratic principle by which we can counter these developments and keep things in check? What if this pyramid structure is not the best way to ensure a better future for all? Shouldn't we at least be concerned?

Now we are getting to some important questions. How negative is the effect of 1% in power? Can one stay in a position of world power with 100% good intent and morality? Is it humanly possible to have so much responsibility without misusing the position, for gain? Are the powers that be simply incapable of creating conditions that will support a balanced life on earth? Or are we asked to see the dark side in the evolution of mankind, extreme narcissism, which always urges to more control and power? Is there an agenda to stay in power no matter what, and if so, to what further extreme narcissism might that lead? Or can we stay in power, following random narcissistic actions, without any controlling plans?

Those questions are likely discussed by the philosophers, political experts, historians and psychologists, but the fact is: a relatively small number of people influence our lives. That should be of interest to all of us. Instead of looking at data, we will focus on the tactics used, past and present, so to recognize their actions. Do they form the foundation on which our systems are being run? If these tactics are recognized, do we agree to allow them to continue – and who allows it? The one that allows it is one who can change things.

I never felt very engaged politically, but I am highly sensitive to injustice and non-transparency. I cannot stand it when one person gets cornered or ridiculed by the masses. At the same time, I don't really understand it when people worship or follow others blindly.

The moment I put more trust in someone else and believe he or she will come up with a plan, I give my power away. And the opposite is true as well. When I put energy in hatred in evil that is happening, I drop in frequency and actually give it more power.

With so many confused information streams out there, learning to observe and discern has become key. It took me quite a while to see through this effect of focussed energy, since ignoring what is happening isn't a solution either.

Humanity is too much out of balance and has been for too long, if not always. I can rest and accept that as a fact, but it doesn't make sense to me. I can't see why we cannot live in balance, in peace and empowered.

So many inexplicable things are happening. In my explorations many topics seem to be highly sensitive and non-transparent. Free energy, climate change, natural health solutions, theories on viruses, 9/11, 5G, vaccine programs, treatment of cancer, these are just a few. Experts suddenly disappear or are blocked. You can call it conspiracy if you like, but then, who is conspiring against who? Isn't it more helpful to find out (together) why these topics are so sensitive, instead of pushing people into divisions, without any dialogue?

What surprises me most is that people accept the well-known flaws of the system without questioning it. Whether it is a politician who lied and is re-elected again, or a tax haven created for big corporates and foundations, or lobbying that only benefits big business. Questioning that, am I suddenly weird, sceptic, a conspiracy thinker, or what other label is there? What is wrong with a fair and transparent system that benefits the people?

To me, it is evident that bad intent exists. It happened in the (recent) past, so why wouldn't it happen today? A leader being smooth and charismatic doesn't mean they're empathic or trustworthy. Why do I see connections between different fields of interest, where others do not? Once my view expanded, my connection to humanity grew more passionate and I have never felt more alive. As if a veil lifted.

Ten tactics of control

Use of manipulation, the main tactic that underpins all others

To stay in power you aim to get what you want in the way you want it, also known as manipulation. How do you maintain control over all industries and politics? You need at least six strategic positions:

- you make sure you are the largest stakeholder in every large corporation of each industry, through a web of investment companies;

- you make sure you can act above the law by controlling the highest court and/or by having enough influence to change law;

- you control or at least highly influence mainstream news (through point 1);

- you control belief systems through education, science, and religion;

- you control the monetary system;

- you control security and defence to secure yourself against whoever is the enemy.

Someone who uses manipulation knows that winning trust is more important than anything. Besides, you cannot stay in power if your actions destroy everything. The list of positive contributions to our societies by the same top 1% is longer than that for negative ones. What's more, those using manipulation to influence others are often not aware of it. For them their behaviour feels normal and their actions make sense. They have an objective to gain: to stay in power, to earn more money, to have more influence, to secure their resources, to win a war. Which is not the same as good intent for the benefit of many.

People believe in people, they seek safety and invest trust in public figures. Once we have identified ourselves with a public figure, we are inclined to believe in their good intent and disregard negative possibilities, especially when the public figure has mainstream support. We trust that justice will prevail, if needed. And *those two things* are exactly the reason why it is so difficult to see through manipulative behaviour.

You cannot legislate power away, because power
leads to evil and evil is in ourselves
(greed, lust, false egoism, manipulation, narcissism).
That is why power structures rule the world and have done for centuries.

Evil has been part of our history so why wouldn't it be present today? Perhaps the greatest self-deception of all is thinking it won't happen under our watch. We use various states of denial to justify what happens, but more of that later. Why are we in denial of evil? Because it is the reflection we don't like to see in ourselves. We all have some of it, subtly for most of us but nevertheless it is there. Even though no one intends harm to other sentient beings, we do allow animals to live horrible lives for our food supply, we allow soldiers to fight our wars, we allow humans and animals to be guinea pigs for scientific experiments, even outside the laboratories, under false notions. We believe it to be okay because we desire safety, new medical solutions, luxury products like make-up, cheaper food and so on.

Law and order are not independent and objective. Like any human, they are susceptible to power and manipulation, enough for the ruling elite to stay in control and get away with crimes, lies and fraudulent actions. Who do you think makes that possible? Somehow no judiciary system has been able to correct manipulation and evil actions. And what about us? We are part of it as well. We simply elect them again or play along in ways that allow them to retain their position. Occasionally someone gets sacrificed and doesn't make it back, but then we judge the person and not the power structure that made manipulation possible. Why do we allow it?

Even *if* our judiciary power is independent and not influenced by any leader's position, we still have to face our own mirror and look where we are selfish, narcissistic, manipulative, and egoistic. We have to acknowledge our own role in all this: we allow injustice and avoid our responsibility.

The collateral damage that comes with evilness is not something our rationalizing mind can sweep under the carpet. The only antidote to manipulation is in taking ownership of our lives and responsibility for every action we take. That will mean being highly uncomfortable for a period of time, changing habits, beliefs, and most of all, daring to be different.

To recognize the next ten tactics, we have to look at our own lives and behaviour. Try to recognize how each tactic plays out in your life, in your job, the education you had, your society, the authority you trust, the networking dynamics in which you play a role, the language you use against others or the selfish decisions you make.

1. Choose those who keep you in power

When you are power hungry you make sure you stay in power. The easiest way is to secure the family line. Children of top wealthy families grow up with the expectation they will follow in the same tradition. Stepping out of a strong family network is not easy. Of course that alone is not enough to sustain a strong powerful position.

How to find the right new candidates that keep you in power? The network is everything and with power and influence you might put anyone in a strategic position, as you see fit. What is better than to have several networks, breeding candidates so you can select whoever fits best with your ideas and can be your puppet? Networks that breed for potential top-level are networks for life. That is why they continue for generations. These networks use strong imposed rules and values, group pressure, hierarchal structures with exclusivity and penalties for dissidents. The higher you get the more common it is that blackmail is used, which makes it almost impossible to leave. To become a perfect candidate you need to show a readiness to comply and obey. Because most people join these networks at a relatively young age, for example at the start of university, their willingness to belong is strongly driven by a desire for social connection and future career prospects. Also targeted are people from unstable backgrounds, who feel lost and have a strong desire to belong to a social group or make career.

Not everything in these networks is negative. They create opportunities for career, connections for life, personal development, sharing ideals or new visions. Still, it is questionable how authenticity, independence and inner freedom is developed through the strict rules of a network, its values and social codes.

2. Lobbying

While many acts of immoral manipulation are executed behind closed doors, lobbying is the most known and openly accepted one. We find it completely okay that our politics are influenced through the lobbying of all industries and networks, in a process directly linked to money, position and bribery. While we allow this, our democratic voice hardly counts. Lobbying can influence elections, parliamentary agenda, and changes in law. Even when a president is elected without fraud, the role of economic hitmen can force countries in debt so external organizations can take over local economies and ensure valuable resources stay in the right hands.

Of course, not all lobbyists are ruthless influencers. Lobbying can benefit charitable initiatives. But while there is a power pyramid structure, the lobbyist's manipulative networking keeps the layers and hierarchy in place.

Whenever we compromise our own sovereignty, and our inner alignment, for the sake of greed and vanity (our false ego), lobbying becomes manipulative and compromising.

3. Keep fear alive

From a western perspective, China and Russia are portrayed as threats to (national) security, lawful economies, and 'western' values. This justifies the basis of intelligence organizations (for example, the CIA and British Intelligence), military budgets and a whole industry built around security and defence. It encourages nationalism and people readily give permission to radical measures, such as war, that cause harm to many innocent people. Whether the threat is real or not, the people never really know because government information is seldom transparent and not investigated by many. The problem with labelling groups, terrorists, nations, or viruses as a threat, is that we never lose the label. Once something is labelled a threat, it is never released, by those who created the stigma! Societies are convinced to never live without fear and always need a protector. Would we only open ourselves to healing our relationship with fear, we would never give any such leader the power and authority to rule over us.

Fear is the foundation of most governments.

John Adams

4. Divert attention

As explained before, we have learned to approach anything in life in fragmented parts. As a result, we mainly focus on symptoms and hardly ever on the cause. We have a hard time seeing the whole picture, as our lower vibrating frequency prevents that. This fragmental approach can divert the attention of a large group of people from any agenda. You keep them busy around a common supported subject (and in fear) by using framed language. Then you make sure to direct the discussion to symptoms and avoid the cause. You create buy-in for something that would never happen under normal circumstances.

An example

In the first month of the global pandemic in 2020, the majority of people did not believe a vaccine would be the only solution, that lockdowns would last more than a year, that a 'testing society or vaccine passport' would even become a reality, that curfews would be accepted in modern western countries. So how is this possible? We are fighting over symptoms (highlighting exceptional examples of illness, subjective statistics, cases, hospital beds) and we lost track of the real cause: weakened immune systems, despite the fact that it was clearly stated on day one of the outbreak and soon confirmed after the events in Italy. The moment a government would emphasize that anyone with a healthy immune system experiences little to no effects of viruses in general and this one in particular, we would all be working to improve our immune systems and supporting extra measures for those whose systems are compromised. We might still have a relatively high number of people falling ill, but the panic would not be throughout the entire population and measures would be more targeted. Focussing on strengthening our immune system is a more proactive and healthy approach to a solution than mass testing, isolating, destroying economies, and creating multiple sources of stress for everyone. So, what has been the real reason for distracting our attention? Is it a coincidence that in 2020 the world seemed to be covered with 5G towers, we're being pushed towards a cashless society, forced into new untested medical injections labelled as vaccines, and, under the premises of health we are asked to share more private data than ever before?

Example 2
Events of 9/11 caused a wave of fear across the world. We allowed war to start in Iraq under the false notion that there were chemical weapons in the making. Once war began (well, we started earlier in that region with the Gulf war), the whole region was soon in a state of conflict. The non-Islamic world developed a fear of the Islamic world and their terrorist groups. Soon we were involved with a wave of migrants who were looking for refuge. And today? No terrorist attacks, no big news on the migrant crisis. As we diverted our attention to the pandemic, other issues faded into the background, but we are more divided than ever over the Islamic religion, the culture, and its believers. And we know that the initial reason to invade Iraq was based on a lie, so, what is the real reason for these wars? To create more division? To introduce more laws to limit our freedoms? To protect oil interests?

A terrorist attack or a pandemic creates chaos and confusion that leaves most people in a state of insecurity. The fear 'it could potentially happen to me' makes people submissive, less able to think objectively. Our alert, conscious mind goes off-line and becomes numbed while it is searching for a solution without any precedent. When the mind goes offline an opening into our unconsciousness is created, to imprint a new belief system: e.g. vaccination with a health passport is our way out of the pandemic, or stricter controls are needed to prevent more attacks on airplanes or depopulation is needed to combat climate change. These new beliefs release the mind, as it has found a way out of the fear and therefore it agrees to a solution it never would have without the fear. Slowly the chaos diminishes while the new reality becomes fact. The chaos and panic has drained our energy and none is left to remember how it started or counteract its effect. With the war on terror we never released our fear, even though the 'feared enemy' has been dismantled. The same is happening with the virus threat, we might never lose the fear of other viruses and variants.

Meanwhile, while we're all in a state of collective fear – completely absorbed by news headlines, no matter what the cause – revised solutions, changes in law, adjustments to our freedoms, can be rolled out without the masses noticing. It is like a magician's trick. We are intentionally distracted, to look at one point, while the trick itself is rolled out before our eyes, but we are too occupied to see any of it. Later in this chapter we will find how to get ourselves out of this deception.

5. Mind control

The use of mind control happens at different levels. Any forced belief system is a form of mind control. Any method of education that focusses only on cognition and downgrades other talents is a form of mind control. The intentional use of images, storylines, narratives or framing of information in public media, be it movies, documentaries, or news, is a form of mind control. The language used by governments and mainstream media contains many words that emphasize fear and are the opposite of empowering. Words like 'can, could be, possible, will lead' are all indirect statements but we perceive them as fact and so the seed of fear is planted.

Although history and today's world (in all segments!) show a lot of intentional framing, it is up to the receiver to perceive it as mind control. The state of being (in that moment) in which a person receives the messages defines how susceptible a person is, which is directly related to the level of frequency. Anyone in a lower vibrating fear frequency cannot distinguish context from message and loses objectivity. Fear is used to manipulate and is an effective way to control groups and societies, without any existence of real danger. Those in fear are easily manipulated by whoever promises safety from the threat. It is easier to control people in fear than those who are self-empowered and independent.

When repetitive messaging is used on a large scale it becomes mass hypnosis. The hypnotized cannot think for themselves and follow others blindly. Anyone who is captured by mass hypnosis would deny it, being unaware. Mass hypnosis captures the mind *and* shuts down our social intelligence: a combination of our common sense, knowledge (IQ) and emotional intelligence (EQ).

Mind control uses different approaches and messaging that levels with the average intellect and social history of the group.

There are various related tactics:

- fractioning, message intensity steps-up gradually (to ensure acquiescence);
- create a 'yes' frame of mind (to have buy in);
- reward obedience (show proof that it works);
- threaten with a consequence (if you don't comply then ...or if you do comply then...),
- the illusion of choice that leads to the same desired result (the follower thinks that he is still in charge);
- social proof (use of popular public figures who promote the desired narrative),
- scarcity and inequality (not enough for everyone, those with money can get it first);
- and the strongest one of all, social pressure.

6. Social pressure

The pressure of group thinking is an effective way to influence behaviour. All it takes is a common idea that we are responsible for each other, that the needs of the group should prevail over the needs of the individual. People within the group keep sharing the common narrative, echoing the same message (often with little personal analysis) and soon the belief is seen as a truth. Then the social pressure increases as the group feeling grows stronger. Phrases like: we are in this together, together we can solve this, are constantly repeated.

Soon anyone not complying is labelled as anti-social, deemed responsible for increasing the problem and excluded from the group. Sounds familiar? Topics like climate change, terrorism and Islam, racism and cultural stigmatization and Covid-19, all show strong group behaviour with social pressure. When in this process, institutions (schools, police, public transport) media and businesses are involved in the same narrative, it puts pressure on individual thinking. The *fear of standing out* as an individual with authentic ideas increases when the main narrative is supported by a larger group. No one wants to feel excluded or ridiculed.

Social pressure works well around subjects where the individual has little knowledge or cannot find conclusive evidence. The experts are seen as authorities and all we can do is echo their statements. After a while no-one knows if there really is still a threat and progressive insights are not relevant. Everyone is focused on one group solution.

To enforce dictatorial regimes, social pressure is used in the same way: create group coherence and obedience, step by step, on the premise of fear of something unproven (religious dogma, for instance). Group coherence creates taletellers, who will work within the group to correct or exclude those that don't comply. Once the majority is indoctrinated the new reality has become mainstream. Then, anyone not following is excluded – their own fault for not complying.

When the social pressure is high and the consequences of not complying are scary or unaffordable (we cannot lose our job), people are willing to do anything, including giving up their friends, compromising their ethics and even sovereignty, to stay within the safety of a group. If this is combined with other tactics like framed mind control, we risk being completely unaware of what we really desire for ourselves and for our world. There are many examples in our recent history of how readily people can exclude groups: Apartheid in South Africa, racial segregation in the US, and the events of World War 2.

Despite these well-known examples, what happened back then happens again, as long as we don't see through these tactics.

7. Ridicule, suppress or eliminate anyone that stands out

Our fear of being different starts at a very young age. We do our best to fit in. Using ridicule and mockery is therefore a tactic to silence anyone who threatens the top of the pyramid. When you control all the means, news feeds, online info, and law, it is so easy to isolate one who stands out. It sends a direct message to anyone else: you better comply and don't think too critically. The fear of being different or having another perspective has grown exponentially through use of social media and online platforms where anything can be twisted, exposed, or framed. In 2020, having different opinions divided close relationships. Now it is you against your colleagues, you against your family or even you against your loved ones. The fact that we cannot share our feelings or viewpoints without being judged or ignored is the real cause why those in power get away with a false notion of protection. The voice of authority has become more valuable than the viewpoint of a person you love.

To ridicule a person for whatever reason is so commonplace that we are hardly aware of it. Whether we know the person or not, we feel entitled to express whatever we think, if not directly. We love gossip. When it is a public figure it is based on hearsay, mainstream news, or social media. All of this interaction is happening in a low vibrating frequency. The more tension there is in a group or at societal level, the more we look for the bad guy on whom to project our fear. Hate speech is therefore more common today than ever before. No matter what a person has done, anyone who uses expression of hate, speaks from a very low frequency.

The fear of speaking up, disagreeing, is present at any level of the pyramid. When you are part of the top 1% you have to comply to the rules of the group as well. Throughout time there have always been those who blew the whistle or fought against the system, but they either didn't live long or were not supported to make a fundamental breakthrough. And we, the people, soon forgot about our heroes or didn't believe they were heroes in the first place, as we went on with our lives.

The real power of freedom is felt by those who dare to speak up and share authentically. There is nothing more empowering than sharing your wisdom. And that is exactly what is used against us. Were we able to speak freely and share a variety of perspectives, we would become too powerful. Therefore it is crucial to understand the essence of what's written in chapter two: Being. Our deep inner alignment and finding our own true expression is what will break the spell of any control tactic.

8. Divide and conquer

We think in 'black and white' or 'for and against'. From a young age we believe we have to choose a side, which only reinforces our feeling of separation and keeps our inner fear alive. By choosing a side we feel safe again. That is why the tactic works. All you need is a subject that can never be proven, agreed upon or resolved and that will keep people debating and fighting! When you have the means to influence both sides, you can even create the problem, blame one side and come up with a solution.

We know we are divided over several subjects, what we don't realize is how it disempowers us. There is nothing wrong with more than one opinion or a good debate but *the way* we debate creates a negative force: argument against argument, proof against proof, fight against fight. Our energy is focused on winning, in a win-lose dynamic, which makes the force negative.

As long as we don't see that we are falling for these negative opposing forces we will be subjected to being divided. A group divided is easier to handle as it is weaker. Any topic that divides us on a grand scale should cause alarm, as it is most likely not about the subject itself. The moment we can see that we need to reposition the field of forces and realize from what state of being we share our argument, we can shift from problems to solutions. The solution is not in the argument itself but in the energy with which we drive the debate. When we approach any 'opponent' with an openness and curiosity to learn from each other, it shifts the debate from fear-fear (which gives more fear) to love-love (which gives more love). It shifts from win-lose to win-win. In a win-win dynamic no one can divide us.

9. Propaganda and censorship

Pay attention to any content that is censored;
it always indicates a threat to those in power and knowledge
you likely need to know. Truth does not require censorship,
lies depend upon censorship of truth.

Daniel Larimer

To steer the narrative one needs to have control over all major sources of information, online and offline. Mainstream news is owned by a few corporations using numerous uniquely branded broadcasting and publishing outlets, creating the impression that our mainstream news is always objective and diverse (this counts for all main news channels in the world). When you control them all it is easy to share one message, especially when you establish international intermediate sources, like news corporation Reuters. Compare news items over one major subject and you will find literally the same sentences on each channel.

Obviously not all news is completely one-sided or misrepresented. Nor does this mean that there are no objective investigative journalists anymore. Controlling the narrative means pushing certain ones through, altering some to its convenience and blocking those that expose the truth too bluntly. Or corner messages and the messenger in a framed negative label. Use ridicule, denigrate opponents, and create confusion by emphasizing words that make people doubt alternative information: call them weirdos, conspiracy theorists, or paranoid quacks. To complete the confusion, make heroes of others who play roles in changing the world. Some are the puppets of the top, others are activists against the top. Most people will accept those who are supported by the mainstream narrative. That is how people remain divided, arguing over details and symptoms, never to see the complete picture.

> *Those who tell the stories rule society.*
>
> Plato

Throughout history, the level of 'freedom of speech' indicated the extent to which civilians were free in their society. Where propaganda and censorship were used, societies were suppressed. It is no different today. To argue over freedom of speech is almost impossible when we are in a strongly divided society. What is not seen is that fear clouds the objectifying of information.

> *Information in itself is never a threat,*
> *how we perceive information makes us susceptible to it.*

Information is only a threat when we follow it blindly, when we echo each other's message, when we lose our inner compass, when we are receptive to sound bites. The main argument for censorship is that information feeds extremism or instigates violence. If that is true, can we then also be honest with ourselves, that information can feed fear and instigate hatred? Can we admit that we have then believed in such hatred? Can we then also admit that we often blindly accept what we read or hear, without being open to other perspectives?

The real cause of hatred, violence and separation is not the information itself but the intent with which it is written and received. It is always on the receiver to take responsibility for interpreting information as objectively and discerningly as possible.

The first step towards a transparent society is to learn to objectify information, read different and opposing viewpoints, refrain from judgement, stay open and curious. That will counter the power of framed information. We will realize that finding truth is perhaps a utopia, and less relevant to our gaining transparency.

10. Keep the world in scarcity

Money has become the basis of our economy. We simply need it to live. What better than to create a system based on scarcity and debt? Only a relative few will be able to get to a level of wealth and the rest keep struggling all their lives. The top of the pyramid has been in control of our banking system and money supply for some centuries. Early in the twentieth century a change was made that easily keeps people and countries in debt.

> ### A short, simplified explanation
>
> *Our monetary system is based on the principle that debt is needed before we can circulate money in our economies. To that debt, interest is added which increases the debt. There is no actual value linked to these two inventions. Almost the full 100% of our circulating money is a **debt**, loaned again and again. We basically create money out of thin air and those in debt pay to those who are in charge of creating and circulating the money. Which creates a strong dependency in our monetary system between the 'creator' of money and the ones who are in need of money.*

This system with its rules is openly known and accepted by many but hardly ever questioned as to whether it is a fair system we should keep in place. Crypto currency creates a first break from this old system but are we sure it is completely free of power control?

The dependency gives money the energy of scarcity, which is the cornerstone of our (global) economic model. It defines demand and supply. Scarcity is directly related to fear. When there might not be enough of something you need, you fear you won't have it. This is the trap we are in, collectively. The economist will argue that is just the way our model works. The model itself might not be wrong, the question is: does it work in all our favour? Perhaps it did in the beginning but now it is safe to answer that question with a 'no'. Could we say that it doesn't work in favour of 99% of the people, of which only 50% have enough to live 'comfortably' – just one percent of the world's population have more wealth than the other 99% combined? (Bloomberg and World Bank)

With the power of a few, they act above the law, not accountable,
practice double standards, apply law to the weak
but the strong are free to act as they wish.

Richard A. Falk

The double standards Richard Falk is referring to is the main issue of our system, not money itself. If we can create money out of thin air and our economies accept it as a valid currency, we can choose to divide it more equally. However, those in power define the rules and those rules are not equal to all.

More alarming is that if you control the money supply, you are also in the position to devalue money whenever you like. It is the perfect way to control the masses, while everyone depends on money to live.

A lot of people are aware how our monetary system works. They are aware that it is not backed up by any standard of value, like a gold standard. Many are also aware of leveraging power and influence to avoid tax. But those who are aware often live comfortably enough not to feel the pain and suffering this system gives to the masses. The same riddles always come up: 'it is what it is, that is how it works, I cannot change anything, it is up to anyone to create his own wealth, I worked hard for mine, money makes money', and so on.

The fact that I'm not offering a solution to all our worldly problems is the response I receive most often when I raise these issues. It actually annoys people to go into any depth because it feels useless to them, having a discussion doesn't help.

I feel their resistance.

I know this feeling of powerlessness so well. Once I had opened my eyes to the problems in our world it felt painful and unsolvable. At times the shift to a new paradigm seems impossible, but as soon as I scale it down and focus in the here and now, something shifts within me. When I look at my own life and feel where I find flow and excitement through my inner alignment, I immediately sense expansion. Then everything seems possible and so evident. It really is a shift in frequency that makes all problems solvable.

I feel their denial.

Denial of things we don't like to see, hear, or admit. I don't expect anyone to be surprised at what is shown in this chapter, but it is a whole different ball game to admit that it might be used against us. Perhaps it really helps to keep it small-scale and to yourself. Like I did, at first, I just explored and didn't share much with others. With each dot I connected, the picture became clearer, and my knowing that the shift comes from within only anchored me more – a solidness that feels so liberated and empowered.

Why are we not breaking free from the power pyramid construct naturally?

*One single tactic is innocent in itself, all tactics combined feels like
a strategy, a strategy is always designed to achieve an outcome.*

At the end of this chapter there is an impression given of how our societies feel today. It is not an absolute version of our reality but it gives an idea how narrowly focussed our societies have become, through our fragmented approach. We don't question our institutions, dogmas, educational systems, news sources and our authorities. Yes we have intellectual, philosophical and political debates, but that is not a given for the masses. We are not raised that way and our school systems don't stimulate controversial ideas, empowerment and authenticity.

To break through a power construct, one needs to feel empowered and courageous enough to openly question the status quo. Whether we can see the tactics combined as a planned strategy or not, it is clear (and, history proofs that again and again) that power and control is contagious and addictive. All tactics are only possible when those in power are in the position to define our reality.

*When you define what is the truth,
you can define the beliefs that create the reality
and keep people stuck in the spell perpetuated by themselves.*

Remember that history is told by the winners, not by those who lost. To understand where we are today we need different perspectives on our history. Our online world is the greatest enabler to reveal what has been hidden for so long.

Our co-dependent relationship with systems and ruling power has intensified since 2020. Governments became more directive, introduced more rules, quickly changed laws and people have become more obedient. Within no time economies shut down, small businesses and jobs were lost, people fell into despondency and depression due to isolation and loss of faith in the future. Billions are in lockdown with minimal access to social life; students and children are told to keep their distance, toddlers grow-up without a stranger's smile, and the majority of people submissively wait for it to be over. But we are also showing signs of breaking free from our dependency. Scientists are more divided, many question the pushed single solution and the lack of data transparency. Ordinary people became freedom fighters, documentary makers, self-taught journalists or new thought leaders.

Each crises also gives rise to opportunities. The great thing about our forced pause in the year of 2020 is that we realized that much of our materialism is not at all necessary. We learned again to value what is important in life. We found new ways to work, from home, more flexibly. We realized we don't have to jump into an airplane for every business meeting. We value our family time again, being at home with our children. We are super creative beings, we will always find a way!

Nevertheless, economic and emotional crisis is unavoidable and at an unprecedented scale. Of course, the threat of a virus coerced many of us into compliance, but has it really been necessary to take such drastic measures? We all long to return to a normal life. But what if that doesn't happen? What if that is not meant to happen?

Let's pause to reflect

Before we continue, let's pause. Can you feel the point at which you get into denial, as it is all too negative, too sceptical? Do you find your mind (or your whole system) shifts into resistance?

The purpose of this book is to expand our awareness and raise our frequency. We first need to acknowledge what it is happening, because it will push us out of our state of denial, which is our biggest collective challenge. Denial keeps us in a low vibrating state where we tell ourselves we feel comfortable, but are we really? By denying world challenges, we deny ourselves free will (more later about denial).

We are collectively at a crossroads. How do we evolve, to a life in alignment? What is the new direction our leaders are taking? What's their focus? On what dynamics and tactics will it be based? Driven by what? What is it we desire? What is the consequence of our own role?

More globalization and centralization

Our systems and leaders seem to drive in the direction of defining, more and more, what is allowed and promoted and what is not. Partially this is a consequence of our move towards globalization in recent decades. One of the points high on the list of the top 1% and supported by practically all our governments is the accomplishment of UN-Agenda2030 (the successor to Agenda21). It has been included in many business plans, school curriculums and news items for some years, so apparently is not a one-off idea.

The Agenda2030 finds it foundation in the seventeen Sustainable Development Goals (SDG). This is a list that describes a planet in complete balance. End of poverty and famine, climate issues solved, planet resources balanced, inequality overcome, women empowered, everyone educated, no more human trafficking, no more genital mutilation, and so on. The 17 goals solve all our worldly problems. Great! But it also gives rise to questions like: how do we realize this plan? Is it achievable? What is the strategy of the UN and its supporting leaders and who else is involved? And what tactics will they use? What role do we, the people, play in this change?

There is another movement that plays a dominant role in our world dynamics: the World Economic Forum (WEF) and its famous elite events in Davos. Their mission statement says: 'The World Economic Forum is the International Organization for Public-Private Cooperation. The Forum engages the foremost political, business, cultural and other leaders of society to shape global, regional and industry agendas'.

WEF has designed many detailed scenarios and technical solutions that show how our planet will look in the near future, which comes down to: we own nothing ('national ownership'), we live in cities controlled by technology, we are all happy and we operate fully with rational minds. In return we get housing, healthcare, our basic needs and jobs. The vision of the WEF is that we cannot sustain our way of consuming and in order to become sustainable we need more top-down surveillance, social control and high-tech solutions. Another dominant player in the global arena, the Rockefeller Foundation mentioned in a scenario report: we need highly coordinated strategies, through strong political and economic alignment, for addressing urgent worldwide issues. If we leave it to individuals and local communities to find new solutions, we will end up in an economically depressed world.

Agenda2030, the WEF and the major wealthy foundations all show similarities in direction and intent as well as in collaborating parties such as national leaders, large corporations, IMF, World bank etc (the same top 1%). They all agree on the same idea. In order to create a sustainable planet, more top-down control is needed, technology is the enabler and transhumanism the solution. Is this just a coincidence or the best way forward?

Do we, the people, even realize what is meant by 'technology as an enabler' to gain a sustainable planet? Looking at the rapid advancement of just one example, Synthetic Biology, where life is redesigned at DNA level with new biological systems, we must wonder if we like that direction, as a global solution. Synthetic Biology is GMO 2.0 which means more technical modifications to our foods, like beef substitutes while consumers enjoy the same taste (these are not the soya products we have in store today). Is this a curse or a blessing? Is this a great solution to address climate change or are we moving towards transhumanism through artificial food and chemical solutions? What does that do to our conscious awareness and our natural health, in the long term?

If top-down control is not the objective but global sustainability is the main goal, there are two major prerequisites: *all* countries in the world must agree and fully collaborate, and *funds* of 2-5 trillion dollars a year must become available, according to the World Bank.

How will all countries align and collaborate?

The first point requires a huge shift the world hasn't seen before: eliminate wars, align on migration issues, share resources more equally, solve conflicts over land, trade, and religion.

In short, all countries must align, agree, and resolve everything before 2030. The agenda doesn't give details of how this shift will happen, nor how countries will align and collaborate, other than 'they will'. Although the agenda was already known and active before the pandemic of 2020, somehow the pressure to comply has hugely increased since 2020 with widely used new slogans: 'build back better' and 'the Great Reset'.

The agenda requires such a huge shift that it gives rise to many questions:

- how are we going to align all these nations while each economy is facing a crisis or will our financial institutions solve this with more loans or printing more money?
- how will it be possible while there is still war in the middle east and high tension in international relations?

- where is the evidence that nations are willing to set aside disagreements and go for one happy planet?

- how will collaboration look like and based on what terms?

- is money the driver and these plans more like business deals, made in full sovereignty of all parties involved? Would that be enough to achieve the end goals?

- will we still keep our cultures and traditions or will we become one homogeneous population?

- who will lead all this, chosen by who? Based on what authority?

Who is paying for all this?

The second prerequisite is the funding. Who will be paying for all this? The wealthiest elite or the common people, through increased taxes? The plan gives a clear indication that domestic resources of all countries 'underscored by the principle of national ownership' are central in the pursuit of sustainable development and achievement of the SDGs, generated by economic growth. With the shutdown of economies, the threat of shortages in food, global logistical issues since 2020, that is going to be even more of a challenge in years ahead.

Whether Agenda2030 is dominating and overruling all nation's agendas or it is just an exercise by the UN to propose a direction, we cannot deny the moral pressure put on our societies by country leaders: we have to build back better, we are doing it together and together we win. There is nothing wrong with a coherent plan of collaboration and an aligned intention to solve world problems together, but only if it is fully transparent and undertaken in free will by all. In fact we *all* need to collaborate to make this happen, not just the wealthy and powerful top 1%. However, collaboration is not the same as demanding compliance through social pressure, restrictive laws and imposing taxes.

Authority and centralization made us lose our sense of morality

Globalization means centralizing systems, governance, industries and making our world less diverse. We can buy the same brands, products, or food anywhere in the world. Costs, the driver making business more efficient, moves labour from developed countries to less developed countries. It might strengthen our economies but it weakens our societies. Where in the past one income was enough to sustain a family, now two incomes are needed. There is less time and energy for raising children, social community service or leisure.

Our industrial growth in the twentieth century has shown we can produce anything, at low cost and high profit. This was very much a necessity, for our economies to grow and meet the needs of many. The gained wealth and material comfort, for those in strong economies, has resulted in huge imbalances across the planet. The opposite is true as well. In the last century our progress in science and technological solutions was exponential and is still growing rapidly. We travel the world as if riding a bus, we meet people online, create new connections and learn more about other cultures and civilization as a whole. Knowledge on any topic is online, one click away, and influences our education system. Progress in health science has made possible surgical procedures we couldn't dream of twenty years ago. China's rapid economic growth demonstrates efficient centralization, as it becomes a dominating force. It is completely understandable that we don't want to go back to how it was 30 or even ten years ago, having experienced the comforts of technological progress.

Progress is the essence of evolution and technology is just as important a part of this as is the raising of awareness. But are we aware enough to handle our godlike technologies? And who defines the ethical norms of what is possible? Where do we compromise for comfort, ego, and materialism, paying the price with our individual freedom?

And who profits from all this? It seems that globalization has made corporations more dominant and powerful, the wealthiest people become more wealthy and the lives of the majority are marginally better in material gain but more dependent on the strategy of those in power (scarcity dependency). The largest profits gained by the wealthy few are made in the waves of global turbulence. Economic crises provide the best opportunity for making huge gain, especially for those who were aware of an imminent crisis and were quick enough to take advantage: the crash of 1929, the crisis of 2008, the increase of wealth of trillionaires during the Pandemic, or the profits from war and its aftermath.

Another important consequence of centralization: anyone in charge of large numbers of people knows that you can't afford empathy or be too closely concerned with the well-being of each individual. In other words, with large groups people become numbers. You care less or are not willing to see the collateral damage your actions cause to individuals (human or animal). We see the same happening in large corporations where the top has little idea of what is happening on the floor and another round of layoffs is based on numbers alone. Another example, closer to home: the majority of people eat meat, fish and dairy products as a normal diet with little awareness of the suffering of billions of animals each year. Our consumption requires highly efficient industries to serve our needs, where empathy towards the individual animal has no place.

Being overwhelmed by facts and figures makes us indifferent

We have created a global economy with global challenges to match. The numbers behind these challenges are massive and beyond comprehension for most of us. The impact of decisions and actions are equally enormous so it is hard to grasp the meaning and impact of it. Naturally, when challenges go beyond our understanding or sphere of influence we feel less engaged or involved. Then there is no option other than to echo what is said and accept that those in power know what to do. Increased taxes, health measures, new laws, less privacy, all receive our consent with few questions asked. Imagine what would happen if you personally had to sign for each change in the law, or pay new taxes each month in person e.g. to Agenda2030. Wouldn't we want to have more information and influence on how this plan is rolled out? And wouldn't we like to be sure that the top 1% contributes in equal ratio, so we really do solve our issues *together*?

Focus on one solution for all

Centralization also assumes that only a relative few decide what are the best answers and solutions for everyone, disregarding numerous other solutions. The past century shows many examples of solutions that were not allowed to come to fruition. To name just two: many scientists have built on Tesla's invention of free energy and others have found working solutions and new (low cost!) health solutions, proven to heal serious diseases in a natural way, but these haven't reached the people. Those experts and specialists have been ridiculed, imprisoned or worse. Why aren't we exploring new solutions in open debate or at least given the option to choose? What is main showstopper for new ideas that could be less profitable, besides the most obvious one: money?

Laws and morality

Centralization and technical innovation also lead to an increase in interconnectivity which calls for more global governance. That means we will cede greater authority to those in charge of defining and constituting the sum of laws, policies, and institutions in international systems, which affect practically everything in our lives. Authority is the right to rule. Or as the dictionary shows us: 'the power to enforce laws, exact obedience, command, determine or judge'. In other words, the right to forcibly dominate others.

> *The people never give up their liberties,*
> *but under some delusion.*

Edmund Burke

We have created a delusion around authority. First we convince ourselves that we need many different laws and regulations. Secondly, we convince ourselves that laws are made under an honest democratic process, hence we should obey these laws. Thirdly, we accept that governments consider themselves above the legal responsibilities that 'the people' are expected to observe. In fact, through their position of authority, governments use law to decide our morality. As Mary Ruwart stated:

> *Government tries to make the immoral, moral*
> *by giving it the blessing of legality.*

What is immoral is taking away our freedom, that is our birth right and not a constitution or a law. Yet our governments have us convinced that they can make new laws that limit our rights to work, travel, breath freely or live where we like, under the flawed morality that we are responsible for each other's health, each other's safety, each other's contribution to pollution and so on.

Some questions to ponder: how is it morally right, that millions lose their jobs or businesses while a few trillionaires increase their wealth by more than 27% during a pandemic? How is it morally right to have soldiers fighting in wars while the ones sending them to war gain more wealth or power? How is it morally right to justify violence and hatred under the auspice of revenge, someone being different, outspoken, or having a different ideology? How is it morally right to force people to have injections, under threat of exclusion from access to normal life (jobs, restaurants, education), when it is our birth right to have sovereignty over our own body?

Morality and law, always apply equally to everyone. It cannot vary depending on the position or institution. If one person cannot legally stop another from taking a drug that he believes will help him, no government should do that either. If one person cannot legally force another to live healthily, no government should use legal measures to enforce health solutions. We have disconnected ourselves from natural human moral principles.

All of our actions are coming from honest truth, causing no harm or loss to the rights, freedom, life or property of other humans or sentient beings.

With this lack of inner connection we have allowed our governments to make so many layers of law, under the false assumption that they need to protect us, because we can't live by our moral principles. And, if we cannot live in freedom ourselves, we don't trust that someone else can. If we all were born, raised, and supported through all our systems in the *natural moral principle*, we would barely need any laws to protect us. This might seem to many of us like an impossible solution, but that is more a matter of perspective and vibrating frequency.

Authority triggers obedience

Authority has led to obedience, which is the silent way of giving our consent. A child gives his silent consent when he obeys the rule of his parent. He was never asked if he agreed. The authority is within the role of a parent, at least that is how we believe it works best. Whether we agree with this aspect of raising children or not, we are not the children of our governments. We are all grown-ups, adults of equal position. We seem to have deferred to to the notion of a false consensus in our democratic system. We are hardly aware of our consent. Through not owning our role and responsibility, we step into the role of the child and expect our parent (government) to take care of us, in return for which we give our consent.

The obedience to authority shows a highly co-dependent relationship between governments, institutions, and their nations. It creates room for manipulation. Any co-dependent relationship requires emotional growth (on both sides) as we have seen in the previous chapter. As long as we, the people, stay willingly in the role of the child, many decisions can and will be made for us and we can't blame anyone but ourselves.

Social pressure leads to false morality, especially when under a 'health emergency'

We can debate global issues quite objectively, but when our lives are at risk we lose objectivity and can be deceived through social pressure. In 2020, under the threat of a pandemic, our governments, national and global health institutions have shown what authority can lead to in just a short time. Many of the described tactics of power have been used: they have ignored transparency, blocked open debate, allowed censorship, and by law have taken away our basic rights of freedom. Is this the best approach to a health crisis? The fact that we cannot debate a serious matter, openly, is immoral in itself. There is no basis in moral principle that make open debate of serious matters harmful to others.

Across an entire planet all governmental actions have been focussed on symptoms and not on the real cause. When faced with a global health threat we would expect military to build emergency hospitals, free supply of immune supportive substances and stimulus, and open debate with experts seeking solutions. None of that has been done. All actions were (and still are) focussed on spreading fear-based narratives, separating people, discouraging and even forbidding social activity and restricting our freedom, even within our homes. These are plausible precautions in an initial phase, when there is panic, but not after a year, with all our knowledge of medical science combined. The *non-transparency* is alarming, not the subjective driven discussion about whether more people are ill. That comes second to transparency. It is a highly sensitive subject and has driven families apart in a way no other subject ever did. That in itself should ring alarms bells!

Under the false notion of giving protection our systems made illegitimate legal rulings and convinced people that it was right to do so. Using social pressure they set us up against each other. Social compliance is given the weight of 'morality', but it is based on false principles. Governments are not responsible for our health, they are (in our current model) responsible for offering the best system that supports our health. They work for us, on our behalf.

People might still argue: you risk doing harm to others if you walk about 'unprotected' while there is a dangerous virus around. How true is this? The false principle is the twisted version of cause and effect. The cause is that we have lived in unhealthy societies for ages. We have given consent to many unhealthy developments, like the stimulus of processed food, indoctrinating children with snacks and sweets, healthy organic food being unaffordable, dependency on chemical medicines, chemicals in our drinking water, chemicals on our crops, promotion of addictive substances and systems (like state supported gambling) and a stress causing monetary system. These all have a negative influence on our immune systems and wellbeing. No government has ever warned us about these negative influences, they allow corporations to provide them. We have all supported this, many still do, without serious concern. Now we suddenly care? Because a virus is contagious and all the other things aren't? Perhaps we need to define contagiousness. The dictionary tells us: a) carrying or spreading a contagious disease and b) tending to spread from person to person, like contagious laughter. When more than 90% of the people are blindly copying habits/actions/reactions of the mainstream narrative of a dangerous disease (definition b), and 98% of the people seem to have little to no reaction to the dangerous virus (definition a). What is then really the dangerous contagium here? And who is responsible for the fear driven narrative? And who is responsible for receiving it that way?

The misuse of 'responsibility' is another sign of co-dependency. As we wrongly make our eldest child responsible for the safety of his younger sibling, so our governments have us convinced that we are responsible for the behaviour or health of others. None of us is responsible for the health of another human being and the justification of the virus is one of ratio not a moral one, where our ratio confuses cause and effect (weak immune system versus danger of a virus). We are responsible only for our own health. There is nothing wrong with taking your own precautions where that feels right for you, that is an adult position. Like many do in flu season. The moment we accept the pressure of 'responsibility' we have become the child in the co-dependent relationship, due to our own fear.

Emperor with no clothes

Immoral practice runs deep and at the same time it is more visible than ever, almost as if it wants to be exposed and dismantled. Remember the story of the 'Emperor with no clothes'. Once you see through the narrative, it is just as obvious as the nakedness of the emperor. That is why we are at a pivotal point in history. We are about to break through the immoral power structures that have long been dominant. The moment we say 'no' to these immoral systems, they will dissolve. For that to happen, we need to awaken from our blinding cognition and break the spell. Let's start by coming to our senses. Common sense is not an act solely of the mind, it is the interaction of the heart (sense) and the mind (logic). The interaction is most important, or we are easily misled by the mind.

Denial is our challenge

You might think this whole chapter is too negative, too sceptical. There are amazing people doing amazing jobs, creating beautiful projects, working hard and who love to share their wealth. This is absolutely true but that vibrating field of higher frequency is not yet on a large enough scale. People are good beings by nature but much of our good nature is suppressed, for various reasons explained here. However a level of scepticism is needed to see through the tactics of power and to overcome denial. It is temporarily an enabler, to ignite a spark within us and see through the tricks everywhere. Our scepticism creates distance and objectivity, necessary to get ourselves out of the trap of 'turning a blind eye to evil, as it can't be that bad'.

> *When there is a consistent suppression of prosperity*
> *for all of humanity and it only gets worse,*
> *we cannot deny what is and has been happening.*
> *That should make us all sceptical.*

Our problem is not lack of understanding, intelligence, or the overwhelming nature of our global challenges. Our problem is denial. Denial is pervasive in societies today, and much used as a survival mechanism. If we would allow ourselves to sense into all the misery and imbalance in the world, most of us wouldn't be able to cope with it (at first!). We use denial to protect us from feeling the suffering. Even though we have learned to shut down our feelings, we still have them as we are by nature empathic beings.

There are three levels of denial:

· literal denial, claiming that something did not happen or is not true;

· interpretive denial, claiming that what has happened is not what it appears to be;

· implicatory denial, denying or minimizing the moral implications of what has happened.

Therefore, denial includes cognition (not acknowledging facts), emotion (not feeling or being disturbed), morality (not recognizing wrongness or taking responsibility) and action (not taking active steps in response to knowledge). (Source: Sirriyeh/Cohen)

Denial is what creates the gap between the mind and the heart and blocks our common sense and social intelligence. Try to feel into this question:

Can our institutions and governments have bad intentions,
to secure their position to stay in power?

Cognitive dissonance, when we lose our inner resonance

Denial is one of our many defence mechanisms, as we will see in more detail in the next chapter. There is another mechanism that works collectively, as one big shield, and is very much related to denial. It is our cognitive dissonance reaction. As the word already shows, it resides in the mind. It is the inability of the mind to see another perspective on a situation, being strongly focussed on receiving confirmation of its beliefs. This is unrelated to your level of IQ or your level of awareness. We all are subject to cognitive dissonance reactions, to avoid any perspective that makes us too uncomfortable. The main thing that blocks us: we think of ourselves as honest people who can see through deception. Admitting that we might have been wrong is a tough one to make.

Because we have become mind-driven societies, this effect happens on a massive scale. The simplest form can be recognized when we buy something that is expensive to us. Receiving confirmation that we bought something for the right price and of a good quality, puts us at ease. We don't like the uncomfortable feeling we might have made a wrong decision. Then we would feel like we failed ourselves and have been betrayed by the party or information source we trusted.

Even without a valid confirmation, we defend ourselves for our actions, convincing others more strongly that we made the right choice. Deep down we ignore the itch that something feels off, we know we made a wrong decision but fear to admit it.

This effect runs deeper than most of us realize. It is a mixture of trusting and not questioning the source, the repeating of a message and the rationalizing mind that finds reasons to confirm the message. When actions are proven to be inhuman, corrupt, based on lies, we have a hard time acknowledging that the person might not be so trustworthy or so knowledgeable after all. We prefer to follow the safety of the large group, mainstream opinion, to define our reaction. Here the cognitive dissonance creeps in. For example, if a person with authority does something illegal and the same system decides he can stay in his position, we're inclined to still trust that authority. We might support this with reasons like: 'well, he is elected again, so he must be alright'. It is irrelevant whether there is enough evidence against this person. We find reasons to decline the evidence. That is how politicians or other well-known figures can get away with immoral and harmful actions. Our rationalizing mind prefers calm waters, rather than risk a system to be questioned. Then what? That question is too big, so we avoid it. We don't feel sufficiently empowered to make any changes.

The cognitive dissonance reaction is highly active in a lower vibrating state. When there is fear, we lose our objective and critical thinking abilities, as all our energy and strength is focussed on our old instinctive reaction of fight, flight, or freeze. In this state we are highly sensitive to the effect of a repeating message from trusted authorities, as that feels like a safe way out. Combine that with cognitive dissonance and a whole world is hypnotized. As we don't dare to question the source of authority, we give away all our power and our sovereignty. Questioning it would not only risk the fall of the authority we have trusted, but with that our whole view on life will have to be questioned. Realizing and admitting that our laws and judiciary system might not be working objectively is perhaps our greatest deception. Because if that is not working well, who or what is protecting us?

> *Our biggest challenge is to acknowledge to ourselves that*
> *evilness can happen under our watch, as it will imply that*
> *we have to come up with a reaction ourselves.*

Meeting this challenge, we would realize that we don't know how the real quality of trust feels as we have not been taught to use our own senses. We would have to admit that we have been betrayed by those we gave our trust. Having been lied to on purpose is worse than believing in the lie and the consequence of it. This is such a collective theme that it goes beyond our personal experience. It is deeply imbedded in our DNA. A tough one to break through without the sense of Self as we have nothing to fall back on. Therefore we prefer to believe the lie, again and again. We seem to go back and forth between two lines of thought about ruling systems, our government and its institutions:

> *'I don't want to believe they are immoral, so I defend it by thinking: all*
> *people do their best / it is not easy to be a leader / they have good intent /*
> *there is no harm in having money / we know it gives power, so what?'*
>
> *and/or:*
>
> *'I cannot do anything about the system, so I ignore it by thinking: we know*
> *those in power aren't honest or trustworthy / they simply have money to*
> *rule / it is all corrupt and that is just how it is and that will never change.'*

Meanwhile we wait until the authorities we trust will set us free. But what if they don't? What if nothing changes? This is how free nations turn into dictatorial regimes. The people trust and wait.

> *From* **They Thought They Were Free: The Germans 1933-45** *by Milton Mayer:*
>
> *(quoting a German civilian during the war)*

"One doesn't see exactly where or how to move. Believe me, this is true. Each act, each occasion, is worse than the last, but only a little worse... You wait for one great shocking occasion, thinking that others, when such a shock comes, will join with you in resisting somehow... But the one great shocking occasion, when tens or hundreds or thousands will join with you, never comes. That's the difficulty. If the last and worst act of the whole regime had come immediately after the first and smallest, thousands, yes, millions would have been sufficiently shocked... But of course this isn't the way it happens. In between comes all the hundreds of little steps, some of them imperceptible, each of them preparing you not to be shocked by the next...

And one day, too late, your principles, if you were ever sensible of them, all rush in upon you. The burden of self-deception has grown too heavy, and some minor incident... collapses it all at once, and you see that everything – everything – has changed..."

And so will history repeat itself again. Each time we tell ourselves, 'but this time it will be different; this time the new solutions of those in power, we have given our authority, will make a difference; this time the new ideas are really based on social improvement for the benefit of all'. Until we realise that *no outer authority* will ever release us or save our planet and bring it into balance and peace. No power pyramid construct will ever have us *all* thrive!

Knowledge is the antidote to fear

Ignorance is the root of misfortune.

Plato

If no one will save us, we will have to start acknowledging that we are the change. No new law will create peace on earth, neither can we push it away believing it is utopia, to live in peace and prosperity. But where to start? Will it change anything if I know more? How can I, alone, change anything?

These are understandable questions. It is a choice that comes from within and starts with our sense of responsibility. And isn't it our responsibility? If not to ourselves than at least to our children and the next generations to come? If you are young, don't you feel the urge, that what doesn't feel right cannot continue?

What makes us powerless, is that we don't know how to solve it. However we don't need to find a solution first to make the shift happen! We need to be willing to open-up to more than one perspective, become curious again, start the dialogue, explore. But never forget, self-honesty, reflection and a humble attitude is most important in those dialogues.

We need to recognize the dynamics and tactics for ourselves, otherwise we'll never believe it. Perhaps it was not just the solo action of a narcissist like Hitler, Stalin, or Mao. Perhaps there is a storyline that leads to a master plan, perhaps not.

The real challenge for us is seeing through the whole play. Actions with immoral intent need to be cunning or else they will not be successful, especially when a relatively small group of people aims to stay in power. Therefore it is not enough to follow one line of the story. Compare it with a thick knot, with different lines you need to disentangle. It is not enough, only to discuss the details of a virus, the flaws in our monetary system or climate change. Nor do you need to understand all these complex matters. Just look at the big picture, the common actions, the tactics and then start connecting the dots.

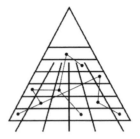

A few guidelines to get you started:

- listen to various sources, channels, messengers, both for and against your current viewpoint;

- be aware of your comfort zone, whether it needs proof from science or proof of credentials to establish authority or activism or political colour. Challenge your comfort zone;

- keep sensing the message in the words 'does it make sense', 'is it morally right, or is it twisted?'

- listen to language - what kind of words are used in statements, how often is the same statement repeated in various channels?

- sense how the info makes you feel, how the messenger makes you feel. Explore that inner process. Sometimes it triggers, other times it feels untrue, other times it feels like hope;

- don't draw conclusions on if it is true or false, just be curious about information, try not to dismiss any of it;

- refrain from echoing messages without your inner check, stop complaining as that only keeps the low vibrating frequency charged;

- take a pause from news in general and practice more of your inner alignment and sense your inner truth;

- reflect back on the ten tactics stated in this chapter. Do you recognize any of these? Do you see commonalities and patterns?

- without going deep, find links between the dynamics in all sectors: monetary, health, telecom, energy, economic, and so on;

- try to stay open to many messengers, including the ones you dismissed before. Try to define the role they play: saviour, authority, activist, populist, influencer, the (fake) philanthropist.

It can help to pick one subject, explore the information, the dynamics and the players in that field, and then move on. Connecting the dots is like attempting a giant puzzle. Perhaps start at the corners but don't create boundaries by fixing the side pieces first. The goal is to get an objective idea of a larger field, impartially observing and taking note. The Self is not part of the puzzle, but is the one who makes the puzzle: your inner alignment with what feels right and wrong. Therefore in creating this puzzle for yourself, you cannot ignore your own belief systems, your own patterns, your own programs. The more layers you go through, the clearer the field (or puzzle) becomes. Soon you will feel more liberated, as if a veil is lifted, and your frequency will rise instantly.

There is nothing to fear. More transparency in information will empower us, enable us to sense into the depth of deception from a holistic perspective. We will soon realize that we can only be deceived by others when we deceive ourselves, a very humbling, honest truth. Once that realisation sinks in, the spell is gone, immediately. They cannot hide any more tricks and tactics, playing their game, we simply see through it all. Their game becomes our game. Once you see through it, it is like the character Neo seeing through the dynamics of the matrix (movie The Matrix, 1999). He gained what seem to be inhuman strength and resilience to fight those in power. We don't have to learn battle skills like that. When our frequency rises we stop giving our consent to that which doesn't feel morally right. No shots need to be fired. Our revolution will be of a completely different kind. It is the combination of the rebel (r) who dares to speak up and the evolution of our inner work. In this process of dismantling the power pyramid, we will make mistakes or read information wrongly. That is all okay, it is a lot to unravel. More important is that we unite, open the dialogue, explore, and share.

We are not the victim, we lack responsibility

The shift in dynamics is realizing that we are the 99%
and 'those in power' are less than 1%

When we are starting to see through the whole play, it is really time to be honest with ourselves. We haven't excelled in living a conscious life either. We might blame those in power, but we all have traces of selfishness and self-righteousness. In our more developed countries we consume too much, misuse the planet, are never satisfied, complain too readily, waste more food than the hungry need, consume animals without caring how they live, exploit the sea without caring for balance, want food to be cheap, ask for state income without owning our issues, ignore those in need, want to live longer, tolerate prejudice, and so on. Corruption, immorality, egoism, lies, secretiveness, hypocrisy, all have to be eliminated, on all sides, in every detail. Acknowledging that we are not the victim will raise awareness, our vibrating frequency.

No matter how much manipulation is used, no one can ever claim power,
power is always given to a person or a system.

That is great news! If we gave power to the 1%, we are the ones who can take it away, with just as little effort. The solution is not only in grand revolutionary movements. The solution is in tiny little actions, but the crux is in it being by the masses. When we all take tiny little actions, within our own reach and ability, we create a ripple effect and soon the whole system will collapse, making space for a new one to arise. It is as simple as not complying with rules that feel immoral, rules that take our freedom away and rules that feel patronizing. That is why the pandemic is a great time to learn more about ourselves. It is as if we are presented with a huge mirror and those in power will keep imposing more restrictions until we say 'no'. The way we keep ourselves small is equally how our power structures keep us small. We are all invited to make little changes and recognize where we hide behind external authority, afraid to speak up or stand out.

Revolutionists are always seen as heroes with hindsight,
let's not repeat history again but learn from our freedom fighters.

Let there be no mistake, we have advanced immensely! We continue to learn and it is said that all of human knowledge is compounding every three years. In other words, we will learn more in the next three years than we previously learned in our entire recorded history. The next shift is in inclusiveness, putting ourselves in the middle, act from there by taking full responsibility for restoring human sovereignty, morality and ethics.

Our future depends on how divided we stay

Human evolution is undefeatable. Our natural frequency, that has been suppressed for so long, is breaking free. That is the power that is feared, our natural empowerment. A higher vibration does reveal a different reality, heightened intuition, different timelines, and other psychic abilities. Those who do experience it are so thrilled and excited about new times to come.

The roaring twenties are years of practice while the world is on fire, holding presence in the eye of the storm. Now, it is up to the masses to decide which timeline to choose. What an intense ride it is! Seeing the world deeply asleep, oblivious to what is really going on, has been unimaginable and deeply painful. No one has any fault in this, it is a result of old systems that have been in place for ages. It is so important to understand that. Being awake is not a superior position, only a different one. It is our natural state, we can all reconnect with. That is why waking up, raising our frequency, is a choice. What always rules is free will. Giving consent to immoral systems is our free will and so is breaking free from them. It is a choice and there is no judgement of any choice, but there's always a consequence.

We really have a hard time acknowledging to ourselves where we are dishonest. How easy is a little lie? How inconsistent we can be, accusing others of something when we aren't much better ourselves. It happens at all levels. Our constant need for confirmation of our existence is the biggest form of self-deception, and such a painful one. As long as we don't recognize that the validation for our existence lies within ourselves, we will give our power away. But the validation is right there, within us.

The moment we trust ourselves, our capabilities, find trust in life and in others, everything will shift. We are no longer focussed on outer authority but will find our inner purpose, our inner excitement, our creativity. All of that will unleash our potential. The solution is not in having millions in the bank. The reason why you are not doing 'that' tomorrow, is because of many other reasons that come before money. All of 'that' is our suffering. That is what we desire to be liberated from. We allow suffering to happen because we are stuck in our own suffering.

No saviour

Now, after 2020, our world is in chaos. It has shown us our deepest fear for our own power. Perhaps Covid-19 is less a classic virus than a metaphorical one. We are all forced to face our weakness (as in not healed) and there is no single cure for such a variety of expressions. For some the dis-ease is physical, for others it is psychological, emotional, or spiritual. It feels that 2020 has shifted life for everyone in some way. It pushes us *all* into purging our pains, letting go of anything that no longer fits our evolutionary growth.

We all live our own life and can only heal that which blocks us from thriving, at an individual level and *that* will have its healing effect on the collective. Understanding the direct relation between the individual and the effect on the collective is where we will rise from our misery. That is the ripple effect.

It is essential to realise that there will never be a saviour out there who will lead us in our evolutionary growth: nothing will save us, no vaccine, no agenda, no leader. That is the whole point of this shift. It is up to us, the masses, to shift the dynamics of the game that has been played for so long. We need to shift the pyramid construct, shape a new way of living and collaborating on this planet. We have to start thinking 'circular' instead of 'hierarchical'. We won't be helped by a new leader at the top of a new pyramid. That will still leave us unempowered. In fact the whole concept of leadership must be redefined.

Our path to liberation is to unite. To find each other in common goals that feel morally right and to serve the real meaning of 'sustainability' and 'for the good of all' – and not in the ways they are used against us today. When we unite we still have our different roles to play, but gradually the darkest roles will disappear. This is a wakeup call for all walks of life.

The silver lining is so bright

When we are truly driven by our own gifts and unique expression,
the 'needs' of the individual, we naturally live together
in harmony and we all will thrive.

The great reset, as promoted by the top today, will be the one we will experience, but not in the way it seems to be proposed. There is no way back to how it was. Those 17 beautifully defined goals are definitely within our reach, to be realized if we do it our way and in full freedom. All it needs is for us to take ownership over our own lives, be responsible for any and all actions we take, including our thinking patterns and the belief systems we have unconsciously been hiding behind.

Once we awaken and realize we are in the driving seat of our lives and our future, we will rebuild our planet in equality, restore balance and peace. It seems like a huge shift if you feel you are on your own, but we are not on our own. We are with 99% of the total population, that is more than 7.5 billion people. All it takes is a full 'yes' to yourself, your loved ones and to your future and just make a start from the point where you are today. Every little step contributes – don't wait for another to make a start.

When we collectively rise in frequency we will *all* be in the top, which means the top becomes as wide as the bottom is today. Then there is no pyramid shape any longer. There is no power-based hierarchy needed, to live in harmony.

Before we dive into the new dynamics of our next paradigm, we will first have to release the old. Those dynamics that no longer work for us will have to be left behind. It starts with more transparency, firstly to ourselves, that will unravel everything. We don't have to wait until we clear all blocks within ourselves, opening up to the idea that everything can shift is a good start. That is what creates space, the needed space within you to let go of the old and become curious about the new. Start by releasing your inner voice, telling you: 'I am too insignificant to make a change' and 'it is not up to me'. Remember that all we need to do is to create small circles of higher vibrating frequency fields.

Our world today

We live in a world...

- *with an economy system that values everything in commodities and shareholder value. Fresh air is about the only element that is exempt, anything else has a price tag or a condition (which is always related to shareholder value). We lost our human value of pure existence.*

- *where consumerism makes people crave more (material wealth, gadgets, experiences) that fuels the economy and increases value for shareholders.*

- *where we create obedient followers through education in memorizing, analysis and logic, more than authentic and empowered young ones who question and learn to take action.*

- *where we create achievers who exemplify competitiveness as the basis of success, keeping everyone in a win-lose dynamic, with less value accorded to other talents.*

- *where we limit potential by using low, middle, and high levels of education based solely on IQ, so only a minority reach the top.*

- *where creativity, art and craftsmanship are treated as lesser talents.*

- *where consumers lazily accept prepared food solutions and have little incentive to educate themselves on healthy diet.*

- *where we allow foodstuffs to be modified unnaturally, and promote addictive snacks to the young.*

- *where the entire food chain is controlled, to keep people eating unhealthily and in need of an unaffordable healthcare system.*

- *where we curtail the biodiversity of crops, making land infertile, dispossess small farmers and allow corporates full monopoly.*

- *where a health system solves 'any ill with a pill' and ridicules holistic approaches as pseudo-science or quackery.*

- *where societies combine science and religion, to drive the need for 'something' to hold on to. For the scientist it is reason, logic, and proof. For the religious person it is the creator, 'out there', who leads, defines, and gives life.*

- where science is the only valid approach to defining truth, but we've forgotten that science has often been proven wrong in the past.
- where any invention that threatens the wealth of large corporations is stopped before reaching the public (e.g. free energy, healing solutions for cancer).
- where we only use the fragmented approach, so will never understand the fundamental holistic nature of life and will remain dependent on fragmented solutions.
- where the monetary system forces people (and countries) into debt through loans, interest and inflation.
- where our financial institutions are not likely to support new ideas but bring up conditions that are difficult to meet and discourage many.
- where we are unconsciously subjected to mind programming through movies, television, news, documentaries with ideas and plans of action for the future of humanity.
- where we allow top-down regulation to increase, through temporary laws that are not removed when their initial reason expires.
- where we make rules and laws so complex that no one really knows what they're agreeing to, on the premise that it is for the safety of the people.
- where those in power control law and justice, so they can get away with anything others can't
- where those in power sustain laws that give them freedom to create money out of thin air and tax-free constructs to move money around.
- where half the population lives in poverty, the other half hardly cares and wastes three times the amount it would take to solve famine.
- where respect for life has been erased by wars.
- where most people have good intentions but little awareness of the consequence of their actions. Where the false ego is served at the cost of many and all, regardless of whether you are in power or a follower.
- where ...

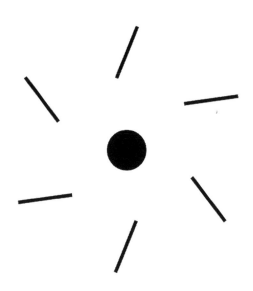

RELEASING

ALL THAT DISEMPOWERS US

5. RELEASING

The shift from conditional to unconditional

Correcting oneself is correcting the whole world.

Sri Ramana Maharshi

The three previous chapters come together in this one, like a grand finale and the core of our shift. Embracing the past and lovingly letting go of what no longer serves us, personally and collectively, and opening our arms wide open to the future. The current dynamic is from outside-in, where we let an outer authority define our lives, whether that authority is old family patterns, identity elements, emotionally immature relationships, co-dependency or controlling systems. To complete the shift to the new dynamic, inside-out, we need to hold still and be purely present, and breathe through all the dense energies we feel.

Well, if it were that simple we wouldn't hesitate one moment, right? It is that simple, but often not so easy at first. There is no story, no discussion, no mutual understanding, no digging up old historical facts, no endless science debates, nothing is needed to release that which holds us back. In fact, we could skip this whole chapter and repeat the same routine, again and again: hold still, be present, breathe into what feels dense until it releases.

To release something is not the same as to reject it! When we let go of relationships we understand that we need to release our attachment to the relationship, but often we reject the person. It's the same with our systems and institutions. We reject the political colour but not the foundation of our system, until we realize that we will have to release all attachment to how it is currently allowed to run.

We are so used to how things work in our daily lives that it is tough to let go of the safety it gives us. At first, this detachment feels cold and distant, as if you reject everything and push people away. The contrary is true. It is the shift from conditional to unconditional. Once it is truly released, the deep connection is felt again. You never lose a system or a person, you release the dependency, and that will set everything in motion. When you are no longer dependent you are free to rebuild or reshape the old into the new, that feels more in alignment. Releasing is what creates the shift of energy in our vibrating frequency, to an irreversible one. It is literally clearing our cells so more light shines through.

Although in essence it requires nothing but presence, releasing will go in phases for most of us. You can compare it with a rope that is fraying. The outside releases first. Those are the beliefs and attachments that are most easy to let go of. However, at the core of the rope, are the last ones to release. Whenever there is still a fibre attached, there is a condition on the connection, the belief or the pattern. No matter what the connection is. There is something there that still rewards your holding on to the attachment. And weirdly enough, that benefit can make you struggle 'forever'. For example, the benefit from staying in your comfortable job weighs stronger than going through your fear, to stand up and share your voice.

Something in you knows that when the rope (the energy cord) is finally cut through, you will fall with it. Nothing to cling to, but nothing sticks either. Pure liberation, but scary if you don't know what is next. The acronym for *faith* – Full Assurance In The Heart – might help to feel the difference with *fear* – False Evidence Appearing Real. Without faith, we have lost our hearts and are stuck in fear. When we are stuck in fear we believe false evidence and convince ourselves it is good enough to be true. To fully surrender to what feels like 'nothingness' is what requires ultimate faith, the trust that life will catch us.

But where to start and not feel overwhelmed by this process of clearing? For example, if the previous chapter felt somehow a reflection of our reality, now what? How to shift a huge complex integrated system with many flaws, immorality and injustice? Where to start? We often feel powerless, unable to make any contribution, which draws us back to our safe bubble while we keep hoping that someone else will do the job for us and will save us.

It is also understandable that you have a different perspective, experience, and ideas of how our societies work. Perhaps you find that our systems are not that bad and you believe in democracy, where human errors are inevitable. Perhaps you have full trust in a better plan this time. Perhaps you believe you are above the systems, so they will never hurt you, nor do you feel the need to change anything. Perhaps you feel inadequate, not smart enough or not influential enough to make the slightest difference. Perhaps you feel it is not up to you to define how our systems work. Perhaps you don't feel you need to change or rescue the world – others will, you trust.

However, don't underestimate the value of questioning something! There is nothing to lose by questioning something. Open yourself up to another perspective. That attitude in itself is the first release and sets things in motion.

Wherever we are in the spectrum of perspectives, change is inevitable. It is true of all times that (sub)systems change. We are no longer hunters or farmers. It is a natural process that comes with evolution and a never satiated hunger for growth. Each new phase is preceded by a shift in consciousness. At society level we went from family bands to tribes, to empires, to nation states. Our economy changed from foraging to horticulture, to agriculture, to industrialization. The power structures changed from tribes, to local, to national, to global. In all these changes, the role of religion played an important role and changed as well. However, with each breakthrough, it was (and still is) *our consciousness* that drives change, although that never receives much attention in our history lessons.

Often, with hindsight, we allow ourselves to acknowledge the shift. How exactly it changes might feel a big mystery, because we act from yesterday's logic. We don't know the new, so we reconfirm the old, until ... well, until what? According to our history, any big shift came with destruction, turbulence, chaos, and pain. No pain no change is always true. But, we don't all *feel* the necessary pain at the same time, to trigger change within us. As long as we don't allow ourselves to feel the inner push, we ignore change, which will collapse us inwardly instead of the evolutionary drive to expand ourselves. It is up to you to define your way. Taking 'the easy way out' and doing nothing might feel easy but will probably make your life complicated and painful. 'The hard way in', as shown in this chapter, might look tough at first, but as soon as you make the choice life feels empowering and light. What do you choose?

The double awakening

Egoist archetype

The big theme we need to face is the dance between the false egoist and the victim. Neither can exist without the other but both will lose their dominant role in our new paradigm. The false egoist archetypes, in all their colours, play their grand finale right now. Don't mistake this with the essence of ego serving the Self. The false egoist is the one that serves the identified persona, the inauthentic one.

In various perspectives, they mirror humanity, how victimized and dishonest we are with ourselves. We fail to see through the dynamics, that it is the false egoist that 'tricks us' (often unconsciously) with a narrative convenient for them (= narcissistic or selfish). We prefer to believe the narrative (= outer confirmation) instead of finding our inner truth and breaking free from our role as victim. The victim is just as egoistic in his role, as he expects an outer authority to solve his problem. One is the dominant and the other the inferior egoist.

In other words, as long the false egoist archetype in us 'acts', it is not acting from inner authority. It chooses the false safety (or position) of an outer authority over self-honesty. Just to restate, an outer authority can be anything for anyone: a belief, a leader, a doctor, a pill, a guru, a fear, dominant family structure, religion, money, the safety of a relationship. And often it is a mixture of many of those.

To clear our false sense of egoistic and narcissistic human traits, we are brought down on our knees, to acknowledge we all have some of it in our DNA. It blocks our ability to connect with others in a true empathic way.

We are a fractal of the whole.
We can only understand the whole through understanding ourselves.

Our role in the power pyramid

Wherever we are in the power pyramid is where we place ourselves, unconsciously (through our thinking and behaviour), in any given *moment*. At any layer the effect is the same, the false egoist seeks outer authority, from a layer above him, to confirm his behaviour and looks down on the layer below. Even the top layer finds its confirmation in a religion, higher authority, or belief system. Like we, at the bottom, look down on animals and our planet. Any power we give to an outer authority diminishes our own.

To *feel into* the power dynamics of the pyramid, we only have to look at our own behaviour in our societies. It is deeply embedded in our social structures. We can feel superior or inferior to others for their colour, attitude, looks, level of education, place of birth, family-line, political viewpoint, level of success, level of awareness, position, health and whatever else. Each time we judge another person or a group we place ourselves higher or lower in the hierarchy. We readily generalize about groups of people: 'they are lazy, violent, simple, rich, arrogant, in power, evil, not to be trusted, victims, need our help...'. Often the judgement is based on a few experiences in the past or stories we heard. One lazy person makes a whole country lazy, or one political conflict makes all parties involved bad. Of course we are familiar with the idea of racism and discrimination but this is way more subtle and automatic.

When we are part of any system, without awareness of its hierarchal power effect, we fall prey to judgement and comparison. Is the hierarchy in itself the problem? No it is not. Nature thrives on hierarchy. No flower feels superior or inferior in taking more or receiving less sunlight. All flowers evolve in such a way that they can shine and contribute while being part of the whole biosphere. We, on the other hand, need outer authority and power to shine and we let the same forces influence our sense of self-esteem. A flower is not sensitive to this dynamic. It just is. It is our unconscious, programmed way, of how we put experiences and ideas in a power-based hierarchy by giving it our coloured value, that we are asked to release. Ultimately we are asked to release all attachments to anything, to perceive life as truly interconnected.

Our way out of it

The dynamics that work against us at a world level, are (in subtle ways) the same dynamics that stop the flow in our personal life. The moment we truly acknowledge that everything needed to shift is within us, including our complicated systems, we suddenly feel so empowered. We only have to turn the pyramid shape upside down, to see the perfect model that shows us the result of releasing.

At the smallest point, at the bottom, we vibrate at the lowest frequency. When we release whatever holds us back, we spiral upwards, as we raise our vibrational frequency. The more we rise the wider the shape gets towards the top, the more we create space and expand our awareness. The further upward we go the wider our range of perspectives will be, and the easier it is to find new solutions. As we have seen, when we vibrate at a higher frequency, our actions will benefit others and no longer be at the cost of others. When enough people raise their frequency, even if only slightly higher than it is today, the power pyramid will start to dissolve.

To be willing to release anything at all, we need to acknowledge that we have a problem in the first place. Now here comes the challenge to all walks of life, including the so-called spiritual communities. Even when we do our inner work and optimize our personal lives, it will not be enough for the paradigm to shift or to free us from our slavery-based system. We need to include, acknowledge, and release the problem of our power-based systems, as well and shift our actions. We cannot ignore it and hope our higher alignment, of love and light, will solve it. It is not enough to only shine light if you don't direct your light on the darkness you want to dissolve.

We cannot ignore the problem we created collectively as we're always an integral part of the collective. As long as we don't awaken to our own role in this dynamic, where we give (subtle) consent to what is happening, we will *recreate* the same reality collectively. Our little lives might improve, but it won't make the world a better place. What happens in the collective happens inside us, in a similar frequency! But as we know now, our inner reflective system is cunning, in hiding what we don't dare face.

I could never imagine that we would collectively be challenged in the way we are in 2020/21. I could never imagine that part of the personal awakenings process is the systemic awakening. But since the systemic dynamics are played out so vividly during this pandemic, I realized its link. Observing how the government and its media just got away with straight lies was unimaginable. Of course it was not all a lie, but the created chaos, confusion and mind programming, made me realize the theme of trust underneath it all. So I looked within my own life and what trust means to me. On what elements do I judge a source to be trustworthy? What does it mean when something feels off? When am I too sceptical or too suspicious? I learned to sense my own inner guidance. Each time I try to sense the energy and intention of the messenger, filtering through the words to sense what feels true for me. Not easy at first as it requires a neutral state of being to begin with.

Parallel to the world events, the theme of trust played a big role in my personal life, within my relationship, my online business and travelling. I experienced directly how a negative narrative in my mind influenced my reality. I learned to trust that not all information is what it seems, but that my interpretation depends on my state of being in that moment. When I am vibrating low, I see a negative narrative confirmed, when I feel very aligned, I see a positive one. Is this what is meant, with shifting realities? Really, try it for yourself, it is very insightful once you observe the difference.

I also learned that we all walk our own path at our own pace. I learned to let go of my old pattern of trying to control the outcome and reverse the process, trusting that if I need to know something it will be shown to me. I learned to trust that if my intention is clear and focussed, the outcome will be aligned. Not always easy but it does work that way.

I felt challenged in different ways, seeing the world problems enfold. How much destruction do we allow to take place? How much of our freedom will we give away? How long will humanity act out of fear and false ego? What is my role here? How can I contribute? Should I trust evolution and wait? To me, it is not meant for us to wait and see. We need to learn to act differently at all levels and in detail. Learn to reverse and live from within. Stop giving our power away. Each day I don't contribute to this shift, the dominant forces of our system gain more power and we become more enslaved to their control.

I cannot let this happen for our future and that of my children. I know how powerful we all are! Our heart is 100 times more powerful and the magnetic field up to 5000 times stronger than our brain (Heartmath Institute). I experience the difference and feel I am only at the beginning. The more I align with my natural heart frequency, my field of influence grows exponentially.

That is the ripple effect. In the same way it creates ripples of fear today. Each day it is finding balance between learning what is evolving worldwide and finding my own role, authentic voice, and inner power. Trusting that we will shift it and it is up to me to hold my vibration high and neutral. I create my circle of influence and I sincerely hope you will expand yours as well.

Does that mean that we all have to become leaders or influential game changers? Or does it mean that we all become saints? No it doesn't, but we need to open up to the dialogue, of what has made our world so inhuman and do we want to keep it that way?

When we allow a system to exist that shows ugly traits like corruption, lobbying, inequality, human trafficking and more, we must look at our own life, where it is that we fail to see something in our own behaviour (where we act in a low vibrating frequency). It's not easy to acknowledge that you might have behaviour that is dislikeable, but we all have some. Or as someone said so bluntly: it is better to be fucked-up and willing to change than perfect and pretending.

You are not alone is this process of collective release. For decades, radicals and lightworkers are finding each other in the desire to create and shift systems. This movement is growing day by day and, since 2020, exponentially. Perhaps not so visible on mainstream channels or in your local neighbourhood but, if you start looking, you will find likeminded people. Bear in mind, we are all recalibrating and finding our inner truth – no-one is sure how it all will unfold.

To let go of the controlling power dynamics, the best and only thing we can do is stop supporting it. Stop giving it our power. Stop acquiescing to regulations and decisions that divide us.

Simultaneously we do our inner process by releasing whatever, for us, is no longer in alignment. The more observant we become, the easier we release. With each release, each purge, we bring in something new, an element that works for us, that will support our growth in empowerment. Remember this journey is about manifesting a better life, unleashing our gifts and the potential we are born with, so we will liberate ourselves and thrive!

Again, that might sound like such a huge task, to release *all attachments*, that it might put you off completely. But it doesn't have to be a tedious one, neither does it have to happen all at once, to feel any benefit. Any bit of release gives expansion. Join together in small groups. Sharing insights, experiences and reflections supports our process, to learn and explore new territories. Together it creates new ripples of consciousness. Of course, each one has to do their inner work, but the safe space, feeling supported and held in your process, as well as your contribution to others, is where we will work with more lightness.

We are all equal but not the same

A dear friend of mine, who sadly passed away, advised me to read the book by Frederic Laloux, Reinventing Organizations. The whole book was one full 'yes' when I read his view on the new organizational paradigm.

Laloux confirmed to me what always felt so wrong in our organizational structures and its disempowering dynamics. I knew my purpose: shift the power dynamics of our systems.

At the time, in 2014, it was commonly acknowledged that the hierarchal leadership model was reaching its end. However, letting go of control and giving rise to self-management at the workplace was something no one was really ready for, or I wasn't ready to deliver the message. For more than a decade attempts have been made but it merely changed the organizational structure and pushed more work onto the workforce without giving them the trust, power and ownership to make a real difference. The top-down power and control mechanisms are still in place in most organizations and institutions, stuck in various belief systems and ego structures. The current pandemic shows that clearly: forcing employees to comply with new regulations, overstepping workplace ethics and constitutional law.

My view and purpose hasn't changed, I am more passionate than ever. But what I needed to do first was sensing all the subtleties of big themes, like power, empowerment, trust, ownership, potential and responsibility within myself. I cannot convey a message I haven't experienced myself. The shift we are about to make is more profound than I realized in 2014. How exciting, to experience this!

The statement 'we are all equal but not the same' touches me to the core, as it gives an answer to why we are not all thriving and why we struggle with the theme of power.

We fear being seen as equal to any other human being, as we think that means we are the same. When we have strived so hard to be different, to become someone, we have a hard time giving the same position to someone who hasn't walked the same path or put in the same effort. We define equality by our position and knowledge, and have come to the conclusion that we are not all equal. But that is not what is meant at all. We are equal but not the same, as we are all unique. To reach our (business) goals, all people involved contribute to the end result. That is what makes us all equal. We are equal in the way we contribute, just as the opposite is also true: one weak link makes the whole chain weak. Acknowledging that we all have our unique contribution, in diversity, is where we shift to new models and a new paradigm.

Releasing our feeling of being superior, or inferior, is needed to see the potential in everyone. We feel better about ourselves when we find proof, through comparison, that the other is less good and, unconsciously, we fear their natural power and potential. As we have been driven by our IQ focus for decades, we rank people accordingly. It has created a whole set of beliefs: e.g. a person with a low IQ is less able to self-motivate or self-organize. The belief remains that these people need managers, team leaders and other restrictive structures, like time consuming report systems, to perform. As long as we hold on to a belief like this, we will find proof of it. We use terms like 'low education' and link that to inferior abilities and gifts. Unless you have an extraordinary proven talent or you are a self-made successful entrepreneur. Achievements give proof of our value. But if you are a hard-working low-educated employee you are stuck in how the (belief) system values you.

Just imagine the impact of the IQ standard, on our societies. It is no wonder that research shows we are only using 50% of our potential. Imagine what will happen if we unleash the gifts and potential each person brings to this world?

We are used to thriving economies,
which is not the same as a society where everyone is thriving.

Our intellect has given us major growth in wealth, science, material abundance and comfort. It has also shown the downside of this single focus: *an intellectual crowd creates weak followers and false leaders.*

An empowered leader is one who chooses people with better and diverse gifts to join his team, who has no fear of the power and talent of someone else, as he values his own empowerment, and that includes acknowledging where he is less talented. He holds visions and is a servant to unleashing the potential of all. A weak leader is one who needs power to control others, as he is not able to acknowledge his own empowerment. He holds vision too, but uses force to manifest the outcome to his expectations.

What the power pyramid shows us is that power is not the same as empowerment. We don't desire the same role, the same position. We are not all born leaders but we all want to be meaningful, valued and able to do what we love doing. That is what fuels our empowerment and makes us thrive. It is known that money is not our driver in life. Being meaningful is where we find joy and inspiration.

What if we have a system without money and we all have more than enough of what we need? How would we value our contribution, ourselves? How would we feel if we have the same abundance as someone with less 'capacity'? How would we create a sustainable living? How can we create a life that feels truly meaningful? Will we feel motivated? What is needed to find our passion, purpose, and gifts? Can you feel where our friction is?

We are definitely not all the same, in fact we don't even value prosperity or wealth the same, but to embrace diversity and move towards equality we have to release many attachments. When we unleash our true power, we need to redefine our ethics, to use our power wisely.

Free will and accountability

To release what limits us in our growth, we need to become aware of our free will and how it underpins everything in life. Free will is the reason you cannot change the other. Just as no one forces you to think, feel or act.

Free will is also needed to release your inner blocks. No healer can do that for you, at most he can facilitate you in the process. Although free will is so fundamental to our lives, we are hardly aware of its principles.

Our organized societies have become quite complex, based on endless rules, regulations, laws, and governance. We mostly take it for granted, as it is convenient and necessary, at least we believe so. It feels too complex to organize it ourselves, or in different ways. It is when your think in millions in one country, but it becomes a lot easier when you think in thousands in one community or entity. Our desire for globalization, our greed for materials and comfort, has made our world more complex than needed or perhaps even desired.

Whatever organizing model we choose, our free will always defines our reality and not the other way around. Even when that model or system has us under control, it is still our (collective) free will that creates the system and our personal free will to give it our consent. In essence, nothing happens without our knowing. All plans, ideas, laws, and sensitive information is made known to us (not always in straightforward or regular ways). Simply because it is a basic rule on this planet: nothing can happen without our consent.

As long as we stay unconscious of this basic rule and our automated consent, one can take advantage of our free will. Take harmful chemical substances in our products as an example: as long as we buy it or accept that it can be sold, we give it our permission. Of course, it should not be the job of the people to check everything. We should be able to trust the parties we select, to be honest and humane. However, when we have seen enough proof that our current systems are failing upon us, we *must* become aware of our (implicit) consent and the free will that allows consent.

It is not relevant to blame anyone for how things are, it is to reverse what is humanly not right and see where we are dependent on an outer source, belief, or authority. That starts with acknowledging that we are accountable for our *own* actions and choices we make (free will), not for the actions or feelings of another! Don't mix the two, as that is a false socially-framed pressure, as we saw earlier, but it runs so deep: we are not accountable for the ones who are born less lucky, not for the situation itself, but we are responsible for our own actions, that keeps the dynamic in place that creates these bad situations (our consent). No one is accountable for unhealthy choices but ourselves (free will), but we are responsible for keeping the system alive that promotes an unhealthy lifestyle or feeds fear (our consent). Can you feel the difference?

When we are accountable we need to be independent, otherwise we are restricted in our freedom to make our own choices. A general basic income seems like a great idea, to take away the pressure of earning money for our basic needs, but if we don't receive the freedom in return, to unleash our full potential, it can become a bad solution, with more dependency on the system that provides it. We might even feel agitated by reading 'we are responsible', as we don't feel we can make a change or create a solution. That is the very trap from which we are breaking free. We don't have to create one new overall solution, we can make a start by owning our lives, every little bit. Feeling where we don't move out of a conscious free will is where we can start exploring, by making a fresh conscious start each morning (see next chapter).

Are we loyal to the right one?

In our childhood we learn to be independent. Most of us don't learn that it is our free will that drives our lives, instead we see independence mainly as a financial thing. We follow an education, find a job, raise a family and hopefully do well enough to live (financially), independent of our parents or other sources.

In chapter 3 we already saw the challenging triangle to becoming emotionally grown up. As long as we are not aware when, as adults, we step into in the role of a child, we stay sensitive to those who act as a parent. That happens within our family systems, as well as, on a larger scale, with those we obey in their role of power. To put it bluntly, as long as we act as obedient children, our governments (and all systems, bosses, institutions) act as controlling, dominating parents. Since both are adults in this relationship, both are responsible for keeping the dynamic in place and potential misuse of the relationship.

How can we recognize the behaviour of a child? Not able to take full responsibility, dependent on financial support, emotionally unstable (complaining), takes shared ideas and beliefs as truth, sensitive to programming and fears punishment. How do we recognize the behaviour of a controlling parent? Decides everything for the child: nutrition, limits of freedom, defines rules without dialogue or mutual agreement, dictates beliefs and values, defines the desired future, standards for success and so on.

When our governments keep telling us what to believe, what to choose, how our freedom is defined, how and where we can live, we are treated as children and not as adults.

Key to any child-parent relationship is loyalty. Loyalty weighs more than trust. A parent who is lying or abusing his child still receives loyalty. Why? It is a consequence of continuing symbiosis, the 'umbilical cord' that is still connected and keeps the relationship co-dependent. Loyalty is a beautiful quality but only in grown-up relationships, based on equality. If the relationship is not based on equality, blind loyalty can leave room for manipulation, without either one of the parties being fully aware of this dynamic. Blind loyalty becomes a false loyalty, as we lose being loyal to our Self.

Adults now are not rebelling against things that are wrong. People are being pushed around, denied normal interaction and they are just following it like sheep... following authority without considering, what if they are wrong? What if it is not in my best interest? This is very dangerous...
Good people, people who think they are doing the right thing, community-wise. But they might be devastating both the community... [the economy] ... and their health as well. Just following without questioning.
... yes, we are at war with a virus, but war should not eliminate basic human rights.

Vera Sharav, holocaust survivor and activist, 15 Oct 2020

Growing up means we all have to face ourselves and become responsible for our actions and our own issues. We will have to open up to the dynamics that dominated us for a long time and see that we don't need 'parents' anymore but that we are fully capable of defining our own lives and ways to organize ourselves. The other side, the dominating parent, will have to learn that power is inflicting the sovereignty of the other. The good news is that only one side has to break free from this symbiosis to release it.

Entering our teenage years we try to break free collectively. The rebel in many of us is awakening, feeling the desire to break free from the childhood phase and define our own identity. An identity not based on a new ideology, even that seems like old thinking, but based on our inner movement. In the terminology of awakening this is the Self and our sovereignty. That is the one who deserves our loyalty first, before anything or anyone else. Now, in teenage times, millions of people are searching for truth and 'fighting' for freedom, eager to define the new paradigm and impatient that it is not happening yet. Just like any teenager who feels grown up as soon as he smells adulthood and freedom. Finding our inner trust and authenticity is the basis for making a solid movement. We will see that those to whom we have been blindly loyal are also trapped in their role of ego and misuse of power.

Growing up is not fighting against the parent but finding equal ground that dissolves the unbalanced relationship.

Any form of release starts by owning our own stuff. We must stop projecting our issues onto the collective reality screen. Where we don't own it will appear again in our life, in a negative or painful way. This is not to create a doom scenario, it is simply how the universe works. The energy we exude is the energy we attract and receive. When we rise in frequency we attract more of what is aligned with our Self. Becoming loyal to our Self, in a pure way, not in vanity, is what empowers and grounds us, providing the basis for creative energy from within. When we release something old, that no longer serves us, we bring in something we desire and wish to experience more of. In this way we start to project more of the desired reality on our collective screen that supports our personal life and the way we live together. Small inner changes make a huge shift together.

In the remainder of this chapter an overview is given of how we can recognize 15 dynamics that no longer serve us within ourselves and within the systemic dynamics. With each purge we raise our vibration. That creates the ripple effect, by connecting our smaller ripples we create bigger ripples. Simultaneously we release the old and create the new paradigm.

Will the current power structures disappear? Who knows? That is completely up to us and what our desired reality looks like.

> *With more understanding of what is really happening in our collective, I learned to understand what detachment means. Letting go of anything that keeps me trapped in feeling (emotionally) dependent on something or someone outside myself. Through detachment I realized what connection means. I cannot be truly connected to someone I feel attached to (dependent). Nor can I be my authentic Self when I feel attached to the acknowledgement of others or a system.*

A never-ending process of release, it seems. Sometimes I went through dark nights of misery not understanding why it happened. Often there was no personal pain or story, it just felt very dark and intense. I learned what surrendering really means. When I feel I am being pulled down, deeply sad, I lie on my bed. I am present with the pain but don't do anything. I just sense and use my breath in the area that feels painful. Or breathe deep into my belly, the solar plexus. I still cry at times, that really helps me to release what feels blocked. Feeling the intense pain in the world right now is so palpable and through my tears I can release the attachment. It is almost impossible to explain at what depth this pain is felt at times.

People close to me don't get my urge for crying. They translate it as drama or it makes them uncomfortable. For me it is a way to release and go deeper. After a while, there is stillness and its feels calm and peaceful again. At times, during a process like this, there is a huge insight. Then it feels more personal. I suddenly see through my own automated pattern or behaviour. This moment of epiphany feels so great, energy rushes through me. In those moments I can feel a physical block being released, like a pain in my hip or knee.

Does it ever end? I don't know and don't need to know. The best thing to describe these low moments is a temporary discomfort ... hahaha, what a ride it is. I don't avoid them as I know they serve a purpose and the feeling afterwards is worth all the inconvenience. Each time it feels lighter, more liberated, and more energized. And the best thing is, these moments are getting shorter and shorter.

I know now that my mind is really the only place that keeps any form of suffering alive and I am so happy that my continuous practice to make the shift out of the controlling mind has worked! I can make a shift in any moment and I am no longer dependent on my outer circumstances. That is pure liberation to me.

Fifteen dynamics that disempower us

1. Release the fear, embrace your authentic self

When we choose the 'easy way out', life becomes complicated, when we choose the 'hard way in', life becomes simple. It is such a great paradox!

To go the hard way in, we need to face our fears, shadows, and traumas. We need to deal with our conditioning, beliefs, and programs. The result is a pure and grounded life with unlimited possibilities. Peace, calmness, empowerment, neutrality, excitement, passion (and so much more) are results of 'the hard way in'. Paradoxically enough this 'hard way in' is way easier than the 'easy way' out. The hard way in will bring us soon to our inner Self, our inner connection, and raises our frequency.

When we choose the 'easy way out', we are the victim of our outer turmoil. We are sensitive to labelling, comparing, judgement or fighting judgement. We are sensitive to opinions, agendas, suppression, and manipulation. We look for outer confirmation, to confirm our identity and even our existence. Even if we don't want to acknowledge that we suffer, we still do and our unknown fear creates a whole series of events in our system. Reactions, like a brief moment of stress, is a contraction that creates the fight-flight-freeze effect. It unleashes a catabolic energy, a natural reaction of our body to be able to defend ourselves. It's a very powerful energy in its purest form, but being in this state too long and too often, is draining on our system. We don't recognize it as such, so it feels normal to feel fearful.

The trick of it all is that most of us don't have any real fears. We mostly have imagined ones that only live in our mind. Even the fear of death is an imagined one. No doubt we feel sad losing life, losing our loved ones, but what is it that we fear of death itself? The pain, the inability to breathe or not knowing how it feels?

Feel into what it is you really fear. That eases the system, as it becomes less abstract or elusive. We all die, that is for sure. We can fear it and choose the 'easy way' out, which makes death and life complex, or we can embrace the idea and choose the 'hard way' in, which makes it simple and pure.

> *I grew up in a small village. I must have been around 10 years old. Each village has the 'mean gang', boys and girls who always make trouble or worse. I saw them on my way home. Nervously I smiled at the group. One boy was sitting in a wheelchair. Suddenly they were all around me, accusing me of laughing at an invalid. Then they started to beat me with a stick. I have no memory how badly it hurt. It certainly didn't feel life threatening, but the fear of being attacked and feeling defenceless was huge and remained with me for a long time.*
>
> *I haven't done active trauma work on this but since 2012 my fears in general have mostly vanished. It is honestly a fact: what you exude is what you get reflected back. It is a tough one to accept that our (unconscious) fear provokes aggressive behaviour. In the same way, our dogs smell who is nervous or frightened which triggers in them a reaction to be dominant.*
>
> *These days I can walk in a foreign city, like Lima, which has the reputation of being dangerous, without ever feeling slightly uncomfortable. Of course I walk in the safest districts, but still, I can be seen as a 'rich, easy target'. When I do feel tension creeping up, like all the security checks in airports these days, I pause and objectify the situation: old pattern, tensed people around me or is there really a threat?*

When we fear the unknown, we make the subject too big, too complex. We use 'container' labels, to name something without defining what it is. Covid, cancer or any other disease known to many, will have many nuances to it. The danger of 'containering' is that we lose our objectivity. Instead we fear the worse outcome, which gives an unnecessary stress signal to our physical body. It only makes the immune system weaker.

Trust is the way to face the unknown. Finding trust within, will create a different world out there. It really helps to reconfirm and repeat this to ourselves, each day we get up, first thing in the morning, simply say it out loud to yourself in front of the mirror. That is how we reconnect to our free will, our inner drive, our passion. That is how we find our individuality, our authenticity, our own colour, or whatever name we want to give it.

> *My biggest challenge was to step in my own power and own my perspectives and express myself authentically.*
>
> *Since I was young, I was never outspoken in my thinking. My early youth experiences, (I am the youngest of four) and being told I was 'too young to know', gave me a fear of speaking up, of being ridiculed or dominated by smart speakers.*
>
> *As a quiet listener I developed a heightened sensitivity to the inauthentic expression of others. As if I could smell it when someone is bragging or telling a story for convenience, or pretending to be happy while I felt his sadness. But then what to do with that? You cannot call someone out on his inauthenticity. It doesn't work that way. It only creates resistance and denial. Not being able to deal with these inauthentic energies, came with a lot of frustration and anger. It is actually my anger that gave me my biggest breakthroughs. As anger brings a certain fearlessness. Through these outbursts I realized I needed to focus on my own authentic expression, I needed to know my own colour, my own passion, and not wait for the other to shift. The moment I do speak more freely, people not only react differently, it gives them the space to open up as well! We are all so caught up in each other's pain.*
>
> *Although I am not always proud of my anger outbursts, I can see its purpose, it opens up the throat chakra and it helped me in finding my voice, more than many other approaches in finding my voice.*
>
> *Authenticity, being me, speaking freely, is still a bit challenging for me, but now I sense the difference! I know when I come from a need to be right, unable to express my perspectives in a neutral way. I had to overcome my*

fear of being ridiculed or denied by my family, my partner, my friends for being too outspoken in my views or too pushy in my ideas. The words can be the same but the energy with which I share the words can create a totally different outcome.

Writing this book has given me a platform, learning to share my ideas and release my fear of being rejected for it. As I know sharing my voice and message has been my biggest challenge, I also know it will be my greatest gift to the world.

In the world we live in, we are almost all fearful of being our authentic powerful self, which is not the same as confidence, charisma, or eloquence. True authenticity and pure empowerment is scarier than anything else. We all have areas where we still hide, fear being judged or different. There we compromise ourselves, which feeds the fear in its low vibrating frequency. Perhaps not having lived authentically is why we fear dying, as we might not have had the best out of life!

The moment we show up authentically, pure light shines through us and we feel immediately empowered. Authenticity means combining and filtering all we learn and experience through our own source of wisdom. That is what makes each of us unique. You can be the best scientist, businessman or spiritual teacher, as long as your expression doesn't come from within, you are pushing or promoting the knowledge of someone else. Authenticity doesn't have to show grandeur, extravagancies, that is all programming. Authenticity is simple and pure. It takes time to sense and explore our inner wisdom and fully accept ourselves for who we are. We judge ourselves in the same way we judge others and we fear being judged.

Next time notice when your throat gets a little blocked, your voice moves up a tone or becomes squeaky, or you feel a pressure on your chest. You will learn to notice when something is off. Don't ignore the sign, just pause a little and observe. What is it that was said, what is it you said, what did you give into or what is it you didn't do, or ignored?

Overcoming any imagined fear is a first step in doing something you never had the courage for. Proving to yourself you imagined it works better than endless inner analyses. Be okay in making mistakes, like showing up too much of the 'new' you, being too angry, too outspoken, or too radical. It will soon become softer and more authentic. Be gentle with yourself in finding your new Self. We are breaking free from ages of programming. Quite a job, but a great one as it feels truly liberating and of course shifts our frequency.

2. Release your need to fall back to false egoism, to open up to empathy

A well-meant joke is still a bad one if it hurts the other.

> *My youngest has a strong radiance and personality. She handles jokes well and in a smart way – still they often hurt, especially when she was young! She connects with people easily. Naturally born with a high EQ, she knows how to use her insights very well in social settings. Unfortunately, it attracts people who love her energy but aren't always emotionally as mature as she is. Her natural empathic abilities shifted into becoming a pleaser, adjusting herself so the other feels their needs being met.*
>
> *Different events traumatized her in such a way that it diminished her self-esteem. She can talk about her own challenges as if I am talking with a psychologist. Healing her pains and shifting it for herself, is of course a whole different ball game. But with her clarity of mind, I have no doubt she soon will. #proudmom*

How often do we laugh at the expense of others and even our children? Making little jokes that hurt and aren't received as funny at all? How often do we gaslight the feelings of the other: 'ahh, don't be so sensitive, it was meant well'? Or 'we all have good intent, I only mean it well...' Who is the 'we' and 'I' here? How often do we confuse 'my good intent' with 'I need to make sure my intention is met, my bad joke is laughed at'?

In little innocent actions, and with good intent, we hurt each other unintentionally. That is exactly our problem. 'Not intentionally' and good intent grates! If we are unaware *who* we are serving, the false ego or the Self, we can't tell if we hurt the other or not. However, we can be sure, if the other feels hurt, the false ego was at play!

A little remark that feels painful, a leader that pushes a plan or a brave soldier that kills to defend his country. We so often excuse others for their behaviour by telling ourselves it was meant well. When we do that we are coming from false egoism, hoping that it will not be as bad as it looks or sounds. That is how the abuser stays the abuser, the bully remains the bully and the victim the victim. Next time you hear yourself saying or thinking: it is meant well, pause for a moment and feel where it is coming from. Do you hope it is more positive than it feels? Did you mean it well, but you realize you were pushing your point?

We believe we are social beings but more often than not we do things for others to feel better about ourselves. Or, we make short term decisions only for our own comfort ('I know it is wrong but I am done with the subject'). Or we take over conversations the second we get the chance ('oh yes, I have had that too...' while the other is still in the middle of a sentence). There are so many ways in which we show ourselves to be selfish and egoistic. The defence mechanisms, shared later in this chapter, provide a good start for some self-reflection.

When we include ourselves and the other equally, while leaving the responsibility completely with the individual, we will start to feel what empathy really is. Only then will we unravel how sensitive we are to false moralities, when social pressure is used to follow ideologies. By telling ourselves 'it is meant well', we are actually saying: I mean it well if I put pressure on others to conform, as that makes me feel safe. Can you see how easily we depart from our inner truth?

Releasing our false egoistic traits underlies all releases in this chapter. It is our big shift towards pure empathy. There is no single way to get started with this release. We all have our own flaws. Start by recognizing when the other person feels hurt by your actions, stop using any reason as an excuse for others, refrain from judging and comparing or stop pushing pressure on others to conform socially. In short, let the other walk his path and you walk yours. By observing our own reactive patterns, we can make a conscious choice to change our behaviour and stop repeating the cycle.

We first need to be aware of ourselves, to sense others objectively and openly. Pure empathy is new to us all. We are only making baby steps, embracing this new quality.

3. Releasing the role of victim to become liberated

It took me a long time to see my own inner conflict, where I choose the role of the victim. When no one shows interest, my strength becomes a force and my natural balance shifts to superficiality (arrogance) and I bathe silently in being the victim: 'no one is interested in me or no one sees my qualities'. Not outwardly, as I dislike drama, but inwardly. I push people away, confounding my desire to be more connected. Until I fully understood how dishonest I was with myself, I projected my need onto others and expected them to confirm me, not my wisdom but me.

Even when I could observe myself doing it, I still had a hard time breaking through that pattern. By nature I have a radiance of self-confidence but only recently I can see when it shifts to arrogance, it shows in my facial expression, my tone of voice or even my presence.

I really needed to shift the movement: express authentically and be okay with what comes back from the outer world and let go of my own judgement of myself. That requires refined self-reflection and awareness of my frequency at any given moment. As soon as I feel it has dropped, I need to refrain from all projections and only sense and breathe to release the tension. Hahaha... I still 'fail' at it every now and then but now I can admit it.

The ones close to me have all been great teachers in revealing this dynamic, perhaps without even being aware of their role. I learned to shift into more lightness, to embrace everything in life with more joy, 'be less serious and keep it simple'. I read it once but there is really no discrimination between laughter and tears, or between making a mistake and excelling.

We never consciously choose to be weak, we don't desire a struggle in life. Still, we feel sorry for ourselves or we pretend to be in control of it all. The areas in life where we don't thrive, where we don't feel free, we choose to ignore or keep complaining about. We either take the role of the caretaker, the problem solver, the accuser, the arrogant or we choose the drama side of things, all states of the victim. The false ego and the victim go together but show up in many colours. Some act repressively (inwardly, drama, victim), others are more reactive (outwardly, manipulative, control, knows best). It underpins any block we want to release. The state of the victim is born in the mind, in our selfishly driven thoughts, but it is deeply stored in our solar plexus, where most of our emotional pain is stored. It is the same with the subtle undercurrent of fear, both feel so natural that we think it is part of us.

In our inability to deal with it, or even to recognize it, we stay stuck in reacting to what is happening outside of ourselves. One day we will realize that there is no outer source that can resolve this issue. No new job, new partner, saviour, or any amount of money will solve stuckness. Neither do we need endless sessions of therapy trying to figure out how it all happened. The power is within us, to release ourselves from this state.

What we do need is self-reflection and self-honesty, to become conscious of our own thinking, feeling, and acting. Through self-reflection we can unravel whatever doesn't flow naturally. Our ability to self-reflect is an absolute necessity in our collective shift to awaken. Becoming conscious of our actions is where we can decide to change our patterns of thought, ideas, and perspectives and thus our (future) actions. When we become conscious of our own dynamic, we can observe the dynamic of the collective and its ruling systems. There is this constant movement of zooming in and out, to reflect and observe at all levels.

Collectively, we will move out of our victim state. It is an evolutionary force. That is why there is no battle to fight. We cannot fight with evolution, we can only deeply trust it and move with its waves without resistance. Release comes in waves, iterations are necessary. It all sounds like heavy duty. It is and it isn't, at the same time. We cannot force ourselves through a deep dark hole, but we can learn to play. Embracing both sides of the polarity, the good and the bad times, is where we feel the lightness of it all. It is a shift from approaching life with heaviness and concerns, to lightness and simplicity. Gradually we embody our new liberated state.

4. Release scarcity, own your actions and focus on trust

Wealth is not our issue,
the corruption and power play used against us is the issue.
That is why we are not all living a prosperous life.

We live in the frequency of scarcity – fear of not having enough. How we relate to money is the best example of how scarcity is expressed in our daily life. Our currencies are created in a frequency of scarcity and we keep feeding it. Within the current monetary system there is still enough space to create an income and find resources, easily and in flow, than most of us are able to do today. But money is not the only area. Releasing this energy of scarcity is a tough shift to make, as we lack inner trust.

Instead of becoming aware of what pulls us down, we try to control our material world. We think in possessions, achievements, securities, and risks evaluations.

We use our cognitive (rational) mind to find confirmation and believe we are well prepared for whatever might happen. Any time we fall back into scarcity, we close our hearts and our minds take over. We are literally forcing an outcome that feels safe again, if only for a little while. This endless mechanism of control blocks any natural flow and we lose touch with our intuitive knowing. Without this, our *inner tuition* or guidance, we are sensitive to being programmed. It doesn't matter whether we have more than enough or nothing at all, we *force* ourselves through life. It is the same force that is used against us.

Immense wealth or an elite position make it seemingly 'easy' to stay in power, however, those high up in any pyramid structure use force to stay in power. They fear scarcity more than we do and use our fear to stay in power. In terms of energy, the *fear* of scarcity is the only fuel for force and control. Without fear, force becomes useless.

Scarcity is related to a lack of trust in life, in its broadest sense. This idea that life is not supporting us is deeply rooted in our feeling of not being good enough to live, or more existentially, there is no reason for our existence. In our daily life it translates into the idea that life might not give you what you need or desire. Whatever that is: the right partner, enough food, enough money, a nice fulfilling job, the right friends, inner peace, knowledge, happiness, good health, supportive parents, and so on.

Blaming anyone for keeping our world in scarcity is not serving any purpose either, neither is it changing anything. It is our own free will, to keep ourselves caged in any belief of lacking something. It is up to us to release this low-vibrating energy.

When a force shifts to strength, power shifts to empowerment, it becomes a natural quality serving equality. This requires a fundament of trust. We can all sense the difference between force and strength, the latter immediately straightens our spine, aligns us with self-esteem, self-worth and self-assurance. Trust can only be sensed, it is a sensation of deep inner solidness. That is always there, independent of possessions or circumstances. That is why this alignment with the Self is our fundament for anything.

From the basis of trust we can open ourselves up to prosperity. We don't have to wait for systems to change, the process is reversed. We change, and so will our systems and our lives. Prosperity is so much more than being rich. It relates to any area in our lives: richness in friendships, flourishing nature, feeling vibrant, freedom, a phenomenal relationship that touches your deep inner core, inner wisdom and so much more. Once we unlock our ancient patterns of keeping scarcity alive, corruption will dissolve by itself. We simply don't allow it anymore, as we won't feed it. We won't re-elect a president that has been fraudulent. Why would we, once we acknowledge the effect it has on us?

Overpopulation and climate change are big container narratives, fixed within mainstream opinion and based in the same frequency of scarcity. No doubt these are our next two big topics. Let's be more aware of how we approach our dialogue around these topics and refrain from copying one-liners or basing our discussion on one or two parameters to confirm the threat (or the opposite). The complexity of these two themes is linked to so many different aspects in our systems and our own choices, that we might remain stuck in argument alone.

We are the problem and the solution. When we stop arguing and focus our energy on our actions, to support challenges we want solve, and stop buying into fear narratives, we will find a natural balance on earth. Only then will we discover if there really is a scarcity issue. If so, we will find a humane solution once we include all perspectives.

5. Release the fear of change, bring in the explorer

> *'The moment I cannot recall my pain I felt so vividly, I know it is healed.'*
>
> *My eldest daughter made this beautiful statement, reflecting back on a trip we made, the four of us, to Peru in December 2020. She continued: "Back then, I felt so sad, angry and frustrated, due to so many changes in my life, that I can hardly believe I feel so different now. My life feels so great, with many beautiful friendships, lots of activities and fun!" She said it with such laughter, realizing how big the shift was, she had made all by herself.*
>
> *Three years ago, she challenged herself to pursue a full bachelor's degree in another country. Quite a challenge for someone who could not even change the interior of her bedroom, as she felt so attached to keeping things as they are. The first two years were a struggle, often asking herself why she pursued this path. The desire to find new friends, the pressure of trying to fit in, in her new environment, emotional entanglements with home (we just divorced) and keeping a long-distance relationship healthy. After a while she understood and felt that it is all up to her. She is the change and that created a huge shift, releasing many old patterns. What an inner power to experience this so consciously when you are only 20 years old. #proudmom*

Most of us fear change. At the same time we can also be excited about change, but only when the outcome is positive, according to our expectations. The funny thing is, we create all of our outcomes (reality), and more often than not, situations that don't serve us at all.

We don't fear change, we fear that the expectations of our mind aren't met. This the reason why we are not capable yet of using our manifesting powers to work for us all the time.

228

We also long for change. We can't stop fantasizing about new ideas, longing to be acknowledged, have new experiences, be famous, successful, gain financial freedom, perfect partners, meaningful jobs or what have you. But, to shift these ideas into reality make us freeze. What if it might not come true in the way we expect? As soon as there is an expectation in the sense of 'what if it is not happening', we drop in our frequency and we manifest the outcome in our reality that confirms the 'what if'. The disappointment blocks our exploring nature and we go back to normal life.

Change the way you look at things, and the things you look at change.

Wayne Dyer

2020 Made us all realize that there is no 'back to normal'. It has changed many lives in so many ways that countless books and movies will be written. No one knows what the outcome will be, we all have our hopes and expectations that it soon will feel safe again. How we define 'safe' seems to be more divided than ever – and yet it isn't at all. We all desire a world that will have improved considerably, compared to what it is today. Without useless wars and loss of innocent life, with restored nature and sea life, more equality, the end of famine, and so on. Where we feel divided is *how* we will get there and *if* life will improve. This is where we block the natural process of change. We either leave it up to others to solve it for us or we fight against it. Neither approach will get us closer, because we focus on expectation.

Change requires the quality of the explorer, our natural curiosity. It is our fuel for living. Life would become such a bore if there was nothing new to experience and each day an exact copy of the previous one. But none of our days are the same. It is a matter of perspective and of wonder.

Wonder is the magical touch. Wondering is not the same as getting lost in a daydream fantasy. To wonder one has to be present, in the now, while you explore what you can observe, with all your senses. Or how new ideas *sense*. As a simple example, you can fantasize about a brand-new car with all its details and see yourself driving in it. Or you can wonder what the experience feels like, being in the car of your dreams, without knowing anything about the brand, model, or specs. In the first you already have the solution, in the second you only know the experience and there can be many solutions.

When there is no predefined outcome, but a perceived feeling of how we would like to experience life together, we can open up the dialogue on how to get there. Most likely we will come up with an explosion of possible solutions and ways to get there. Wonder and exploration sparks our creativity and resourcefulness.

Whether it is a group process or an individual one, whenever you feel a little lost, stuck or unsettled, be curious, explore and wonder. Question yourself, how you feel around something and what it is you would love to *feel* different. We have a world to explore, people to meet, jobs to love, inner work to play with, character traits to soften. Can you feel your heart expanding when you become the explorer? It requires some practice at first, as we are so inclined to think: 'it will never change'. We have to take baby steps, especially in the more sensitive areas around our core theme. Shift from '*I desire*', '*I want*' to '*I am curious*', '*I am open*', from contraction to expansion. No predefined expectations, no list with requirements of your ideal partner, no fixed solutions. Only sense and wonder. You will be amazed how energizing and empowering this is. This is only a first step but it will make such a shift.

6. Releasing the era of reason and opening up to universal intelligences

On average, in a relative low vibrating state, we can only be open to another viewpoint if it is not more than 10% different from our current ideas. Just pause and realize how challenging life is when we want to bridge two opposing viewpoints! Imagine our world challenges!

Seeing through a destructive and corrupt play has little to do with being intellectual or academic. Neither does it have to do with calling yourself spiritual. There are people with master's degrees who never see through it and school dropouts who see through the deception immediately. There are those who talk about love and light while their actions still favour their false ego, not willing to look at what is happening in our world.

How is this related to the reasoning mind? We all have some belief system we hold on to. We see life as we are. We choose to ignore what we don't want to work with. It can be a short-term selfish reason or a deep pain we don't want to see or release. Our reasoning mind is our saviour from this, as it comes up with an answer that suits us. Those permission slips are used by all walks of life.

The reasoning mind needs facts to prove his point. No matter what area you look at, knowledge and understanding is what drives us: science is based on facts and proof, religions on written words of a saviour, and our spiritual world on teachings of love and light.

Knowledge comes from knowing, wisdom comes from not knowing.
Richard Rudd

As the reasoning mind so often cuts off new input, we miss many opportunities, ideas, and other input, to enrich our lives. As we have been pushed in this era of reason to use our brain, with its logic, facts, and analyses, most of us (and especially the more highly educated ones) are restricted to the limitations of their mind, while holding on to knowledge and (past) proven experience and methods. We are not allowing other sources of wisdom to enter our reasoning.

Yet, we all know that the epiphany moment, the great breakthrough, seems to come out of nowhere and is a result of an open question (contemplation is a great practice for this). Well it isn't out of nowhere, but it is not coming from the mind or brain function alone. It is as if a new circuit is made, new dots are connected, information is received from a different field, other than our brain, and suddenly it makes sense. For that to happen, we need to be in an open state, to receive without the dominant interference of the *reasoning* mind.

When we introduce a speaker, listen to teachings, or read a book, it is again the reasoning mind that searches for proof that the person has credentials. to confirm their authority and accept the information. We are not used to wisdom, as in 'not knowing'. Why do we see the wise children, the extraordinary talents, as exceptions instead of examples? What if we could open ourselves to universal and natural wisdom that is available to all of us, independent of IQ?

The metaphoric mind is a maverick. It is as wild and unruly as a child.
It follows us doggedly and plagues us with its presence as we wander the
contrived corridors of rationality. It is a metaphoric link with the unknown
called religion that causes us to build cathedrals – and the very cathedrals are
built with rational, logical plans. When some personal crisis or the bewildering
chaos of everyday life closes in on us, we often rush to worship the rationally
planned cathedral and ignore the religion. Albert Einstein called the intuitive
or metaphoric mind a sacred gift. He added that the rational mind was
a faithful servant. It is paradoxical that in the context of modern life we have
begun to worship the servant and defile the divine.
The Metaphoric Mind: A Celebration of Creative Consciousness

Bob Samples

The crisis Bob Samples refers to is the belief (or persona) that gets triggered and pushes us into reasoning that controls us. Reasoning happens in a lower frequency than the state of love. Food also has us drop in frequency, especially the poor nutrition we consume today.

Anyone who has ever experienced a period of fasting, knows how clear our thinking becomes when we eat very little or nothing. A lower frequency makes our system more dense and it is difficult for the light (carrier of information) to come in. The epiphany moment is like a ray of light rushing through your system, a direct embodied experience of an intuitive mind.

A reasoning mind is based in emotion, despite the fact it might appear aloof. Therefore it is not the same as a neutral statement or an observation. As soon as we react with defence, offense, or disregard something, emotions are involved and we can be sure it was our reasoning mind that was talking. Someone can be very open minded in many different areas, but completely narrow minded on one topic. The reaction always shows where it is coming from.

The moment we open up to our intuitive, exploring mind we are able to see a broader view. This bird's eye view has a widened perspective and is able to connect dots and see through complex matters.

Our mind is not the bad guy here, on the contrary, our mind is essential to our lives. It holds beliefs, creates our reality, and alters our state of being. When we fiercely believe something that limits us, we can use the same focus to believe in something that works *for us*.

The mind plays an essential role in the health of our immune system. Wim Hof (the Iceman) has dedicated his life to showing the world how a simple breathing exercise and exposing our body to low temperatures builds a super-strong immune system. In his practice he uses the positive effect of stress, by bringing the mind intentionally into this state. The powerful catabolic energy, the adrenaline that releases, puts our system in the well-known fight-flight-freeze state. Being in this state and holding our breath for an extended period, gives our body the perfect setting to heal what is out of balance. This 'stress state' of the mind is very different from being emotionally in a state of stress!

The power to keep the mind focussed, combined with our natural self-healing mechanism is not only physically healing , but releases old ancestral patterns and woundings as well. In other words, the healing gets to the core of our DNA.

There is so much for us to learn and to discover. Science, universities, education systems will always be part of our world, to gain progress and learn new skills. But can we include and open up to extra fields of information, to accelerate our growth? Can we shift from needing to know (narrows the brain) and also include practices that open us up to not knowing, to wisdom? What other intelligences are within our reach, that we are hardly aware of? Let's explore and be open.

7. Release through the gentle push of triggers

A trigger is as if a button is pushed inside you, that makes you feel uncomfortable and 'triggers' an *offensive or defensive* reaction pattern. Triggers serve a purpose, for growth. The moment we realize that only our ideas, beliefs and feelings are being attacked, and not who we are, we can stop taking things personally. It is the persona that defines input as personal or not. It is our attachment to this persona, or elements of it, that causes the trigger to be felt. In other words, not everything that is said to you, that you read or hear, triggers you. Only those remarks that trigger an old pain.

A trigger can even arise by itself within your thought patterns while you drift off into memories or fear a future event. A trigger shows you where you are taken out of balance through interpretation of your beliefs and past events. The intensity of your reactive response shows how painful something still is for you.

When we feel triggered, we immediately narrow our viewpoint and lose our empathic abilities. Becoming aware of this effect gives you a flow of opportunities, to release old dense energy. Some events that trigger a mild reaction can be released more easily. Others push our core pain body and need some iterations before all sides are polished.

We can learn and shift fastest when we look at our patterned reactions, how we do things, not just the trigger moment itself, as we are not always aware of it. We are very skilled in distracting ourselves. When distractions become dominant repetitive patterns they are called addictions. In essence they give the same *temporary* benefit, not to feel the trauma or pain that lies underneath all distractive patterns.

Addictions and distractions show up in many different ways. Not just in drugs, alcohol, or food. Many people find it really challenging to be alone or without a partner, so they move from one to another and often have the next already 'arranged' before breaking up. Other people dive into work and use numerous excuses for why work always gets a higher priority. And of course our youngest addiction is to social media, mobile phones and binge watching. Even a need to always care for others shows distractive patterns. Procrastination is another well-known distractive pattern that blocks many of us from getting things done in a smooth and energized way.

What basically happens is that the trigger has us dropped in frequency. That in itself is what makes us feel uncomfortable. The drop in frequency is what requires our attention so we don't fall for the trap of the story. Freeze, the moment you feel a distraction arising (you grab your phone while it is not ringing, you want a snack). Go back three seconds and recall what you were doing, what thought came up? Feel where your body is tense or contracted. Working in the moment, releasing the tension or shifting the thought, gives more progress than years of therapy. It requires dedication and willpower to release distractive patterns, because they are so automatic. However your progression is exponential and you are rewarded with a more consistent higher vibrating frequency.

The less triggered we are the more transparent we become. It increases our abilities to observe and be more present in the moment. Don't mistake this with pretending to be okay, pushing yourself into a positive mood or controlling your emotions. That is being indifferent, being less triggered is becoming more compassionate.

8. See through your defensive reflexes to release what blocks your empowerment

Just as we are skilled in avoiding the pain behind our triggers, so we have become skilled in defending ourselves. By the way, a defence mechanism can appear offensive or defensive. But what is it that we are protecting? Our hurt persona and general distrust in life. We don't live in a world where we have to protect ourselves against wild lions, but the defensive reflex is still within us. Once we connect more deeply with the Self, there is less need to defend our persona and we gain more trust in life.

It goes without saying that our defence mechanisms are activated as soon as we feel triggered by someone else. But there is more to it. When we are dishonest we use it to hide our lies, or when we don't dare to admit we are wrong, or when we feel insecure, or when we feel judged, cornered or ridiculed, we react. The list of situations is endless.

Whether it is offensive of defensive is quite irrelevant, it is often a mixture of both. Try to find an example of each one listed below, you will be surprised how subtle this mechanism shows up (Q = a first question to reflect upon, when a mechanism is used). Often it is easier to recognize this behaviour in others, than with yourself. It requires quite some self-reflection and honesty, to see your own behaviour.

- **Our rationalizing mind**: avoidance of opening up to another perspective, not able to show any form of weakness, avoidance of inner pain and pretending to be okay.

Q: What do I really feel?

- **Projection**: instead of owning our discomfort, fear, or guilt, we blame, envy, judge, and label others. We 'shadow' project onto others what we can't acknowledge to ourselves: our role, lies, pain, shortcomings, or disempowerment. This gives us short moments of release, as we hope the other will compensate, change, or solve it for us.

Q: What I project onto the other tells me something about myself – what is that?

- **Dominant**: a strong need to share your stories, your successes and dramas (can be online as well). You dominate conversations and often take over someone else's story. There is strong need to be confirmed that you are good enough.

Q: How can I listen more and ask open questions?

- **Need to be right**: use arguments and persuasive techniques to prove our point, until we have won. In those arguments we often use, 'yes, but', which is the same as, 'no, I don't agree or even hear your perspective'. There is a strong need to be heard or seen.

Q: Where is the other person coming from, what is his perspective?

- **Gaslighting**: a form of emotional abuse, by doubting or ignoring the reality or feelings of another person, which makes them confused or frustrated. It is often seen as a tool of the narcissist. However, as many of us lack empathic abilities, milder forms of gaslighting are very common, but harmful, nevertheless.

Examples: 'You are too sensitive', 'you make such a fuss', or 'it doesn't help anyone you feel this way' (the emotional world is made invalid). 'You lied about what happened two years ago'. This is deflection. (using unrelated or old issues to boomerang back the blame). 'That never happened' (denying any form of evidence through anger or deflection).

Q: What makes me so insecure that I ignore the feelings of the other?

- **Control**: any act of control, of your - actions or towards others, shows a sense of distrust in life, in others, but mostly in yourself. You use control to make sure your expectations are met.

Q: Why is it really that important to have it my way?

- **Manipulation**: those who use this will not recognize it, as we think it is only done with a predefined plan in mind, and we can't imagine ourselves acting so negatively. It is not a conscious strategy but an unconscious way of acting to get what we want. Through smart ways of communicating and (subtle) emotional pressure, we make the other feel guilty, responsible or in agreement. A seemingly innocent example is asking leading questions to manipulate the conversation. In more extreme forms, denial, lying, or bluffing are used to force the other to accept your own ideas and preferred outcome.

Q: When am I manipulative in my questions or in making sure I get my way?

- **Repetitive destructive patterns**: our inability to own our actions. Instead we keep hurting others, by repeating the same pattern. For example the partner who often cheats or uses 'innocent' lies.

Q: Why do I keep hurting the other?

- **Pleasing behaviour**: to avoid conflicts, criticism, or rejection. We adapt our behaviour to the expectation of the other by being silent, obedient, confirming, caring, not able to make our own life a priority and so on. The pleaser always comes second.

Q: Where do I adjust, to be liked, to avoid standing up, and stay silent?

- **Dramatic behaviour**: the endless need for attention, by exaggeration, being inauthentically spontaneous, complaining, judging others, being loud. Or the opposite, using a silent negative expression to get attention.

Q: When do I pretend or exaggerate to get attention?

It's a list that could easily become a whole book itself. And no doubt, deepening each point with more examples and questions helps in understanding and recognizing your behavioural defence patterns. But ultimately you need to have a willingness to work with it, and for that you are only helped by asking yourself, again and again: 'How did I react? Where was I coming from? What am I trying to achieve? Which form of defence did I use? What is it I am defending?'

Seeing through the lens of defensive reactions teaches us a lot about ourselves and others. Know that a person in defence is hard to reach. Arguments and quarrels are understandable but often little of use. For example: when you see your partner reacting defensively, realize that there is something else, not being shown or said, that is more important than the reaction itself. Even though it is quite a challenge to refrain from reacting (as most often you are caught up in it as well), try to withhold yourself and show compassion for the deeper dynamic between the two of you.

9. Release labelling and duality thinking, open up to unity

Have you ever wondered why humanity has been at war for as long as history tells us? Why it is not possible for humans to live peacefully together? Because humans are inherently malicious? Who thinks of himself as a malicious person? We don't, we only think that way of others.

Even the one who is proven to be evil or malicious, still doesn't think in those terms of himself, as he has found reasons to justify his behaviour.

Isn't that interesting? So what makes us label others that way? Because history showed us? Because the news tells us? Because we have been bullied at school? Because we have been hurt in the past, so we project our pain by labelling others as perpetrators?

The answer is quite sobering and promising as well: we are constantly forced into duality thinking, to keep us divided. The victim versus the perpetrator, the good versus the bad guy, the beauty versus the beast, the saviour versus the devil, the winner versus the loser, success versus failure, white versus black, men versus women, east versus west, Christianity versus Islam, the protector versus the enemy, and so on.

This is very deep programming that keeps us in our low vibrating frequency. To free ourselves we need to see that we always play a role on both sides. There is no perpetrator who hasn't been (or felt) a victim in his life! Because we all have been hurt, we hurt others.

We might think we don't polarize in our daily lives but we do when we gossip, judge, blame, project or feel superior or inferior. We might think we don't discriminate, but we talk about other cultures in a superior way when we compare ourselves ('they are lazy' or 'oafish'). We think we show compassion when we have pity for those who are suppressed, but we don't know how they feel and what they need, and we actually feel superior. It is even in the 'them and us'. It is deeply ingrained in our language. The programming is that we are forced to choose sides and we use labels to show what side we are on.

The labelling gives a sense of belonging. In choosing sides, we don't unite, we gather in groups to feel safe, which is completely different. We are even programmed to be divided within ourselves, divided from the light that we are. For us to truly unite, we need to be able to see the pure soul in ourselves *and* in our biggest enemy. Just let that sink in for a minute.

Can you truly open yourself up to those who have hurt you most? Or to those who hurt others, in the most evil ways thinkable? They don't have to become your friend. That's not what is meant here. To unite is to step out of the framed thinking of 'good' and 'bad' and see beyond the labels. There is always a reason why we develop inhuman behaviour.

As long as we are divided we have the other to blame for our issues and we'll never heal our deep human trauma. You cannot fight for peace, as that is the same energy used to create war. You cannot heal evil by condemning it.

Being divided takes away our power, our strength. It might feel safe to belong to one side, but it actually weakens us. Once we feel empowered we will unite and see through the old game of divide and conquer.

> *We think we are stuck in 'I am not good enough', but as a society,*
> *a collective, we are stuck in: 'you are not good enough for the group'.*
> *Solving the second makes the first a piece of cake.*

10. Release fragmented thinking, develop a holistic view

While we are in this phase of transition, we can look at the benefit of polarization. Being open to the perspective of others enriches our own view. Can we shift our rigidness and become resilient to what others think and feel, allowing everyone follow their own truth? That shift alone will give lightness to conversations and help deepen our own truth.

Choosing sides made us rigid, only seeing a fragment and not a broader picture. As we don't see the links, we risk leaving out valuable information and the cumulative effect of it. There is nothing wrong with specialism, but we miss the connectivity. This is one of the most fundamental insights. There are so many perspectives to one idea, and it is not important to know or embody them all. Just accepting that there are so many creates an immediate flow of opportunities, outcomes, possibilities.

Take a chronic illness, as an example. The definition in itself is already fragmented. It assumes many things as fixed and unsolvable. But even the most studied and bright doctor doesn't have all the answers, nor does a whole lineage of doctors (trained the same way). There is always another perspective, a different approach or idea of how to look at a problem or dysfunction.

We don't have to solve every issue, it is enough to see through it and understand what is happening. As long as we stay stuck in the fragmented approach, we keep arguing with each other over details. We keep defining more rules and don't see the consequences. For example, we accept laws that allow chemicals to impregnate wood (causing huge pollution to waters around those factories) to build outdoor playgrounds while we fight for a healthy environment. We are excited about the internet of things and don't see the danger of a high-tech frequency network directly influencing the vibrational field of our biosphere. As long as we are stuck in this fragmented viewpoint, we keep talking about symptoms and miss the connectivity that can bring us to greater solutions.

When a planet and its inhabitants are so out of balance, we're not troubled only by the force of power, but perhaps even more by the force of fragmentation. Once you see through this fragmented approach, you open yourself up to a wealth of possibilities. It becomes easier to connect the dots between all events and suddenly you see the role of power play from a different angle. Its purpose is to force us to break free. Force, just like catabolic energy, is very powerful and effective for a short period of time. Through evolution we were forced to straighten our spine, to feel its strength once it was straightened.

How do you open up? Where do you start? Ask questions, assume nothing, and solidify your emotional state in a neutral one (through the core practice). Not to suppress it, on the contrary, acknowledging how uncomfortable it is, is effective in opening more doors than pretending to know all the answers.

11. Release the need for a saviour, bring in inner trust

Throughout time there has been the story of a saviour that rescues humanity. The Jesus figure, the many versions of God, Allah, the embodiment of Magdalena or the guru who guides his followers. It is of all times. The saviour embodies hope and faith that we cannot feel within ourselves. We know hope and faith is crucial to life. When we lose hope or have no trust (faith) in life, for example because a doctor told us we have three months left to live, we literally start losing touch with life.

Gurus, saviours, authorities, teachings, or institutes (and any other permission slip) are here to show us that the trust we put in them is the trust we lack in ourselves. That is their role. Whenever we put greater trust in a figure or an idea outside ourselves, alarm bells should ring.

It is our pattern of escapism. We can still be inspired, triggered, challenged, or guided by them, but the tipping point is to whom we give the role of the saviour. Ourselves or the other? Seeing through the deceit of those you trusted deeply is a painful moment (see cognitive dissonance reaction) but nevertheless one we all have to go through. Seeing how you deceived yourself is equally painful. The ones who awakened to the system aren't necessarily awakened to the Self *yet*, the ones who are awakened to the Self aren't necessarily seeing through the deceit and failure of the system and its destructive power *yet*. The events of 2020 have shown that both levels of awakening are imperative to make a profound shift happen on a collective scale, whatever path you choose.

Frequencies, levels, pyramid, hierarchy are models that give us the safety to know where we find ourselves, even if we don't like the position we are in. It is reassuring. Somehow we have been led to believe that anyone above us is better, knows more, has more power or more authority. At the same time it ignites a drive within us to climb, become better, learn more and strive for that position. There is nothing wrong with hierarchy itself, but if the meaning we give to the structure becomes more important than the structure itself, we are blinded by it.

When we shift, for example, to circulatory thinking, the Self is at the core of one circle. From this core, we 'zoom into' other circles, to collaborate, extend information, assist or facilitate, but we never give our power away to another circle. We will soon feel that there is nothing better or higher, we have different roles, but we are all equal in contributing to the whole. We zoom in and out of circles, not up and down, without outer authority, only outer facilitation. No one is 'better' than anyone else.

When we do open up to a new paradigm, we like to start with the structure and try to fit ourselves into this newly designed one. It is as if we like to see the same solution in a different structure, without changing anything else. That creates resistance, as it won't work. To shift to any new structure, all dynamics (mechanisms, norms and values, beliefs) need to change, or at least be refined and redefined, even without knowing the exact outcome of the new. At the same time, we don't have to throw away the old immediately. It is more a process of release-create-refine-experiment-release, and so on. Eventually a new structure will find its form.

The core reason we love the outer figure, authority, saviour, is because we fear our own responsibility. If there is no leader, who will give us a plan or deal with complex matters? If we simplify law, can we be sure we will live in harmony? If there is no geopolitical structure, how do we organize our trade? How can we be sure that if I move and open up, you will as well? Can we trust our neighbour, our friend, our relative to also move along? Can I trust myself? To rebuild trust is most likely the greatest challenge, at a collective level. By taking baby steps within ourselves, and our inner circles, trust will grow. Create the ripple effect.

12. Release our false need for competition and shift to an empowered win-win

We have been taught that 'survival of the fittest' subjects us to the need for competition, that we will always battle in a win-lose game. But how true is this? The natural hierarchal structure in nature is not a competition as in an active battle. It has a natural structure, in which every element in the pyramid serves its purpose. The 'survival of the fittest' still applies, but this is natural, in an organic polarity with a hierarchal structure.

Our human behaviour shows hierarchal structures as well, but the dynamic has shifted into a synthetic polarity. There is nothing wrong with the concept of leaders and followers. However, we have convinced ourselves that we need to compete to survive, and win *at the cost* of others. There is no natural survival ground for hurting, or worse, killing people, other than extreme situations of personal defence. We have many other means of overcoming a conflict, before a fight or a war.

When the 'strongest wins' through force, it becomes synthetic. It is in our mind, where the need to win resides and where it gives a temporary boost to our system, through the release of hormones. Too much of these hormones can lead us into addictions. The power and status, driven by our competitive patterns, is addictive and keeps the 'need to win' alive. We all use our win-lose battle in various ways. One of the most obvious ones is our need to be right.

The only competition there is is the one with ourselves. That is the eagerness to grow, learn, experiment, improve, learn, and so on. That is the same as we recognize with professional athletes and sportsmen, winning their game is never at the cost of others. They focus on themselves winning, not on the opponent losing (although that happens in consequence). However in our organizational models and our systems in general, harm is done when we try to win *at the cost of another*. Then we shift into separation, powerplay, and feelings of superiority.

The opposite, helping others to 'win' or improve, being of service, is immediately rewarding and even life lengthening. That produces the right enzyme that is essential to the support of the telomerase process in our DNA. It prevents us from aging and declining.

It is simply not human to *like* it when another person loses or gets hurt. Our programmed idea of losing is directly connected with our fear of failing, rejection or not being good enough. Compensating that with winning doesn't justify the win-lose dynamic. All we do is keep the unwanted dynamic alive.

Teamwork, teamplay, synergy, are all based on collaboration and a win-win for all. Competitive vibes between team members, in any team sport, weakens the team performance. Letting another win by playing the inferior person isn't benefitting the energy and creativity either.

To release the win-lose dynamic, we first need to heal, from false ego to a healthy one, with self-care. But let's be careful not to stay there. A healthy ego without empathy still leaves us too self-centred. To really shift to a natural win-win approach, empathy will be crucial. Women and men will be challenged to embody their natural energy. Let's cross-pollinate the pure and embodied feminine and masculine energy. It will create a new organizational and institutional paradigm at its core and dissolves any power-based control systems.

13. Releasing the need for quick fixes, activate our own self-healing abilities

We love quick fixes. We love easy solutions. We prefer to take a pill rather than invest in a breathing method or just take a rest. Of course, our rationalizing mind and our unconscious programming are definitely the big showstoppers, preventing us from activating our self-healing abilities. Yet again, it is too easy to hide behind beliefs alone. More often than not we don't even give it a try. We are not willing to read a recommended book, apply what we've learned or listen to an alternative perspective. We are quite stubborn and lazy.

We pride ourselves on our health science, so advanced that we can live longer. At the same time, we complain and worry about all the diseases we, or other people, have. Either way, it's not in our hands, it seems. Either it's God's will, our DNA, or a solution by scientists and experts.

Where are we in all this? What is our role? We eat and drink unhealthily, we spend our days with stress and little movement, we are separated from nature, we pollute the air we breathe and we expect our doctors to solve our health issues. We accept diseases as something that happens to us. We have been so indoctrinated, with our western vision of health as the only solution, that we don't even doubt or question whether its knowledge might be limited. Those who live holistically, healthy and never ill, are disregarded and simply seen as lucky ones, with a strong system. And yes, our health science has advanced in many areas, but there are so many illnesses that can be prevented and/ or healed by being personally responsible for our physical system. And what about cases of instant remissions, healing of chronic diseases without chemical medication, curing stage-four cancer, and more. Are these all just pure luck?

How can we put so much trust in our health system while it is run by an industry that never really has our best interest at heart, nor defines it that way? Isn't it always about efficiency and profits? Anyone in this system knows the role of the lobbyist, the huge profits health insurance and pharmaceutical corporations make and how little they are held responsible for their actions. So where does that leave us?

If our body can heal a broken bone, why can't we heal cells that are cancerous? Could you be open to the idea that we can change our beliefs and heal ourselves? Perhaps not every disease, but can we make a start, to shift our perspective? Can we be open to medical science that takes different approaches?

We are the ones who are in our own way. This is not meant judgementally, we simply haven't been taught this way before. Resistance to this insight is perhaps logical, but not helpful. Second to that, we cannot expect to disregard our beliefs (with the mind alone) and expect our body to respond instantly, with a solution. We have to believe it in every cell, embody it, truly feel it is a truth for us. Just like the old version was a truth for us, and we have to act accordingly, step by step.

Man is the most insane species.
He worships an invisible God and destroys a physical Nature.
Unaware that this Nature he is destroying
is this God he's worshipping.

Hubert Reeves

We live in comfort and we barely know who we are. We don't know what our bodies are capable of and the genius system we are born with. For example, our skin consists of millions of tiny muscles and receptors that we need to read our environment. If this works freely, we have the optimal basis on which to receive information, to be more balanced and healthy. But when our skin is constantly covered with clothes, or is mainly inside buildings with no fresh air or movement, the skin never gets to exercise its great protective qualities.

In the context of nature, humans are only minority participants, yet we act as if we are superior to all of it. If we could only change our view of our position and embrace the gentle quality and richness nature offers, we would be thriving with nature and not fighting it. Activating your self-healing abilities requires a full 'yes' to yourself. Does that mean you never need help from our western medical institutions or that they are worthless? Of course not, at least not at first (for many of us). But we can make a start and become more responsible for our lives and the choices we make.

14. Release our resentment through forgiveness to upgrade all our systems

Resentment is a huge energy burner. We can hold on to feelings of resentment for a lifetime without doing anything. Just feeling resentful is a result believing that someone or something should pay a price, confess guilt, offer excuses, or restore what was taken. We feel we have every right to be resentful as we were the victim of their action or the situation. It doesn't have to be a person, it can be a government, a judge, a company, life itself or the bad luck we were born with. We might be right, but it doesn't help or release anything. All we do is live in the past and recreate that energy in our daily life, and, as a result, influence our future with it.

Resentment can only be released through forgiveness. The pain once stored is what your body is dealing with every day. As long as there are triggers, you have trauma; as long as there is trauma, you have the opportunity to forgive and heal.

So forgive, mostly yourself. Focus on your desire to liberate yourself. It is less relevant, the choices someone has made in the past, or makes today. You can never influence the other in such a way that it will satisfy you. Do your part of the work.

Forgiveness is releasing our blocks. Gratitude is nourishing and creates more lightness in our body. We need both. There is so much to be grateful for. Even in times when we unravel all the injustice that has been done to humanity. It is amazing to see how our online world has exploded with free information and knowledge, from experts, scientists, Nobel prize winners, journalists, lawyers, and more. We are creating a new world. We are learning that our natural way is to give unconditionally, before we will receive. Our monetary system has forced us into 'getting', instead of giving and receiving. The energy of money will change, once we release its scarcity. Forgiveness of our past and how we used to do things requires a conscious focus, paramount to our shift and awakening.

15. Permission slips are needed to realize all answers are within

This is such a useful insight for our journey. Permission slips are newly discovered truths we find along the way, that give us great new insights and growth. Just be reminded that it is only a temporarily container for our mind, to bring us ease and to gain trust. Even the concept of frequency paradigms, often referred to as 3D, the current paradigm, and 5D, the new, is a way of expressing what we sense, as it is all so new to us.

There is not much difference between channelling, downloading, tapping into a higher wisdom, intuition, or guidance by angels: it is all a reflection of your inner knowing, combined with what we pick up or receive. All insights contribute to the phase we are in, in that moment. Ultimately, we are a vibrating energy field, limitless in its essence – a consciousness.

It makes sense that our human mind needs understanding, a translation to communicate what we perceive in our experiences. Psychologists, spiritual seekers, scientists, and any other experts will debate truths and facts. Each perspective has its truth and each 'level of expansion' comes with new insights, abilities, and experiences. Our perception of a certain level is the perspective of that level, until we outgrow it. There is no Truth to seek, it is a journey of experiences and expansion.

The best thing is, we don't need to know. Embrace and acknowledge each level, its permission slips, with compassion – and stay open. New guides and mentors will be shown to you when you are ready. This way teachers will stay teachers and never become gurus. The seeker creates the guru, making a teacher the absolute master. But who are you making small here? We all are masters, teachers, and students. It helps to be inspired, reflected, guided. as long as we know that all answers lie within.

Choice is our gateway to freedom

To sum it up: we are our own worst enemy, but only if we choose to stay in this role. Choice is our gateway to freedom. The moment we decide to let go of fears and open up to another way of living, things will shift. It is a choice, between love or fear. No one, no system, no authority is to blame, nor to hide behind. The moment we stop living in the past and only relive the previous day, we can change our perception of memories, recontextualizing, and free ourselves from that burden.

Gratitude and gentleness are the best friends in this transition. Releasing that which no longer fits, happens only from any 'now' moment! Let yourself not be deceived by the mind, with its thoughts that would take you back into the past or worry about a future. Be grateful for what there is, right now, each moment. It fills your heart and lifts your frequency. That is the only thing that defines your future, as it is your frequency that creates your reality. Remember, we don't see the world as it is, we see it as we are.

In the next and final chapter we will get a sense how life will change, when you vibrate at a higher frequency more consistently, and the effect of us creating ripples from a higher level of awareness. Will you be part of the frontrunners who will direct the shift? It is a simple task, no big decisions to be made. Only a full 'yes' to yourself, to your loved ones, to humanity and her future.

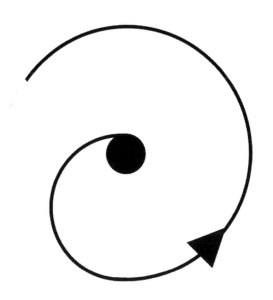

THRIVING

FROM INSIDE-OUT WE LIVE,
CREATE AND EXPAND

6. Thriving

We only thrive when we all thrive

What we have done for ourselves alone dies with us.
What we have done for others and the world remains and is immortal.

Albert Pike

What has been described in previous chapters can be best referred to as the matrix system. The matrix, the construct of life as we normally know it, is a sum of neurological programs, beliefs, ideas, memories, ideologies, control systems, historical data, languages, and values. To perform, live and relate with others, our five senses are influenced, stimulated, and react to the input we receive from life, from our reality. We often don't believe or accept that there is a reality (an existence) beyond our five senses. Our mind, as we have seen, interprets it as perceptions and real-life experiences. We use language to translate it into stories, ideologies, beliefs and ideas.

As we are all brought up and influenced by more or less the same ideas about what is real (beliefs), we create the same reality again and again, collectively and personally. As external input is what drives our lives, we react to what we receive from our collectively created and programmed reality. It is almost impossible to imagine, but we define our realities through the working of our mind, not as a projection outward but from how we perceive the reality (re)created by our (collective) unconscious.

Our outer world is a reflection of our inner worlds combined. If we change our inner world, our outer world will change as well. We need to refine and heighten our (inner) senses, to receive and translate information differently and beyond what is projected within the matrix. This is not by any means a sci-fi story.

By only using our mind (as an operating system) we will stay within the limits of the matrix. Just 'thinking positive' or in terms of 'all is bliss and perfect as it is' is another programmed idea created within the matrix. Without acknowledging the whole spectrum of what is happening (the good and the evil), we cannot shift anything. Once we activate our sensory system and intuition and allow all information to go through us with little resistance, we are able to see beyond the current boundaries. We can objectify what is happening and from there sense and define what feels in or out of alignment (discernment). And more importantly we can focus on what it is we want to experience more of (manifest).

Expansion of our awareness means seeing through the limits of current matrix systems, and where power is misused. Only then will we be able to create a new paradigm with different parameters than the current matrix. But are we stretching our awareness enough to make a fundamental shift? The question that always comes prior to this: do we choose to make this shift happen or are we comfortable within the current limits and its dynamics of power? Are we okay with being compromised in our basic human rights, and restricted in our freedom and prosperity?

If you don't believe any fundamental change is needed and restrictions feel safe, focus on your expansion within the system. Improve your relationships, your work-life balance, unleash your potential by strengthening the connection with the Self. Most importantly, feel into your fears, all of them. Let go of the neediness to copy what others say. Remember anything is a belief system and nothing has meaning until you give it meaning. Live and let live.

Empowerment, embodied frequency and (self) honesty are the key elements to all levels of our shift within and beyond the matrix. We don't even have to fight against any system, all we need is the activation of our inner knowing and, with the same effort, we can create and perceive a new reality. Our minds are more powerful than we can even imagine as long as we don't let them lead the show alone. If we create our current reality collectively, we can choose to create another, one that serves us all better. Same logic, same principle which you can apply now – and in every new now moment.

A new paradigm is a new way of living, a completely new ecosystem on earth with newly defined norms, values and ethics. That will impact all current systems. Whether it is financial, legal, medical, security, education, or food, none of them will be same in our near future. For those who let go of the old, the new will emerge, even if we don't all agree that there will be a new paradigm. Many already do, the ship is turning. How long our chaotic times will last is more up to us than anything else. You are always at the midst of your creation.

Once we understand how manifestation truly works, we know that fixed designs and models can be beneficial but we will risk being limited by the current understanding of our mind. We will manifest more effectively if we focus on sensing the new experience in the right frequency. You cannot just *think* of a new design, you have to become it. Why?

From the centre of your body (heart and solar plexus) we all emanate a toroidal energetic field. This field can reach as far as five miles from your centre. How far it reaches depends on your alignment and frequency.

This heart based electromagnetic frequency arcs out from the heart and back in the form of a torus field (aura). Its shape is similar to a ring-doughnut, with the whole centre of it folding upon itself as in two flowy movements – the male and female aspects of the whole – in opposite directions like a 3D infinity shape. The energy of this torus is constantly refreshing and influencing itself (animal, plants, trees, sun all have a toroidal field). The heart sends out more information to the brain than the other way around. It is about the coherence between the heart and the brain, that increases mental clarity, a higher discernment capacity and a heightened intuition. (HeartMath Institute)

Collective human consciousness affects the global information field. Therefore large numbers of people, creating heart centred states of care – love and compassion, will generate a more coherent field environment that can benefit others and help offset the current planetary discord and incoherence.

HeartMath Institute

But there is more of influence. Sounds, symbols, language, colours, images, geometrical patterns, all create toroidal fields. We see it as a 2D image, like a word, a symbol, or a colour, but it represents a three-dimensional field. Each vowel has its specific toroidal field and thus influences the field of resonance instantly. Can you imagine what words alone already influence? Can you imagine how we are constantly influenced by what we see, hear, sense and vice versa?

That is why it is all about energy, our vibrating frequency!

A vibrant energy full in trust manifests a different life than one that is restrictive and fearful.

Perfect conditions for the shift: from power to empowerment

The challenging times that began in the year 2020 provide exactly the friction we need to push us in a new direction. We need this disruptive energy and the events we allowed to happen show the much-needed reflection of our current state of awareness.

Without a challenge there is no evolution. But how much more destruction do we allow to take place on our planet? When do we stop making decisions for our own egos and comfort but at the cost of others? And yes, you will find reasons to stay stuck in your beliefs but are you ready to look beyond your safe bubble? If there is a real danger, we don't need someone to tell us what to do, we will run, hide, or fight and collaborate immediately. That is a natural reaction we can trust. We don't need a government to tell us what to do, do we?

No one in a position of highly influential power will willingly give it up – there is simply too much to be gained. It never was like that in history, it won't be this time either. Evolution moves from within, not from the top. Therefore we will need to be pushed to our limits until we feel that we are powerful and wise enough to trust ourselves and say 'stop' to those who overpower us. And then it will move.

The fear you experience is related to the frequency
you allow yourself to stay in.

It feels as though there will first be a period of more chaos. It is best explained in frequencies: the low, fear frequency promotes more dogmas, restrictions, measures, and a saviour. The higher, light frequency promotes new ideas, visions, explanations and solutions. But neither feels solid, everything is shaking. We all move up and down within a certain bandwidth but on two different timelines, in two different realities. And there is a group in the middle, not sure what to feel or believe, who've become numb but are shaky, nevertheless.

Neither one is more true, they're just different truths.

At some point in time there will be a tipping point, when one of two realities no longer receives enough supportive energy to continue with its dynamics. This has happened in the past many times, periods of more darkness alternated with periods of more light, only this shift seems to be more profound. The light will win this time because humanity knows deep down the quality of freedom and harmony. Perhaps many have known this in the past, but now we have the support of our technologies. We are facilitated in our worldwide connection. That is what makes the timeline of light so much stronger than ever before.

When this timeline of light becomes strong enough, our systems will no longer receive enough support. Unable to sustain their power dynamics, they will die from within, as a tree ends it lifespan and dies from within. No matter what your reality, life on earth will transition to a new paradigm, but only with those who are able to let in enough light.

Your frequency is your choice

Your frequency is a state of consciousness, of your mind-heart-body-aura, and it expresses itself in your toroidal field. In essence you, the Self, is never changing. When you vibrate at a lower frequency you perceive less of who you are, than at a higher vibration. In a low vibe you live more in scarcity, in a high vibe all is possible. That difference in perception is what you believe to be true and possible.

You know that already, in your day-to-day life. No longer dismiss this as 'just a bad day', but see it from now on as something to work with. Don't simply convince yourself that your positive loving thoughts are of a high frequency. Look at your actions, observe yourself in pure honesty.

You can choose to shift your frequency any time, as you have unlimited potential for high levels of frequency. Stretch your bandwidth by refining your inner guidance, simply through practice and choice. Snap yourself out of low thoughts and ideas and snap yourself out of denial and confirming old patterns. Be as pure in the now with any cell you can sense. Take a deep breath, find an aligning practice that you can apply at any moment. It can be in nature, with animals, in meditation, focussed breathwork, grounding connections or simply in your next business meeting.

Our frequency defines our view on how we can create new societies and ways to live together. The stretch of your current bandwidth of vibrating frequency is defined by your openness to new ideas and solutions. When you feel yourself thinking in limitations you narrow the bandwidth immediately. When you stay obedient to social pressure you are limited as well. When you are open and curious, you expand your view and thus the probabilities.

To think in new ways to organize ourselves, we have to go beyond our current ideologies, structures, and solutions. Democracy, capitalism, socialism, and many more, are all based on the non-responsibility of its voters. We elect but we never become fully engaged. Start by owning your role within the current system. Do you feel aligned with what is decided for you? If you don't, open the dialogue with others, explore, educate yourself and change your actions. Stop giving consent to whatever doesn't make sense to you. If you don't discriminate in your safe social circle, don't cooperate with systems that force segregation on society.

Learn to play with these frequencies and feel what the differences are in ethics, values and embodied behaviour. The words might be the same for any vibrating frequency but the actual lived values and ethics show up differently in a higher vibration with a holistic perspective. The difference is, as was explained before, in the embodiment of the value, to become the language we use in the frequency that honours the value.

Let's take as an example responsibility and ownership, as an embodied value in a higher frequency. Controlling mechanisms like reporting, (prescribed) proof and other ways to check upon others will no longer be needed. We will create societies where people know their natural role, act accordingly, ask for help if needed and contribute to the whole in a way that matches their ability. No one questions that, it will be a given. Societies will consist of many circles, all interlinked with each other, with specialists and generalists, performers, and leaders, like we have today, but communication and information will be transparent. Decision-making processes will be based on tensions felt by one person or a group (circle) and that tension is the driver for a correction, an improvement or a new creation. Solving a tension starts by owning it and then looking for assistance to find a solution. There will be some level of governance but based on supporting growth, flow and creation, not on control and punishment. It will all be based on finding a win-win for all, in any situation. We will still have money, profits, economic dynamics of demand and supply, but the new natural way is to be at service, to improve our collective reality, not benefitting at the cost of others. This is just an example of how things will feel in our new system.

We won't shift overnight and yet, the moment we are willing to do the work, the shift quickly begins. For many of us, already fully engaged in a new way of living with a more expanded awareness, the shift is becoming more noticeable in daily life. Synchronicities are profound, miraculous manifestations occur and the shift from one idea to the next is like creating a new reality in the moment, while the old reality seems to have disappeared.

Frequency and alignment with individual path and purpose

Now we understand more of what a vibrating frequency means, we might wonder why there are people who use corrupt means and seem to be successful. How does that make any sense, in relation to a high vibrating field that is supposed to be flowing, effortless and not harmful for others? Are these people vibrating at a high frequency? No they are not. The nuance is in being aligned with a personal (soul) purpose and living your vibrating frequency. Let's take just one perspective to explain this (there are many possible perspectives).

Take Hitler as an example. Looking at his actions, his overall vibrating frequency was very low, at a level of manipulation with little to no access to a higher frequency of compassion. His individual purpose could be described as leading the world to a very refined superior race that has no flaws or weaknesses. Looking at history, he was 100% aligned with his purpose and for that reason highly successful (at least for a number of years), but in a low vibrating frequency where he had little to no awareness of the consequences of his purpose for millions of people. His low vibrating frequency narrowed his bandwidth to one single focus that the world would be better off with a stronger race, therefore very much aligned with his purpose. Had Hitler been able to raise his frequency, he would have seen the darkness of his actions. If people at the time had been vibrating at a higher level, they would have seen through his manipulative actions sooner and not supported him.

In other words, achieving a goal only for oneself doesn't require an overall high-vibrating frequency. Force and determination can make a lot happen. However, achieving a goal that does _no_ harm to other people, does require a high-vibrating frequency and alignment with purpose to make it happen.

Expanding our awareness means observing the difference between the various roles that are played out. They all show different reflections, to sharpen our inner alignment. Evil is here to destroy itself, but if we are not willing to see that it will take many of us down with its destructive powers. Once we see through these dynamics, we can accelerate our own growth and choose our own path, and soon we will re-create less of our dark side.

Reverse the process: don't give power to others, empower yourself

Where we put our focus is what we create more of. Power is focussed energy. We have little idea how often we give our power away. Remember, most of the time we react to the input from outside of ourselves (outside-in) to determine our (re)actions and feelings. Feel, as objectively as you can, into the following examples:

- when we criticize others, we give energy to what we criticize and give them more power (complain, rage, frustration);

- when we praise others more than we praise ourselves, we give our power away;

- when we ignore evil or pretend it is not happening, we let it exist. Energy cannot disappear, we can only change the direction or the vibration;

- when we project an issue onto our partner, we give more energy to the issue. And as any projection tells us more about ourselves than the other, we feed our inner issues as well;

- any time you *need* the news (or alternative media truth-seeker) to understand what is happening in the world, you become dependent on those views and ideas. You follow and don't lead your own life;

- any time you need a text or meditation from someone else, to feel aligned, you seek answers outside yourself, instead of finding them within;

- any saviour figure we define as more powerful, more enlightened, more pure... we feed on their energy and not our own;

- when we perpetuate ideas that humanity will never change (they will always be lazy, criminal, stupid, irresponsible, selfish) we take power away from humanity, including ourselves. It leaves room for others to take control and overpower the ones we define as weak.

'Trust the plan', whether it is *the great awakening* or *the great reset*, results the same way: you make yourself less powerful and give power to those who lead the plan. Gain information, be inspired, receive support, but don't stay 'out there'. Filter what you receive, make it yours, authentically and keep redirecting your energy, from within. Learn to discern information, refine-sense-refine-sense-refine. Build inner trust and empowerment!

There is abundance in powerful energy! It is unlimited. Those who use self-focussed power with force (the narcissistic / egoistic type), need others to keep feeding their energy. They can't keep it at a high level themselves. A dictator needs followers. Religion needs believers. A singer who is hyped by a record label, needs fans. Only if we *become* the higher vibrating energy, will we not use or need others to stay powerful; we become empowered. No one can *em*power you.

The essence of our new paradigm: thriving

Empowerment is the basis of thriving. See it as all of your cells pointing in the same direction, the direction of your inner calling. We know how this feels, being in alignment. When we fall in love in a beautifully surprising way; when we have made a big step toward a new job that we are excited about; when we have taken steps to overcome our discomfort; when we share beautiful moments with our loved ones; and even when a loved one dies and we feel that birth and death are a natural part of life.

What comes closest to full alignment is when we experience a full body orgasm. Our cells align in that moment, a natural energy that is very healing. Although this feeling is often brief, we know how powerful the energy feels.

When we thrive, everything makes sense. Events happen synchronistically and life feels amazing. When we are in this state, we don't question what happens – life just is. And as we know now, in these moments our lower vibrational shadows are not coming to the surface.

We are the shift!

We don't need to predefine our new paradigm. We shift by becoming the shift we like to see happening. We should not wait for it, nor talk too much about when, if or how it is going to happen. It happens when you are it. Think differently, stop taking things personally, focus, be resilient, be honest, stop denying and raise your vibrational frequency, in each moment. Make the conscious choice and be consistent with it.

A true sign of intelligence is not knowledge but imagination. Without imagination we cannot create anything new but we repeat the same patterns, make the same mistakes and live the same life again and again. When we stay stuck in proof, nothing new will ever be built. To shift, we let go of our need to fit in, the small boxes our society puts us in. We all have dreams but only few of us live them. We all have a purpose, but only a few pursue it.

When life gives us challenges we return to what we know, what feels easy. However, the known easy road will never lead you to your dreams, as that is impossible. Dreaming is not about the future, that's a huge misunderstanding. Dreaming is living the miracles in the present and *that* changes the future.

When you raise your awareness, you will find opposition, especially from those close to you, because it reminds them of the lack of it! Don't let that distract or discourage you! Stay true to your path, to what is right for you. Those who matter will come around eventually and those who don't, no longer matter. Live your life fully and don't apologize to mediocre minds for living a thriving life. This is not selfish or superior, it is just not useful to keep adjusting ourselves to those who cannot shift. When you walk your talk, others will be inspired.

This might all feel very conceptual, but really isn't. By embodying it we create new ways to organize ourselves. Take action yourself, it can be small or on a grand scale. Soon many initiatives will show up in your field, joining forces. There are already so many great ideas leading us to new ways of living together. Become the new essence, the higher vibrational field from within which we all move. That is how we create new ripples of higher vibrational frequencies. The final pages of this book will describe what some of these new essences will feel like, to help you in your focus.

Our gifts and potential = empowerment

Thriving is tapping into a field that is bigger than ourselves, and bigger than we ever knew, which is why it feels so overwhelming. In our thriving moments, we feel that our persona is only a small part of our ever-expanding self. This is a natural energy that moves mountains. It merges with a soft compassion, a desire to serve others and be meaningful. That is true empowerment. That is where we shift (authority) power into empowerment.

Our place of birth, in today's paradigm, does have a great influence on whether our paths are easier or more challenging. We aren't all born lucky. However, to live a thriving life, to be awakened, to shift into a higher frequency – these are choices that we can make, independent of where we're born and how that birthplace affects our life path. Are you born lucky? Don't use the situation of another as an excuse not to do your own inner work and unleash your potential. Once we release our potential, we contribute to the path of others.

Thriving is being aligned with our core passion, purpose, and gifts, but these words block many of us. The quest can seem too profound, as we feel we fail ourselves when not finding it. Where to start? Where to change, if what your life is currently showing you doesn't feel aligned? Make your life a living workshop by playing with it every day. It is as if, without expectation, you open yourself to questions.

Living Workshop

1. Reflect back on your youth. What is it that you loved doing? How did you do things? What role did you pick up or was given to you by others? Don't dive into the stories but feel into the experiences. What feeling did it give when you felt in your element as a child? What motivated you? Play with words and sense.

2. Then look at your childhood pains, objectively. See the patterns you developed to avoid pain or where you tried to fit in. Flip the coin and see the gift in these traits.

3. Then look at your current life. Where is it in flow and easy, what do people love about you and can you define where you show up inauthentically and why? What do you love doing, that spikes your interest, evokes your curiosity? Define what gives meaning to your life.

4. Then, drop the current paradigm requirement list. We are all perfect imperfections. Don't hide behind 'society rules' or lacking the right credentials. The list with successful 'auto didacts' is endless.

5. Create a living mind map or word cloud and embrace all your traits, flaws and gifts.

6. Reflect on whether there is resentment that holds you back, things you haven't accomplished yet or to people who didn't support you in the past (remember the act of forgiveness).

7. Play with this picture for a period of time, adjust, refine, let it rest for a while but each time keep sensing and releasing and avoid any defined outcome.

8. Does the theme of money come up? Where is it you lack trust?

Soon you will see a clearer picture, especially when combined with the daily focus-practice (see below). Last but not least, act consistently! There is no failure, no wrong options or choices. Play, stay curious and educate yourself.

Once you have found your passion, your gifts, nothing feels like work anymore, while you spend more time on it than ever before. You do what you love doing, in the way that is natural to you.

The true act of manifestation

You know how to manifest, you do it every nanosecond, so there is no holy grail to find.

Thoughts create our reality but not every thought becomes a reality. We can dream endlessly of new desires in life but they never happen, and the things we don't want keep happening. So what is the difference? We only manifest what we are, our frequency, including everything that defines the frequency. Where it doesn't feel to be naturally flowing, there is underlying program (beliefs, patterns, old pain) at play and when you give in, you lose your focus. There you feel challenged and that shifts you to desire, denial, expectation, acts of control, force and need.

To manifest more consciously, we need to stay focussed with a clear intention in a completely neutral emotional state and no expectation of the materialized outcome. It must feel as evident as anything else that happens in your life, that feels normal. In that focussed state we *embody the experience* (we become) on which we have set our intention. Not 'I will be ...' but 'I am ...'. And remember, it is your vibrating frequency, of your whole system (body-mind-heart-aura), that manifests the same frequency! You can't manifest a palace if you don't feel that is as evident for your reality and as likely to happen as you manifest the house you live in today.

When you expand your awareness, it is wobbly for a while as you haven't embodied your higher frequency yet. So there is a delay in the early stages. To support this shift for any area in your life that is not in alignment yet, we need a daily focussed practice.

Daily focus (remember the core practice as well)

1. **Align with the Self**: connect with your heart and solar plexus first thing in the morning by focussing on something you feel grateful for, that opens your heart. Stay with this until you feel something opening/softening.

2. **Feel your inner pulse**: what excites you: what do you love to see happening, but not in a predefined idea; focus more on sensing the new experience.

3. **Embody it**: feel into this excitement until it feels very natural to you.

4. **Define an action** (or more): make it more practical but stay focussed on your *neutral* emotional state. Refrain from expectations, negative ideas, detailed outcome, or checklists.

5. **Follow up** on the action, even if it is only for five minutes a day: consciousness in action. Integrate something new, challenge a belief. You must get out of your comfort zone.

6. **Repeat it daily**: a new natural pattern to start the day and extend this on more aligned actions (actions include activating new patterns).

7. **Reflect** daily and adjust.

The goal is to consistently shift the direction and move from within, inside-out. You can integrate this in your work, or any daily activity, even those you like less. Soon you will notice it all is related to *how* you do things.

How we do things makes us thrive, not *what* we do

The essence of thriving is not found in *what* we do, but rather in *how* we act and feel. You can have a major job and influence many, earn lots of money, but if you can't do it in a way that is natural to you, the *how* you do things, it will drain you eventually. That is not thriving, that is forcing. Passion is therefore often misunderstood. We know *what* subjects or fields of interest excite us, we feel stuck in *how* we can bring it to fruition.

The *how* makes your radiance glow, attracts people in your field and that creates success. It is not the same as charisma. Charisma is a skill, whereas thriving is pure authentic expression. We just feel when it is natural. Just as many of us can feel when it is fake or inauthentic. A person with strong charisma can be the greatest liar, whereas a thriving person can only be honest in his expression as there is no agenda to uphold.

Once you find your authentic expression, your natural role, your radiance will start to shine. How do you know? Others will tell you. There is no single formula to knowing your natural way. It requires self-reflection, observation, trial and error in new expressions and actions, and refining along the way.

Connection and empathy

We only thrive when we all thrive!

A balanced emotional state is a prerequisite to thriving. Being balanced does not mean we don't feel emotions. In a balanced state, we develop a high-level awareness of what is going on within us. We are able to self-reflect, and use this skill as a natural navigating tool so that we can release the emotional co-dependency with others and with our systems. We learn to discern. Emotional entanglements indicate it is time to dive within to release old wounds. But that is it. Do the work, realign, and focus. A thriving person takes full ownership of his thoughts, feelings, and actions. Although we naturally love to connect, unite, and belong to a community, it is so important to first solidify our own essence and sovereignty. If not, you will fuse easily with others again, you will project, become selfish or take things too personally.

This whole process requires a new level of empathy. Where the empath sees his quality as a strength and not as an automated pattern to be of service to others. That drains the empath, as our collective field is still too unbalanced. Too little comes in return. Empaths are invited to observe and *only* act when it is requested.

Fearlessness by restoring trust

Become fearless by questioning any fear that comes up. You know now that fear dims your light, weakens your immune system and supports negative-based behaviours of others as well. The mirror effect is always active. What you exude is what is reflected back to you. What you exude is what you attract. More fear, more negativity that confirms the fear.

Fearless is more an act of doing than a state of being. Be courageous and stand up for who you are, what you think and what you love to see happening, be the change. Shift the narrative, from 'it is not possible' to 'I trust...'. We need to restore trust. Once we align more with our high vibrational thriving energy, life will show us high vibrational experiences.

Organizing principles of synchronicities

By its nature, thriving cannot be driven by the mind, as a mindset change. Mindset changes are programmed changes that do help to shift a person from a negative to a positive mindset. However, this constant effort to stay in a positive mindset costs a lot more energy than the natural state of thriving. With a positive mindset alone, there is still an essence of force, to make things happen instead of following flow effortlessly.

One can only experience thriving by unlearning old restrictive patterns, not by replacing old patterns with new limiting ones. Once we have unlearned limiting patterns and move from within (inside-out), our intuition becomes a loud inner voice and guides us to follow the steps of excitement, without really knowing upfront how life will unfold. Only then will we understand the organizing principles of synchronicities.

What we used to call coincidence suddenly makes sense, and feels as though something magical is happening. You meet the right people, you find the right information, you are intrigued by a question. This may not happen in every single event, and often it is only with hindsight that one can see the synchronicity of events that unfolded so logically and beautifully. But after a while synchronistic events feel natural, as if life happens the way you love it to happen. When synchronistic events become less frequent, you know you lost your natural alignment (frequency), time to realign.

New empowered leadership strives for a win-win for all

No one can thrive just by thinking about themselves. That is our old way of defining success. A person who thrives doesn't know envy, judgement, or a feeling of superiority. We can only thrive when the people around us and those we feel connected with thrive as well. Perhaps they might not feel that they are thriving, but we support their process in a way that serves them in that moment, in complete silence or by holding space at a distance. This requires a very fine and subtle sensing capability and an openness to feel another person's needs instead of assuming we know what is best for them.

A thriving person is highly empathic, a core trait for new empowered leadership. True leadership is when the collective is leading itself, through their individual expressions. But before we have reached that level, leadership will still be transmitted through individuals in different roles of leadership, to be of service to the collective in this phase of transition. New leaders have a natural bird's eye view and a clear focus that oversees the consequences of all actions for their circle of influence. Leadership requires resilience, adaptivity, active listening and presence. Choosing our words, gestures, and images wisely, as we know it transmits a ripple effect.

Thriving is letting go of advice as that only gives an energy of feeling superior. Whereas curiosity coming from the heart creates an open tone of voice in our expression.

Thriving is letting go of the neediness to convince anyone. We let go of being right as we shift naturally from a win-lose to a win-win dynamic. It simply makes sense to create an outcome that serves all involved. Our limited mind-based knowledge will be expanded with the wisdom of not knowing. Thriving is living from our hearts with a clear and sharp mind.

Prosperity requires unconditionally giving and receiving

Thriving is finding that state where you live in prosperity, effortlessly, not measured by your bank account, but measured in fulfilment and meaning. And the thing is, that will fill your (bank) account with more than enough resources to make your dreams happen.

Some will have access to large resources to influence the lives of many, others live the most prosperous life by being a mother and homemaker, a support to the local community and by bringing forth wisdom and traditions.

To shift to prosperity is experiencing the natural flow of giving and receiving. To give unconditionally and receive gracefully what comes naturally, without expectations or judgement. This is not so evident for us, as the giving and receiving is not always directly connected. It requires deep trust, that life serves you, or actually that you serve yourself. The shift is in being authentic, unconditional, grateful and without expectations. Play with this, feel into these subtleties and life shows you when you have embodied the shift.

Holistic self-healing

Perhaps self-healing should have been the core of this book, but isn't it evident? Without our body, our vehicle, we don't have a life. The fact that you are here, alive, is said to be a one-in-400-trillion chance. Isn't that a miracle in itself, one we should be in awe of every single second? When we thrive, we are. We unleash the full potential of our highly complex system. We approach problems holistically, own the (unhealthy) choices we make and ask for support where needed. We are conscious of our self-healing abilities, by interacting with our body, in coherence, and treating our body with respect. We drop the programming of aging. Our cells replace themselves repeatedly with completely new ones and we know that the quality of living defines whether that process is healthy or not. Perhaps we can't heal all that is damaged, but we are better served by believing we can.

Holistic wellness will be central to our organizations. Silence, retreating to recharge, will be as normal as a ten-hour fully scheduled workday is today. We will replace the buzz phrase 'I am so busy' with a more refined answer that is beneficial to supporting our sacred presence.

Emotionally mature relationships

Once you realize that each time you say, 'I love you', you are actually talking to your own mirror, and you understand that relationships are about learning to love yourself.

When we thrive, we honour the safe and sacred connection. We own our emotional processes without projecting them onto our partner. In a thriving relationship, we give space and hold space for each other's life challenges without the neediness to change the other. At the same time we stay aligned with the Self at all times. Once we open to the gift of reflection, all of our relationships will flourish.

The partners we meet are the right ones in any phase of our life. As long as there is growth, there is more to explore. Understanding why we fall in love, why we love to be in a relationship, what intimacy means, makes all the difference between an average relationship and a phenomenal, thriving one: 'I love myself ánd I love you'.

Resilient and curious

Thriving is feeling joy, happiness, excitement, creativity, peace. It feels abundant whilst enjoying the simplicity of life. It is feeling light and playful, like a child again, exploring without knowing what to expect, combined with the experience of an adult in an emotionally balanced state.

Thriving is being resilient. The ability to flow with life, embracing the good and the bad days. Being resilient means we are able to sense and respond at a pace that is required in that moment. Sometimes a direct response is required, other times we surrender more and wait for things to unfold, the complete opposite from the over-achiever mindset.

Thriving is flowing through life like a river, with some natural boundaries otherwise it wouldn't be a river. The tension of a limit gives opportunity for growth. Limits challenge us to go deeper and become more aligned with our own truth, our own uniqueness. This refinement infuses our empowerment. In the same way, a river runs faster when the stream narrows. It is a beautiful paradox, we love to be free and we need limits to make us aware of our limitlessness.

Will you be co-leading this paradigm shift?

Can this new way be challenging? Absolutely, especially for those leading this transition in various roles. The older, awakened, generation conveys and holds spaces filled with wisdom, life experience and guidance for the younger ones, to unfold their gifts and natural intellect. New balanced solutions will be created between our advanced technologies and our human nature.

Thriving is becoming who we are, living the gifts, the higher vibrating frequency of our blueprint we are born with, and healing the shadow side of that same blueprint. That requires focussed intention, consistency, and commitment. Not always easy in turbulent times, where we are all learning, experiencing, exploring, releasing. Therefore it is necessary to find like-minded, or better like-vibrating people, who explore a similar path to inspire, exchange, unite, collaborate, and co-create. Your path and that of others will create ripples of higher vibrating frequencies. When these ripples join, we will rise exponentially faster.

It all comes back to choice, your choice, to unravel the veil that covers you and know how powerful you are.

Ready?

And now …

It is mid-August 2021. The world is in complete chaos. In various countries the push for compliance is intense, the restrictions on people without 'proof of health' are getting stronger.

Today I cry.

What happened to our feelings for justice, equality, human rights? It is independent of what you believe to be true or desire for yourself, but we seem to have lost our discernment. In the past we divided by race, colour, social class – now we let ourselves be divided by allowing fear to run our behaviour, ideas and freedom.

Feeling into the consequences of this for my children makes my body contract. I let this negative energy go through me, breathing deep into these contracted areas. It releases immediately. I feel lighter again. I see possibilities, new outcomes.

This is the practice! The only one that has a direct effect. I cannot take a break from this inner work, but once I trained myself in this simple method, it often only takes less than a minute each time.

For years I have been contemplating the most simple way, the one magical pill, that awakens people. And it was there all along, my experience back in 2012 showed the first glimpse to me, but now it has become my new natural way.

It can be yours today. It doesn't have to take you ten years. I took many detours, which was apparently my way to truly understand the depth of life, to be able to share it with you in a simpler form. It starts with a choice, consistent practice for some weeks, and making it your new way of conscious living.

From a higher perspective, it is learning to play the game of polarity. Where the positive and the negative are complementary forces that work together to create balance. I can only play it well if I acknowledge the darkness. Not in a heavy dramatic way, anymore. Just acknowledging it is there for a reason. It helps me to see how it is played, seeing the different elements makes it less dark.

I never realized how deceived I was by the word 'enlightenment'. I always thought it was achieving a life in 'light' with no darkness. Now I realize it is lightness, living life in lightness.

That is the freedom I have been looking for, with both sides of the coin, pain and pleasure. It is the very nature of things.

I have learned, especially the last two years, how I manifest my reality and in which areas I still feel challenged. Where do I still play small? What to do with my frustration and anger, seeing all the injustice unfold? Acknowledging it, but not feeding the low vibrating energy, that is the subtle but profound difference.

You might wonder, if everything in this book is my lived experience, is my life thriving? It is, in so many ways. Thriving is in the living experience, not in what I have or have achieved. And, once I am thriving, life shows me the right way naturally. That is the order, the direction starts from within me.

My life has become simpler and feels richer than ever. Therefore it is really difficult to express how thriving feels other than all that has been shared in this book.

I am now learning to play with time, releasing its beliefs and the concept of linearity. When I approach time vertically, then past - present - future are on top of each other. I can choose to step into the past, which we call memory, but in that moment I feel as if it is real again. The same for being fully present. When I step into the future, I imagine and embody a new reality and with the embodiment I bring it into the present moment. Physically I am still in the same location, the same moment.

The fun thing is, it really works that way. Where I feel challenged is the delay in my manifestation powers. But I think that is due to a lack of pure embodiment of the imagined future. Synchronicity is the perfect example of how the future appears in the present.

With releasing the concept of linear time, I need to release the concept of distance as well. Energetically I experience that as true, but shifting physically is a whole different game.

I am only dipping my toes in this new field of expansion and can see why this cannot become mainstream yet. We first need to grow in our emotional awareness, before we can embrace such a powerful gift of instant manifestation with grace, collectively.

I sincerely hope that this book is a big game shifter for you, as it has been for me. A huge transition embodying a new role, co-leading the world to a new phase, a new paradigm.

*Curious to hear more? Please join me at **www.luciennekoops.com***

Printed in Great Britain
by Amazon